FAMILY LIFE IN
THE MIDDLE AGES

FAMILY LIFE IN

THE MIDDLE

AGES

LINDA E. MITCHELL

Family Life through History

GREENWOOD PRESS
Westport, Connecticut • London

Library of Congress Cataloging-in-Publication Data

Mitchell, Linda Elizabeth.
  Family life in the Middle Ages / Linda E. Mitchell.
      p. cm.—(Family life through history, ISSN 1558–6286)
  Includes bibliographical references and index.
  ISBN-13: 978–0–313–33630–0 (alk. paper)
  ISBN-10: 0–313–33630–X (alk. paper)
  1. Family—History—To 1500.   2. Social history—Medieval, 500–1500.
3. Civilization, Medieval. I. Title.
HQ513.M45   2007
306.8509′02—dc22   2007018268

British Library Cataloguing in Publication Data is available.

Library of Congress Catalog Card Number: 2007018268
ISBN-13: 978–0-313–33630–0
ISBN-10: 0–313–33630-X
ISSN: 1558–6286

First published in 2007

Greenwood Press, 88 Post Road West, Westport, CT 06881
An imprint of Greenwood Publishing Group, Inc.
www.greenwood.com

Printed in the United States of America

The paper used in this book complies with the
Permanent Paper Standard issued by the National
Information Standards Organization (Z39.48–1984).

10   9   8   7   6   5   4   3   2   1

Contents

Introduction: Investigating the Medieval Family

The family in the Middle Ages is a large and complex topic. The medieval world was multi-ethnic, included many different kinds of cultures, and occupied a broad range of geographical regions, from the Mediterranean to the Baltic Seas, and from the Atlantic coast of North Africa to the Central Asian Mongolian Khanate of the Golden Horn. Three cultures dominated the medieval world: the Roman-Germanic culture of Western Europe, the Byzantine Empire of Greece and the eastern Mediterranean, and the Muslim world of the southern Mediterranean, Spain, and central Asia. In addition, a fourth culture, that of medieval Jews, operated symbiotically with these other three cultures, always existing in tandem with them, but often quite separate as to customs and practices. All four cultures of the medieval world will be considered in this volume.

How Historians Look at the Medieval Family

Until quite recently—the last fifty years—medieval historians rarely discussed the experiences of medieval families as a topic in its own right. Family history appeared only in the context of political events, such as the political maneuvering of royal dynasties in western Europe or the Byzantine Empire, or in discussions of medieval legal systems in the context of marriage and inheritance law. Moreover, when families were discussed at all, the only ones mentioned tended to come from the most elite social classes: the aristocracy and the families of kings, queens, and emperors. The urban middle classes and the rural and urban poor were scarcely considered as appropriate subjects for study.

Two elements changed historians' attitudes about studying the medieval family. Firstly, some historians began to use approaches found in the study of anthropology to develop ways of looking at families in the pre-modern past. This anthropological approach encouraged historians to look at families as culturally determined systems, rather than merely as collections of related people. If family structure is affected by the larger culture, then the ways in which families operate and interact are worthy of study. Anthropological approaches also provided historians with methods that could be used fruitfully when studying the medieval family. Families could be discussed as centers of production, as systems for defining social roles, as structures that mirror the larger culture in which the family is embedded. Armed with these innovative methods and approaches, historians began to find family life in the Middle Ages more interesting and worthy of being studied.

The second element that changed attitudes about studying the medieval family was the expansion of archaeology into the uncovering and analysis of medieval remains. For nearly two centuries, the focus of archaeologists was entirely on the ancient world, especially Egypt, Greece, and Rome. Medieval remains were uninteresting to archaeologists who studied the classical world. They merely got in the way of excavations of ancient sites. Ancient artifacts, such as those found in the tomb of King Tutankhamen, were glamorous. The treasures of classical Athens and of the so-called glorious Roman Empire were considered the artifacts of superior civilizations. Medieval artifacts were considered the leftovers of an inferior civilization. As a result, a huge amount of material remains from the Middle Ages have disappeared under the bulldozers of modern cities and the earth scrapers of nineteenth-century archaeologists in search of ancient treasures.

As interest in the social culture of the Middle Ages began to grow, especially after World War II, so too did interest in preserving the physical remains of the medieval past. Local historical societies in European and Middle Eastern countries began to raise funds to preserve crumbling castles. Archaeologists began to use the aerial reconnaissance photographs taken during the war to identify sites of lost and forgotten castles, the shape of medieval agricultural fields, and evidence of medieval peasant villages. Dramatic discoveries of treasure hoards, such as the 1939 discovery of the Sutton Hoo ship burial, which contained fabulous artifacts as well as the body of a seventh-century king of the Anglo-Saxon kingdom of East Anglia, made medieval archaeology more glamorous. More recently, the unearthing of the so-called bog men in Ireland, Sweden, and England—ancient and medieval people whose bodies are preserved because they fell or were buried in peat bogs, which are so dense that air cannot penetrate to the lower layers—has given archaeologists incredible opportunities to investigate everything from what medieval people ate to the chemicals they used to dye cloth and tan leather.

Thus, especially in the last fifty years or so, the lives of common people in the Middle Ages have become much more interesting to historians of the period. This new interest, combined with new ways of looking at written sources—such as the use of statistical evidence to develop analysis and form conclusions—has led to a burgeoning in the field of medieval family history, especially for western Europe. Interest in families in the Islamic and Byzantine cultures of the Middle Ages, as well as Jewish families, has lagged considerably behind research on western European families, but historians are beginning to address these populations as well.

Sources for the History of the Medieval Family

The sources for the history of the family vary widely as to time, level of detail, and availability. Although much information has come to light for the medieval west by picking through legal records, transfers of property (sometimes by means of wills and testaments), and economic transactions, similar work is lacking for the Byzantine and Islamic regions. As a result, our understanding of family life in the Middle Ages is both incomplete and fragmented. We know, for example, a lot about peasant families in late medieval England, but almost nothing about Russian peasant families in the same era.

Since the historian's craft focuses on mining these kinds of primary sources, the ways in which such records are interpreted has also changed over the years. No longer do historians assume, as the Victorian-era ones did, that medieval families were just like ones in the nineteenth century. They recognize that family structures are often fluid, especially in the West, and that changing economic circumstances, the rise of urban communities, and changing social statuses can all alter the family dynamic.

Different kinds of sources provide different windows on the medieval family. Religious texts, such as saints' lives, depictions of the Holy Family, popular selections from the Bible, sermons, and similar texts from the Islamic and Jewish cultures such as the Quran and the body of interpretive work connected to it, and the body of rabbinic literature known as *responsas* present families as part of the socio-religious system, one that reinforces the ideals of the religious perspective. Occasionally, families are seen as operating contrary to the religious ideal, such as in the stories in Christian texts of female saints whose families were resistant to their religious vocations, since such a vocation removed these daughters from the family's orbit of appropriate marriage partners. Legal texts, such as the extensive records of the courts of common law in England and the documents of the Cairo *geniza* (the storage warehouse used by medieval Jews to house damaged Torah scrolls and family archives, which was discovered in a suburb of Old Cairo in the late nineteenth century), emphasize family continuity, since families are most typically depicted as strategic organizations by means of which land, moveable property, and individuals are distributed to new families. Conflicts within and among families do certainly appear in the legal records, but even in those circumstances the structure of the family is taken for granted, as is the mutual consent of all its members. Literary texts, such as western European Romance literature, often present families as obstacles to be overcome: the hero must fight the father of his lady-love in order to win her; the lady and her devoted knight must sneak around her husband—and the knight's lord—in order to consummate their love, and so on. Historical texts, such as chronicles and annals, tend to view only elite families—mostly the royalty and nobility—and only in times of conflict, death, or dissolution, except in those cases where the author of the chronicle was commissioned to write the family's history. Finally, visual sources—illuminated manuscripts, paintings, tapestries, frescos, statuary, stained glass windows, and so forth—usually depict families as static entities limited to two generations, but also present families as cohesive structures whose integrity was necessary to the maintenance of public order.

All of the sources mentioned will be used in this book, as will the work of many other historians. The use of sources in uncovering information about the medieval family is often more interpretive than in more obvious political histories. It is usually necessary to tease out information about the medieval family, to weigh the agenda of the author in depicting family associations in particular ways, to compare different views: none of this information is automatically obvious in most textual narratives. This kind of work, then, requires historians to identify the kinds of approaches they use to interpret the sources with an eye to illuminating the family in the Middle Ages. My approach operates on several levels. Firstly, a significant amount of material presented in this volume comes from direct investigation of the primary sources that most historians use in writing history. Secondly, whenever possible, I have read, analyzed, and incorporated the work of several different historical perspectives on a given topic in order to provide the broadest possible overview. Thirdly, although I have attempted to provide as equal an emphasis as possible on all four medieval cultures, the lack of sources for areas beyond western Europe have made true equality almost impossible to accomplish. When information has simply been impossible to obtain, I have both discussed how the lack of information has an impact on the historical analysis and have suggested ways in which historians speculate about topics when they do not have much information about them.

Dating the Middle Ages

Medieval historians identify the beginning and end of the Middle Ages in different ways depending on the topic and the geographical area under study. The terms *Middle Ages* and *medieval* are themselves artificial categories: middle how? In fact, the French term *medieval* (meaning middle or in-between) was coined in the eighteenth-century Enlightenment to refer to what the intellectuals of that era felt was a dark age between the glories of the Roman period and the rebirth (i.e., *renaissance*—another French term) of classical culture in fifteenth-century Italy. These days, historians no longer believe that the period between the end of the Roman Empire in the west and the Italian Renaissance were dark; nevertheless, the name stuck.

Most historians of the medieval west date the beginning of the Middle Ages to around 500, when the permanent establishment of independent kingdoms by Germanic rulers throughout western Europe seems to have been accomplished. The end of the medieval period in the west is disputed, but generally the year 1500 is used as a stopping point, in part because the Columbian expeditions to the New World beginning in 1492 threw the Old World into a dizzying cultural tailspin and partly because the Protestant Reformation of Martin Luther, which was launched in 1517, marked the end of the unity of the church of Rome.

Historians of the Byzantine Empire in the eastern medieval world work under a different dating convention. Generally, Byzantinists consider the re-founding of the Greek city of Byzantium as the Roman city of Constantinople in 327 to be the beginning of a transitional period that ended with the death of the emperor Justinian I in 565. For them, the truly Byzantine period begins with Justinian and ends in the year 1453, when the leader of the Ottoman Turks, Sultan Mehmet II, conquered Constantinople and replaced Byzantine rule with a Muslim Turkish empire that survived until 1918.

Historians of medieval Islamic culture use an entirely different set of criteria for determining their historical periods. The religion of Islam began in the year 609, when a wealthy 40-year old Arab merchant living in the city of Mecca, named Muhammad, began to have visions that he believed came from God. At the time, Arabia was an independent region that had significant economic and cultural ties to both the Byzantine Empire and the empire of the Sassanid Persians. The first year of the Islamic calendar is the year 622 of the Christian calendar (which, because of European imperialism, now operates as the world's standard dating system). In this year Muhammad established the first community of Muslims at the city of Medina in Arabia. Thus, in terms of religion, the first centuries of Islam should be termed the early period. For the purposes of this book, however, medieval Islam will follow the conventions of most historians of Islamic culture: the period from roughly 622 to roughly the year 1600 (978 in the Islamic calendar), which marked the beginning of the long decline of the Ottoman Empire following the death of Suleiman the Magnificent in 1566.

When discussing the medieval family, the strict periodization of the political historians is not all that relevant. Family structures are remarkably resilient and long-lasting, and social change occurs only gradually. Therefore, it is possible to discuss family life in all these cultures' medieval periods in the context of the ten centuries between 500 and 1500. This thousand years will in fact be the focus of this volume.

How This Book Is Organized

This study of family life in the Middle Ages is organized into two major sections. In Section I, each region or culture under study—western Europe, the Byzantine Empire, the Muslim world, and the Judaic culture—will be introduced in separate chapters. In addition, these chapters are prefaced by one that outlines family structures in the later Roman Empire and the ways in which late Roman culture affected and influenced medieval family systems. The emphasis in Section I is structural. The intersections between law and definitions of family; the ways in which roles of individual family members were defined; the criteria for determining lawful heirs; and the status of women in the family are the kinds of issues discussed. Section II is divided topically. Each chapter focuses on a specific element of family life: domestic space, relations between husbands and wives, the experiences of children, the role of religion, work, and the existence of untraditional or atypical family structures. Each chapter addresses its particular topic in a comparative way. All four cultures' experiences are looked at together. Finally, a glossary of terms and a list of recommended further reading appear at the end of the volume. Maps and illustrations also appear when necessary to illustrate particular issues.

I

DEFINING THE FAMILY IN THE MIDDLE AGES

The chapters in this section focus on the ways in which the different cultures defined the structure of the family. All civilizations have legal definitions of what constitutes a family and how membership in the family affects the ability to inherit property, to contract marriages, and to gain guardianship of children. In addition, all civilizations identify the age at which children are considered to be adults, the roles of men and women in the family, and the ways in which different generations in a family interact.

The first chapter acts as an historical introduction to the rest of the section, in that it focuses on family structure in the Roman Empire and how the Roman models influenced family models in the medieval period. The following four chapters focus each on a specific medieval culture: western Christian, Byzantine, Islamic, and Jewish. All of these chapters discuss not only the issues of the intersection between law and family structure, but also act as introductions to many of the issues that are discussed in greater detail in the chapters of Section II. Historical context is also included in each chapter where relevant, so that the reader is aware of some of the political and social issues that surrounded changes in family structure.

1

The Late Roman Family and Transition to the Middle Ages

Introduction: The Roman Empire in Transition, from Augustus to Justinian I (22 B.C.E.–565 C.E.)

In order to discuss the family in the later Roman Empire, it is necessary to provide a brief overview of the political and economic history of the empire from the reign of the first official *Imperator Augustus* to that of the emperor Justinian, whose reign marks the transition from Roman to Byzantine culture. As early as the late fourth century B.C.E., the Roman Republic controlled territories it had conquered and absorbed as imperial acquisitions. The political transformation of Rome from a Republic governed by a Senate, whose members were appointed by virtue of their election to the position of consul, and an Assembly, whose members were elected by the male citizenry, to an Empire ruled by a single autocrat who passed his title to his successor through hereditary and dynastic succession, did not occur until Octavian, the adopted son of Julius Caesar, was granted the title of *Imperator Augustus*—supreme military commander both inside and outside the boundaries of Rome itself. Augustus maintained the fiction that the Senate was still the supreme political body, but even that propaganda was abandoned by later successors of his own family, the Julio-Claudian Dynasty, which ruled to the year 68 C.E.

Over the next two hundred years or so, the power of the Roman Empire grew as its territory expanded to encompass the entire Mediterranean, western Europe, and the isle of Britain. The borders of the empire were vast and difficult to defend. Its culture was eventually a hybrid of customs, traditions, and religions that owed a great debt to the Greek culture that had traveled with Alexander the Great during his own conquests in the fourth century B.C.E.. Indeed, comparatively few people in the Roman Empire spoke Latin as their native or first tongue. People in the southern and eastern Mediterranean spoke mostly Greek, as well as Aramaic and Coptic (the language of the Egyptian peasantry). In Europe they spoke a number of different Celtic and Germanic languages. In North Africa, peasants spoke Semitic dialects based on ancient Phoenician, the group that had founded the city of Carthage. Latin was the official language of the Empire: the language of its laws and administration. The language of most of its population, however, was usually Greek, the result of the Alexandrian conquests.

Even as the Roman Empire expanded and its administration became more effective, cracks began to appear in the political and military institutions that guaranteed the stability known as the *Pax Romana*—the Roman Peace. The succession of emperors had always been a problem. From the first century C.E., the Roman army began to influence the transfer of power from one imperial dynasty to the next. The period between dynasties tended to be chaotic—the year 68 C.E. is known as the Year of the Four Emperors, for instance—and every successive dynasty struggled to sustain its power and influence while still keeping the army occupied and politically disengaged. The army itself was difficult to control. Made up of troops from vastly different territories within the Empire, it patrolled a land border that in the north went from the Baltic Sea, along the Rhine and Danube Rivers to the Black Sea. In the south, the Empire was bordered by desert and the empire of the Sassanid Persians, who also occupied the eastern border. Only the western border—the Atlantic Ocean—was secure. As a result, the army was huge and was overseen by powerful generals, many of whom had imperial ambitions themselves.

Another problem the Roman Empire faced involved people living just over its borders, especially Germanic peoples who were clustered along the Rhine and Danube rivers, and who were being pushed from behind as more Germanic groups migrated into the European continent: a more or less continuous stream beginning in the second century C.E.. The Germanic groups were themselves being pushed by Hunnic tribes (Mongols from central Asia) from central Asia, who formed alliances with some Germanic "tribes" and who eventually spilled into the European world in the sixth century, in a second great wave of migration. Managing both the population inside the Empire and those just outside it presented huge problems for emperors, their administrations, and the army. The easiest solution came to be to invite Germanic groups to police their own borders: certain tribes were invited into imperial territory as so-called federated troops (that is, resident aliens who were used as military troops by the Romans but who were not headed by a Roman commander) and charged with defending Roman territory against other Germanic groups. As can be

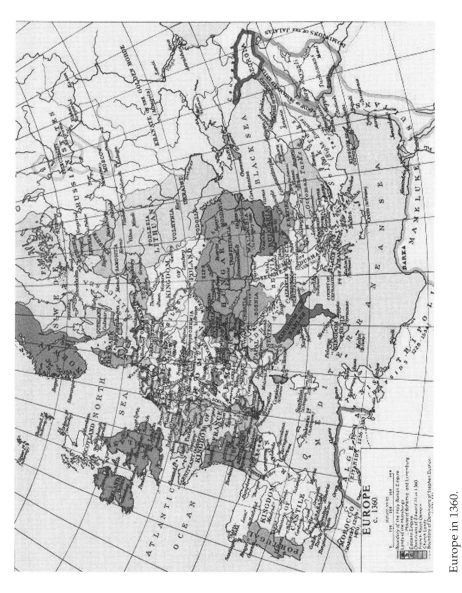

Europe in 1360.

imagined, the system did not work all that well, although its effects would not be felt in the heart of the empire until the fourth century.

When Alexander Severus, the last member of the Severan dynasty, died in the year 235, the problems with imperial succession, the ambitions of army generals, and the pressures on the troops came to a head: the cracks in the imperial system became chasms. What followed was fifty years of virtual anarchy, with generals being declared emperor by their troops; troops murdering newly declared emperors; the imperial administration falling into tatters; even the coinage losing its value because of the adulteration of the silver and copper used to make the coins. Although provincial governments centered in the Roman towns known as *municipia* tried to maintain order on a local level, the disruption of the *Pax Romana* became obvious to all.

In 284, a strong man with an unlikely background—his grandfather had probably been a freed slave—who had risen through the army ranks to a leadership position was able to retain the imperial title conferred on him by his troops: Diocletian (r. 284–304). Unlike his predecessors, Diocletian entered the job of emperor with a well-thought-out plan, which he soon began to implement. Diocletian divided the empire into two halves—the Greek-speaking East and the Latin-speaking West—and further divided these halves into provinces called *dioceses* governed by imperial officials called *vicars.* He also appointed a co-emperor to rule one half of the empire: Maximian, who ruled the less wealthy western half. Each co-emperor, or *Augustus,* chose other generals as their adopted sons and successors, known as *Caesars.* Diocletian chose Galerius to succeed himself and Maximian chose Constantius. This system was called the *Tetrarchy* (after the Greek word *tetra,* meaning four). This system probably saved the empire for at least another generation. Diocletian also reissued the coinage, standardized weights and measures, and passed a law stating that sons had to follow the professions of their fathers: farmers had to remain farmers; shoemakers and wheelwrights had to be shoemakers and wheelwrights; and so forth, in perpetuity. Diocletian might have been an autocrat, but his system seems to have worked and many of his innovations were preserved by his successors.

The Tetrarchy, however, did not survive. Death and dissatisfaction with the system after 304 led to another short civil war. When it was more or less over by 314, the last man standing was Constantius's son, Constantine (r. 306–337). Constantine would take Diocletian's social, economic, and administrative reforms and rework them into an imperial system that survived for hundreds of years after his death.

Constantine is best known for two specific acts: his legalization of Christianity in 313 and his rebuilding of the ancient city of Byzantium, at the mouth of the Black Sea, as his own personal capital, renaming it Constantinople. The legalization of Christianity, which had become an increasingly popular religion in the upheavals of the third century, had few immediate effects, but by the end of the fourth century, it would become the dominant religion of the Roman Empire. The city of Constantinople, re-founded in 327 as the New Rome, was in some ways even more important to the preservation of the Roman Empire: the Empire would continue to exist in the form of the Byzantine Empire, centered at Constantinople, until 1453, when the city was conquered by the Ottoman Turks, led by Sultan Mehmet II.

Between Constantine's death and the reign of Justinian (r. 527–565), the Roman Empire experienced dramatic and far-reaching changes. As the center of the Empire shifted eastward, the importance of keeping the western empire intact faded. Gaul, Spain, North Africa, Britain, and eventually Italy were invaded by Germanic groups who established independent kingdoms in each. The last Roman emperor of the west, the teenager Romulus Augustulus, was deposed in 476 and replaced by Germanic overseers until Theodoric the Ostrogoth was declared king of the Ostrogoths in Italy. Although Justinian had ambitions to reunite the Mediterranean parts of the Roman Empire, the western half was ultimately lost to other groups of conquerors.

Justinian's reign marks the transition between the Roman and Byzantine eras in the history of Rome. Although he spoke Latin, the center of his empire was the Greek city of Constantinople. Everything about Justinian's reign looked forward to the Byzantine world that would follow him, with the past but a nostalgic reflection. The Roman way of life would survive in the east, but only in its Byzantine incarnation.

The Traditional Roman Family

The Roman Empire was a unique phenomenon in the history of the world and the Roman family was no less unique. Since the Empire was comprised of many different cultures, including Italian, Greek, North African, Semitic, Germanic, and Celtic, each with its own particular family and community structures, it is amazing to consider how effectively the Romans were able to export variations on their own traditional ideas about the family into the far flung regions of their empire.

The traditional Roman family could in some ways be considered a peculiar institution. It shared its patriarchal and paternalistic (both terms refer to different aspects of a male-dominated culture) qualities with virtually every family structure in the ancient world (the exception perhaps being Egypt), but it went far beyond other cultures' notions when it came to the role of the patriarch. In the traditional Roman family, the paterfamilias (literally the father of the household) was the absolute monarch, ruling over everyone: not only his immediate family, but over married sons and their wives and children, over the servants and slaves, over foster children and wards, and especially over their wives. According to the earliest written legal code, the Law of the Twelve Tables, the paterfamilias had the power of life and death over all his children at birth, both male and female. Disobedience on the part of the *familia* (the larger household comprising all the people under the rule of the paterfamilias but especially referring to the slaves in the household) could lead to death. Wives were brought into the family through a process known as marriage with *manus*, which made them effectively the legal daughters of their husbands. Similarly, girls born into the *domus* (the Latin word meaning "house" but also referring to the kinship unit we would think of as a family) were distributed to other *familiae* (or, more accurately, *domus*) through marriage with *manus*. This meant that, at least under law, girls and women were only temporary members of their natal families—their families by birth—and all associations with their parents and siblings were, at least in legal terms, sundered when they married into another *domus*.

The historian Keith Bradley has invented a kind of road map that helps to model the Roman family during its eight hundred-year history.[1] First, Roman marriages were always arranged by parties other than the bride and (often) groom. The parents and sometimes guardians were in charge of arranging marriages. Second, once marriage with *manus* became less popular (during the later years of the Republic, as will be discussed in more detail later in this chapter), marriages became more easy to dissolve. Third, in part because of the ease of divorce but more importantly because of the dangers of childbirth and the sometimes significant age difference between spouses, men and women often experienced multiple marriages because their partners died. Fourth, generational differences between spouses could result in children of multiple generations, with younger children being similar in age to the offspring of older children—the younger children and the older grandchildren could be the same age. Fifth, Romans viewed marriage and procreation of legitimate children as social obligations and people who failed to honor these obligations were considered selfish and anti-social. Finally, marriage promoted political, economic, and social networks that were valuable to the families arranging them.

What this description demonstrates is that, even though Roman legal structures made Roman families appear to be radically different from those of other ancient cultures, in broad outlines they were quite similar to most of their ancient neighbors. Families experienced a broadly diverse range of membership, affection, cooperation, and conflict and this range is not often illuminated in the legal terminology of the Roman jurists (specialists who wrote decisions based on Roman law). Like that in other ancient cultures, therefore, Roman marriage and the structure of the Roman family was male dominated and was based on the need to develop and foster social and political networks rather than on the modern-day ideal of two individuals creating a loving partnership between them.

Changes in Marriage from Republic to Empire

The traditional power of the paterfamilias and the exclusion of brides from their natal families that is so absolute in Roman law seems not to have actually operated in such extreme ways in day-to-day interactions. For instance, in the first-century historian, Titus Livy's *Early History of Rome*, his famous episode of the rape and suicide of Lucretia involves her biological father, Spurius Lucretius, as one of the principal actors who revenges the crimes against Lucretia committed by Sextus Tarquinius.[2] If Romans were used to daughters disappearing from the family's associations, then this episode would have made no sense to them: clearly, the practice of marriage with *manus* was not likely to have resulted in the cutting off of all ties to a bride's natal family, as has been demonstrated in some depth by historians such as Suzanne Dixon.[3]

By the time of the so-called Social Wars (in the second and first centuries B.C.E.), indeed, the practice of marriage with *manus* was going out of fashion, replaced by a form known as marriage without *manus*. In this form, the bride retained her biological and legal associations with her natal family and entered her husband's household as a kind of resident alien, connected to her new *domus* but not a part of it.

Marriage without *manus* certainly had advantages for both parties. Unlike marriage with *manus*, which made divorce almost impossible to obtain, because wives could not be returned to their natal families, marriage without *manus* was easy to dissolve should spouses decide to divorce. Finances were kept largely separate, with wives retaining at least nominal control over anything they might inherit from their natal families and their dowries (the property and cash a bride brought to the marriage) were not allowed to be used to pay the husband's debts or frittered away without the husband being assessed a penalty. Wives had the added protection of continued intimate and legal connections with their fathers and siblings, so they had people to whom they could go in cases of abuse or neglect. Husbands did not have to worry about setting a large portion of their estates aside for their wives, since they were provisioned from their own fathers' estates. They also had the bonus of political and social associations with their wives' families, ones that might have been lost in the earlier system.

Marriage without *manus* had drawbacks as well, though, particularly for the women involved. For one thing, fathers could compel a married couple to divorce, something that, in fact, the emperor Augustus did with both his biological daughter, Julia, and his adopted son, Tiberius, the biological son of Augustus's wife, Livia. Most importantly, though, mothers were not considered to be related to their children: all children born in a marriage without *manus* were considered to be part of the *husband's* lineage, not that of the wife. Although this legal stipulation might be seen to have dire emotional consequences, especially in cases of divorce, when a woman would be forced to abandon her children, this also had legal advantages. Since mothers were not considered the legal parent of their children, they eventually could be appointed as guardians of their own biological children in their husbands' wills. There is evidence that this did, in fact, occur with increasing frequency over the course of the Roman imperial era, which suggests that Roman men and women used these legal definitions of marriage and relationship to their advantage. Indeed, it apparently became so common that the emperor Theodosius I made a mother's guardianship of her children more or less a legal requirement when no specific instructions regarding the surviving children existed.[4]

It is likely that the role of the paterfamilias also changed over time and was affected by this new and popular marriage style, since daughters could be retained as members of the *familia* and so could be used for political and dynastic purposes in ways they could not have been before. In addition, the inclusion of a wife, someone in the household who was not bound to the paterfamilias—the bride was subject to her natal paterfamilias, not the head of the household into which she married—changed the family dynamic in several ways. Wives might have been able to have more say in the ways in which their dowries were used by their husbands. Daughters might have been valued more as members of the family since they would not be leaving it after marriage. Sons became more independent and eventually the law of *patria potestas* (the authority of the father) changed, restricting the power of the paterfamilias to interfere in his sons' marriages and even giving both sons and daughters the possibility of *manumission,* the freeing of them from the power of the paterfamilias entirely. Thus, at the time when Rome was acquiring an empire, the structure of the family was changing, becoming somewhat less peculiar in the eyes of its neighbors and more like them.

Roman Law, the Roman State, and the Roman Family

Roman law was the most highly developed system in the ancient world. When the Emperor Justinian (r. 527–565) decided to compile and standardize all of Roman law, the process took six years (from 529 to 535) and about two dozen people to complete. A great deal of Roman law is focused on the family: on the powers of the paterfamilias, inheritance, marriage, divorce, legitimacy, and so forth. These issues became more rather than less important as the Roman Empire absorbed different cultures, especially those of Greece and the Hellenistic kingdoms in Asia and North Africa, and they shaped Byzantine and western Mediterranean notions of family quite profoundly. These will be discussed in more detail in the following chapters, but it is important to note here that this connection between written law and models of the family influenced the debate about family structures and legitimacy in the medieval period and beyond.

The Romans equated the family with the State, and this rhetorical connection was strengthened during the Empire. From the beginning of the rule of Augustus, the emperor (a term that actually designated the ruler's military function outside the city of Rome itself) was referred to as *Pater*

The Ara Pacis Augustae: The Imperial Family. Ara Pacis—detail of procession of Augustus's family. Museum of the Ara Pacis, Rome, Italy. Photo Credit: Alinari/ Art Resource, NY.

Patriae—the Father of the Country. This association of the emperor and the paterfamilias was not accidental. The specific obligations of all members of a *domus* toward the head—obedience, respect, and duty—were exactly the obligations the emperor expected of the people living in the empire. Indeed, one of the most famous monuments from the age of Augustus, the *Ara Pacis Augustae* (Altar of Augustine Peace) demonstrates this idea visually. The emperor Augustus leads a religious procession, followed by all the members of his family, male and female, old and young, adult and child in a profound statement of both religious devotion and family solidarity. Indeed, the increasingly autocratic power of the emperor, especially after the mid-third century C.E., was associated with a paternalistic role for the emperor.

Parents and Children

Ironically, even as the powers of the emperors strengthened, those of the paterfamilias waned. One reason was that social systems derived from the cultures of ancient Greece did not agree with the idea that multiple generations could be held under the authority of a single patriarch, and ancient Greece had provided the legal foundations for the Hellenistic kingdoms of Macedonia, Egypt, Seleucia (which originally incorporated Syria and all of Mesopotamia to the Persian Gulf), Pontus, and the independent kingdoms that came out of the division of Seleucia—Syria, Pergamum, and Armenia—all of which had been conquered and absorbed by Rome between the second century B.C.E. and the first century C.E.. Since the eastern half of the Roman Empire was the wealthiest and most densely populated portion, and the one most influenced by Greek and Hellenistic cultural norms, the typical idea that male children achieved independence once they reached a certain age (around 21 to 30, depending on the system) entered more forcefully into Roman ideas of family. It became common for Roman *patresfamilia* (the plural form) to emancipate their adult sons at the time they married. This turned the Roman system into a more nuclear organization, with the position of the male head of household being assumed by each generation for his own small family. Even though the patriarch might expect a certain veneration—and *patresfamilia* in the traditional sense did retain control of the religious rituals in which the family engaged—he had considerably less power over his sons than in earlier times.

Control over daughters was a different matter. The old, traditional Roman practice of marriage with *manus* disappeared entirely by the end of the first century B.C.E.. Instead, marriages were arranged without *manus*, which meant that daughters were considered still to be members of their natal families. As a result, fathers retained considerable power over their daughters, even when they were married and had children of their own. For instance, fathers could compel their daughters to divorce—a situation that probably occurred more frequently in the imperial family than in more so-called typical Roman families—and they could then marry their daughters to men with better political or financial connections. The great orator Cicero did just this with his daughter, Tullia, and, as mentioned above, Augustus was guilty of the same manipulation of his daughter Julia. Fathers could also emancipate their daughters—and some did—in order to prevent just this kind of abuse from occurring after the father died and the control of his daughter passed to a new paterfamilias, such as her brother or uncle. In addition, as time went on, women were able to designate their children as their heirs, even if the marriage was dissolved or a wife was widowed.

Roman law clearly placed a tremendous amount of power and control in the hands of the patriarchs of Roman families. Is there evidence that Roman men abused this power consistently? Actually, rather the opposite seems to have been the case. Although evidence is somewhat anecdotal, it suggests that both marriage and family relationships in the Roman period were on the whole quite a bit like they were in the Middle Ages: complex and pragmatic, but also affectionate, especially with regard to children. Some of the most interesting evidence about families in the later Roman period comes from the literature of early Christianity, especially female saints' lives.

The "Life of Saints Perpetua and Felicity" is one of the most unusual pieces of literary evidence we have for early Christianity, because it seems to be an authentic autobiography of a young woman who was martyred in Carthage (the capital of Roman North Africa) in 203. Perpetua was in prison with a number of other Christians and awaiting execution with them, but her situation was different from the norm because she was a nursing mother of a newborn who was also in the prison with her. Perpetua's husband never appears in her account, but her natal family figures prominently, among them her mother and her brothers, but especially her father. Perpetua's father is beside himself with grief and panic over Perpetua's willingness to sacrifice herself for the sake of her religion, and he begs her several times to change her mind (he had arranged for her pardon if she would agree to sacrifice to the image of Roma and Bona Fortuna, the patron deities of the Empire). Perpetua is unmoved by her father's frantic entreaties, but she does allow him to become guardian of her son and arranges for his care after her death.[5]

This is an example of a family unit—father, mother, adult children, and infant grandchildren—that operated as a social organism without the interaction of the infant's father or his lineage. It suggests that, by the third century, marriage systems were even more fluid than at the beginning of the Roman Empire, some 250 years earlier, and that families were constituted in more informal ways than the legal system stipulates. Indeed, mother-daughter relationships are depicted as very common in early Christian groups—Saint Jerome had a mother-daughter duo as his principle patrons—as are mother-son relationships, such as that between Saint Augustine of Hippo and his mother, Monica. According to Augustine's *Confessions* (written in the late fourth century C.E.), Monica abandoned her husband (Augustine's father) to follow her son to Rome and Milan. She seemed tireless when it came to promoting her son and, in fact, Augustine rarely mentions his father by name. He also fails to identify the mother of his son, Deodatus, by name, even though he had had a long term living arrangement with her, although they had never formally married, and he claims to have loved her devotedly.[6]

Mother-son relationships have a long history in the Roman world, with perhaps the most famous being that between Cornelia, the wife of Tiberius Gracchus and the daughter of Scipio Africanus, and her sons Gaius and Tiberius Gracchus in the second century B.C.E.. Cornelia, who had raised 12 children only to see all of them die before her, was intimately involved in her sons' social reforms and she even got into arguments with them over which course of action might be best. As the daughter of the most famous Roman hero of the Punic Wars, Cornelia had a certain status (one which she seems to have lorded over her husband) but the relationship she enjoyed with her two adult sons went beyond her stature as kin of the great Africanus.

In contrast, the first century C.E. historian Tacitus's relationship with his father-in-law, Cnaeus Julius Agricola, seems to have been more significant in some ways than his relationship with his own father. Tacitus's biography of Agricola, who had been the governor of Britain during the reign of Domitian and had died in 93 C.E. (about five years before Tacitus wrote his biography), displays not only a sentimental attachment to his illustrious father-in-law, but also a long history of political alliance and connections between them.[7]

We can thus see that even while Roman law might have created hardened definitions of marriage and family and somewhat rigid structures in which these definitions played out, it is likely that the pragmatic norms were more like the intimate relationships between parents and children that appear in non-legal literature. This is not unusual; indeed, it would be bizarre if Roman society had preserved the legal forms in the real world without interpreting them flexibly.

Changes in Roman Family Structures

Roman family structure, especially as the Empire aged, took on some interesting and relatively unusual characteristics beyond the changes in the power of the paterfamilias and the growing trend toward the emancipation of children. For one thing, Roman moralists from the beginning of the first century B.C.E. commented frequently on an apparent decline in the number of marriages and in the number of legitimate children born. Although it is difficult to quantify this alleged trend, since there are no records available to verify whether or not this was actually occurring, one aspect of this situation does appear often in the histories of the imperial dynasties: the adoption of adult males in order to guarantee the seamless transferal of property from one generation to the next. Adoption seems to have been an occasional strategy during the Republic, as a way of providing a son for the nuclear family to rely on. This might be seen as the reverse of marriage with *manus* especially since adoptions often seem to have occurred concurrently with the newly adopted son being married to a biological daughter of the household, at least in the case of imperial adoption practices. Although there is very little evidence of this phenomenon occurring with any regularity among the lower classes, this kind of adoption system was a strategy used frequently by the imperial families. Augustus adopted his stepson, Tiberius, and married him to his biological daughter, Julia. Tiberius adopted his sister's sons and designated them as his heirs. The so-called Antonine emperors succeeded each other through the mechanism of formal adoption and marriage to females in their predecessor's lineage. Adoption thus could create a legal family that was nonetheless not biological in origin. Although seemingly common as a guarantor of imperial succession, the use of adoption does not seem to have been a popular strategy outside the imperial age. Although occasionally utilized by Byzantine emperors, it seems to have died out in the West once the Germanic kingdoms had superseded the Roman imperial administration.

The Status of Women in the Roman Family

The use of adoption when a family does not have any male heirs should suggest quite strongly that females were not considered appropriate members of the family to inherit the family property. This issue speaks to larger one: the status of women in the Roman family. Although Romans did occasionally refer to the wife of the paterfamilias as the *materfamilias,* this was a term that did not resonate the power and influence that the patriarch of the family enjoyed. Women occupied necessary roles in the family, as mother, matron, and daughter, but these roles were buried in the family structure in ways that render them difficult to unearth. Moreover, the significance of these roles actually changed over time, especially with the decline of the political importance of the Senate and the Assembly in the Roman Empire.

Historians often make connections between status and access to wealth. If this were the only criterion by which to evaluate the status of women in late Roman culture, then we would conclude that women had very little status, indeed. Aside from their dowries, which were not controlled directly by wives, women had access to very little property and almost no land. Brides had some right to claim ownership of their clothing and the physical goods they brought to their marriages, but they were not allowed to write wills without the permission of their husbands. Wives also received a small marriage gift from their husbands, but this, too, was only nominally under their control. The ability of women to control property changed, however, if their status changed from wife to widow, especially in the later Roman period, when marriage without *manus* was more common. Widows (and in some ways divorcées and women who never married) could attain a different status, especially if their fathers had emancipated them from paternal authority. If freed from the *patria potestas,* women could own land, engage in business, write wills, and even adopt other adults as their heirs. Although they needed a male to act as their representative when conducting public business (this person was referred to as a tutor), emancipated single women and widows were much freer to be able to invent their own families and to interact with their natal families as more powerful members.

Imperial mothers figure prominently in the histories of imperial Rome. From Livia, Augustus's wife, to Helena, wife (or perhaps concubine) of Constantius I and mother of Constantine I, mothers seem to have played significant, if informal, roles within the imperial family. The roles of wife and mother cannot necessarily be considered as co-equivalent: Livia was very powerful as Augustus's wife but she was far more influential as his widow after his death and as the mother and grandmother of his successors. Emperor Antoninus Pius's wife Faustina was deified (made a god) along with him when they died. As they had been the model married couple in life, so they became the model married imperial gods at death. Julia Domna, the wife of Septimius Severus, was responsible for promoting competition between her own sons and seems to have had significant influence during their reigns. Helena, whose relationship with Constantius was dissolved so that he could marry the daughter of his co-emperor when he was adopted by him, did not apparently play a significant political role during the reign of her son. Her conversion to Christianity long before Constantine's own conversion, however, must have had a significant impact on her son's willingness to embrace the religion, and she became an important patron of the church during one of its formative periods. Certainly, in a non-imperial parallel, Monica's dedication to Christianity had a tremendous influence on her son Augustine's eventual adoption of that religion.

Not all imperial wives and mothers were positive influences on their husbands and children, however. Agrippina the Younger, the last wife of Emperor Claudius and the mother of Nero, is depicted by the Roman historian Suetonius as a horrible scheming murderous harridan who would stop at nothing to ensure that her beloved, if unstable, son attained the imperial throne. Nero apparently returned the favor by having her murdered.

Imperial daughters had considerably fewer roles to play than their mothers. Often they were simply political pawns their fathers used to connect the imperial family to important and powerful men. The daughters of members of the Julio-Claudian dynasty were used in this way. Faustina the Younger, the daughter of Antoninus Pius and Faustina, married Marcus Aurelius when Antoninus adopted him as his son and successor. Perhaps the most significant imperial daughter was Galla Placidia, the daughter of Theodosius I (r. 379–395) and the sister, wife, and mother of four other emperors. Galla Placidia wielded an incredible amount of power in the late Roman imperial system. She was sent to Rome by her brother, Emperor Honorius, to live with Stilicho, the Germanic general who served as imperial governor of the city, and his wife Serena. Honorius had Stilicho murdered in 408, however, possibly with the collusion of his sister, and Galla Placidia was taken prisoner by the Visigoth king Alaric when he invaded Italy and the Visigoths sacked Rome in 410. She eventually married Alaric's brother Athaulf, who succeeded him as king of the Visigoths. He was killed in 415, however, and Galla Placidia was ransomed back to the Romans. Her brother Honorius, who was western emperor, then married her to Constantius III, whom he made co-emperor in the west in 421. Constantius died less than a year later, and popular opinion turned against Galla Placidia, forcing her to leave Rome for Constantinople, the capital of the eastern Roman Empire, where her other brother, Arcadius, had ruled. When Honorius died in 423, Galla Placidia returned to the west and became co-ruler with her son Valentinian III. By this time, the western imperial court was located in the city of Ravenna, on the Adriatic Sea. She was instrumental in sustaining the western empire, negotiating with the Visigothic generals who governed from Rome, and working to prevent the invasion of Attila the Hun. She was also a significant patron of the church, especially in Ravenna. When she died in 450, a magnificent mausoleum and tomb was erected for her in Ravenna. Fortunately, Galla Placidia died before she could see her beloved Italy and Rome invaded by the army of Attila from 451 to 453.

Galla Placidia was probably more influential than any late Roman imperial daughter. As such, her career probably illustrates the kinds of cultural and political changes that occurred most dramatically in the fourth century. Galla Placidia's life also acts as a prediction of the

Portrait of Galla Placidia, from her tomb in Ravenna.

The Mausoleum of Galla Placidia. The Mausoleum of Galla Placidia in Ravenna, Italy.

experiences of imperial women in the years to come: the wives and daughters of Roman and Byzantine emperors after her tended to be considerably more engaged in political activity and religious patronage than those of the earlier period.

Different Family Structures in the Later Roman Empire

People living within the boundaries of the Roman Empire, especially those who attained citizen status (after the year 211 every free person living in the Empire was granted citizen status), were bound by Roman Civil Law and that meant that their own family traditions underwent some modifications to conform better to Roman ideals. Civilizations such as Greece and the Hellenistic Mediterranean already had family structures that were quite similar to those of Rome, in that they were patriarchal and incorporated household members such as servants and slaves into their definitions of family. Other cultures, however, structured families quite differently, and were less conformist in their approaches to reconciling Roman legal categories with their own family traditions.

Three such groups are worth illustrating, since they ultimately influenced notions of the family in medieval culture quite significantly: Jews living in the Roman Empire, Celts who occupied western Europe from Britain to modern-day Spain and from Gaul (modern-day France and Switzerland) to the Balkans, and Germanic groups who moved into western Europe, eventually supplanting the Celts throughout the areas west of the Danube.

Jews, a very small group in the Roman Empire, were granted a semi-autonomous status by Rome, especially in the area of private legal traditions. Judaic law, as outlined in the Hebrew Holy Scriptures, is very strict in its definitions of family, marriage, inheritance, and community, and these categories were allowed to coexist with Roman legal structures in Roman Judea. The only aspect of Judaic family traditions disallowed by the Romans was the possibility of polygamy—the marrying of more than one woman at a time. Since this was a highly unusual phenomenon in Judaic culture, the only ancient examples coming from biblical legends such as the marriage of Jacob to sisters Leah and Rachel and Solomon and his thousand wives, it is unlikely that this was a great hardship to the Jewish community of Roman Judea. Other aspects of Judaic family structure were compatible with Roman traditions: the primacy of the male head of the household, his power over his children, the control of daughters' marriages by the father, and so on. Other Semitic cultures living in Roman Syria, Egypt, and Mesopotamia had virtually identical structures, and were not bothered by the Roman authorities.

Celts, on the other hand, were deliberately and systematically Romanized after the Roman occupation of Iberia by Scipio Africanus and Julius Caesar's conquest of Gaul. The Britons were less acculturated after the Emperor Claudius's conquest of Britain than their continental cousins, but their aristocratic families were also Romanized. Romanization included not only the adoption of Latin as the dominant language (so much so that many Celtic dialects disappeared) but also the adoption of Roman lifestyles: living in towns; governing through magistrates, provincial senates, and assemblies; participating in Roman entertainments; and abiding by Roman law. As a result, those areas most significantly affected by Roman occupation lost their traditional family structures. Nevertheless, in outlying parts of the Empire, such as Britain, and in areas not conquered by Rome, such as Ireland, Celtic family and social structures persisted. Celtic families were very broadly conceived, including all possible extended family members and even illegitimate children. Instead of the nuclear family systems found in the Mediterranean (even when those included servants, slaves, and married children), Celtic society was based upon the idea of clan: anyone related by blood was considered family and patterns of power, inheritance, and association were conceived horizontally rather than vertically. In other words, brothers and first cousins of a particular man were typically considered important social and political associates, sometimes even more than his sons and daughters. Indeed, in the Celtic cultures that persisted into the Middle Ages, all the men and boys in the family—and none of the women and girls—were potential heirs of family property. Marriage was also much more informal in Celtic society, with different kinds of relationships ranging from formal marriage to temporary concubinage (a system of informal, but often permanent, union between a man and a woman) being considered legitimate and the children of those unions being incorporated into the family structure. Even though the conversion of many Britons and Irish to Christianity did affect these structures, they remained essentially unchanged until the Middle Ages.

Germanic societies were closer to traditional Celtic societies than they were to the Roman model. Also based on the idea of the tribe or the clan, Germanic families were also inclusive, polygamous, and more informally organized. Nevertheless, Germanic families emphasized the relationship between the patriarch-father and his children as the dominant structure whereby families were defined, property was transmitted, and associations were maintained. For example, in Germanic society, sons and daughters tended to inherit parental property and cousins or other relations were usually not considered direct heirs unless there were no children available to inherit.

Medieval family structures in western Europe came about as a result of the blending of Roman and Germanic family traditions. The blending was unequal: in the south, Roman traditions took precedence and in the North, Germanic traditions predominated. Nevertheless, it is impossible to talk about the western European medieval family without looking at the nature of both the late Roman Empire and the Germanic kingdoms that began to replace Roman rule beginning in the sixth century, as shown through the written law codes of both traditions.

Legal Definitions of Family in Early Germanic Culture

Germanic law codes, which were written down between the sixth and the ninth centuries by kings of many different Germanic kingdoms in western Europe, are not nearly as detailed as those of the Roman Empire, and they served a somewhat different purpose. The Germanic kingdoms were not highly structured administrations with magistrates, law courts, and complex document-based systems of taxation and justice. They were expanded tribal entities headed by a royal lineage that had attained that title through warfare, conquest, and personal leadership. The law codes reflect the customs of pre-Christian Germanic culture, modified and to some extent transformed, in order to accommodate the Christian religious leaders who did the actual compiling of the laws. Moreover, it is not clear whether these law codes were intended to be entirely enforceable, or whether they were designed to imitate the law-writing tendencies of the Roman provincial administrations they had conquered.[8]

Another issue that makes the Germanic codes different from Roman civil law is that they were ethnically specific: Bavarian or Swabian or Kentish or Visigothic law related *only* to Bavarians or Swabians or Kentishmen and women or Visigoths. Former Roman citizens living in the newly formed Germanic kingdoms remained subject to Roman law. It would take hundreds of years for the two systems to be blended into a customary or common law that related to the entire population of a given region.

Like Roman law, Germanic law was very concerned with defining family relationships and with issues such as marriage, divorce, widowhood, guardianship, legitimacy, and inheritance. Although there were a dozen or more individual codes, relating specifically to all the different Germanic kingdoms that existed after the sixth-century conquests, all contain a number of similar features, with the details being only slightly different. As a result, Germanic law can be discussed in general terms, and differences highlighted only when they are particularly relevant.

As mentioned earlier, definitions of family in Germanic culture were quite different from those in Roman culture. Family was defined both as the nuclear group of parents and children, but also as kinship groups extending beyond the level of grandparents, uncles, aunts, and cousins into even more extended kin. In addition, marriages were more fluid so children considered illegitimate by Roman standards were included in the closest kinship groups. The fluid structure of Germanic families influenced not only the development of inheritance laws, but also what we would think of as criminal law.

As in Roman law, girls and women were under perpetual guardianship of some male, usually fathers, husbands, or sons. The term for a woman's legal personality was *mund* and so her *mund* passed from one family to another at the time of marriage. Unlike marriage with *manus,* however, this did not mean that the new bride's kinship associations were also transferred: she was always considered part of her natal family.

Historians generally consider marriage in Germanic society to have been an economic arrangement: scholars talk about bride purchase and brideprice when referring to the property potential husbands had to give the bride and her natal family in order for a legal marriage to take place. Ironically, unlike Rome, where dowries—the goods and property wives brought to the marriage—were considered the most important economic transaction, they were minimally important in Germanic marriage systems and the brideprice was emphasized. This has led some historians to claim that women were more highly valued in early Germanic culture than they were in Roman culture. Most recent historical arguments, however, suggest that it is hard to make such categorical conclusions based on very little evidence beyond law codes and the occasional political history, such as Gregory of Tours's *History of the Franks.* On the other hand, it is true that Germanic women had a greater economic stake in her family-by-marriage, and this might reflect a different kind of division of labor within that culture. This makes sense, since Germanic culture was agrarian, not urban, and did not share in the Roman obsession for complex administrative systems and hierarchies. This meant that female and male status was not deliberately organized into separate spheres as it was in Roman administration.

Marriage was not necessarily considered a permanent state in early Germanic culture. Although the law codes indicate that husbands could divorce their wives for virtually any reason, wives also had rights within the system and could even initiate divorce proceedings for certain mis-behaviors on the part of their husbands. In addition, formal marriage was not the only option: men and women could engage in more informal arrangements, such as concubinage, a situation in which a man formed a legal and formal association with a woman of lower social status (even a slave) and in which the children of the union were considered to be legiti-mate. Men were also allowed to have wives and concubines at the same time, a phenomenon that persisted in early medieval western Europe in areas of Germanic dominance even after the Germanic kingdoms con-verted to Christianity.

The nuclear family (even one expanded by multiple marriages and concubines) was not the only family system in Germanic culture. The clan was even more important in the political environment than the nuclear family. Clans were defined as larger kinship groups made up of individuals who shared a common ancestor: the Merovingian kings of Frankish Gaul traced their ancestry back to a mythical ancestor, Merovech; their Carolingian successors were in the Middle Ages more frequently known as the Peppinids, a name that refers to their most illus-trious ancestor, Pepin of Heristal. In this larger family unit, all members of a particular generation were considered to have an equal share in the family's political, social, and economic fortunes. As a result, political leadership in early Germanic culture was not passed from father to son, but more typically was shared among brothers, who then fought to gain political advantage in order to pass their power to the next generation. Women in the family unit were also political actors in this context, espe-cially as the mothers of sons who might have a claim on the inheritance. Indeed, there are some indications that Germanic culture might origi-nally have been matrilineal—that families traced their origins through the female lines—and that it became more patrilineal after the conversion of Christianity.

Since the clan was conceived as the fundamental family unit in early Germanic culture, it is understandable that laws governing inheri-tance in families did not privilege one particular member over the rest. Inheritance was partible: all the children of a given father and/or mother received portions of the family property, although often in unequal shares. Partible inheritance had certain advantages, in that it usually required all the siblings to work together to maintain the family's economic and biological viability, and the family's power was not destroyed with the death of a single family member. It had serious disadvantages as well, especially among the wealthier and more powerful clans, who tended to become embroiled in internal conflicts, feuds, and competition over increasingly small portions of the clan's patrimony. Indeed, early Germanic society (at least according to historians such as Gregory of Tours) was rife with cases of fratricide, plotting, and enmity among both male and female members of clans, issues that will be discussed in greater detail in chapter 2.

Conclusion

The family structures of the Roman Empire had a significant influence on those of the medieval world, but they were also derived from distinctly un-Roman elements as well. Medieval culture was a combination of Roman, Greek, Semitic, Celtic, and Germanic cultures, intermingled in varying degrees depending upon the geographical region, and so medieval families combined these elements in their systems as well.

The Roman Empire's family systems were based upon very clearly defined legal structures that identified virtually every aspect of family life, from the power of the paterfamilias to the status of wives, to the position of children. As the centuries progressed, Roman definitions of family became influenced by their contact with other cultures, especially Greeks in the eastern Mediterranean. When other groups invaded the empire, such as the Germanic tribes, their more flexible and informal systems sometimes came into conflict with Roman regulations.

Religion also played a part in the transformation from the Roman to the medieval family. The traditional Roman religion of the gods of the hearth (the *lares* and *penates*) was supplanted, by the time of the fourth century, by Christianity, which was also a profoundly family-based religion. Christianity, however, was soon incorporated into imperial administration and it modeled its own public structure on it as well. Christian leaders began to be interested in regulating marriage fairly early in the history of the religion, as evidenced by the statements of St. Paul in the first century C.E., but they were not able to do so from a position of authority until well into the Middle Ages.

By the end of the Roman Empire in the west in the fifth century, the cultural differences between east and west had become obvious. Political leaders effectively abandoned the west to its Germanic conquerors, preferring to maintain the unity of the more populous and wealthier east. Thus, the city of Rome became the preserver of Roman imperial culture as interpreted by its bishop, the Pope. This was the culture that the Germanic kingdoms of the medieval west inherited.

Notes

1. What follows is a somewhat simplified version. See Keith R. Bradley, *Discovering the Roman Family: Studies in Roman Social History* (New York: Oxford University Press, 1991), 171.

2. Titus Livy, *History of Rome* at *The Internet Ancient History Sourcebook,* ed. Paul Halsall, http://www.fordham.edu/halsall/ancient/livy-rape.html.

3. See, especially, Suzanne Dixon, *The Roman Family* (Baltimore: The Johns Hopkins University Press, 1992).

4. As mentioned by Geoffrey Stephen Nathan, *The Roman Family in Late Antiquity: The endurance of Tradition and the Rise of Christianity* (Unpublished Ph.D. dissertation, UCLA, 1995), 324–326.

5. "The Passion of Saints Perpetua and Felicity," in *The Internet Medieval History Sourcebook,* ed. Paul Halsall, http://www.fordham.edu/halsall/source/perpetua.html.

6. There are numerous translations of the works of Augustine of Hippo. See James O'Donnell, ed., "Augustine of Hippo," http://ccat.sas.upenn.edu/jod/augustine.html.

7. Tacitus, "Life of Cnaeus Julius Agricola, c. 98 c.e." in *The Internet Ancient History Sourcebook,* http://www.fordham.edu/halsall/ancient/tacitus-agricola.html.

8. *The Internet Medieval History Sourcebook* has an extensive section of early Germanic law codes: http://fordham.edu/halsall/sbook-law.html. See, also, a fuller discussion in chapter 2.

2

The Family in the Medieval West

Medieval western Europe, from roughly 500 to 1500, was a vibrant and diverse culture dominated by two particular legacies: the Roman and the Germanic. The western Roman Empire, ruled as a separate entity from the eastern Roman Empire from the middle of the fourth century to the end of the fifth century, was slowly replaced by encroaching Germanic groups who established independent kingdoms in every part of the formerly Roman territory. Vandals occupied North Africa until the late sixth century. Visigoths ruled all of Spain until the Muslim invasions reduced their territory to the northernmost portion of the peninsula. First Ostrogoths and then Lombards ruled almost all of Italy, with the exception of the region around Rome retained by the local aristocracy and the papacy and the southwest quadrant and Sicily, both under Byzantine control until the Norman invasions of the eleventh century. Gaul (modern-day France, Switzerland, Belgium, The Netherlands, Luxembourg, and portions of Western Germany) was occupied by Franks in the north and Burgundians in the south, but eventually the Burgundians, too, came under Frankish rule. Angles, Saxons, and Jutes occupied most of Roman Britain. Portions of Europe not conquered by Rome, or minimally part of the old empire, were also colonized by Germanic groups, either through migration similar to that which brought them to the Roman Empire or through so-called Viking activity: Ireland, England, Scandinavia, Germany, the Danube region, and portions of Eastern Europe that now comprise Latvia, Lithuania, Poland, Austria, and Ukraine. Most of these regions eventually converted to Roman Christianity, although the process took centuries to be completed. Indeed, the conversion of Germanic groups to Christianity was the most important component in their Romanization: without Christianity, most of the regions occupied by Germanic groups would have had only minimal contact with and influence from Roman culture.

Historians usually divide the medieval period into several units: the early, central or High, and late Middle Ages. These units are largely artificial distinctions and are much debated, with political historians identifying specific political events (such as the invention of the so-called Holy Roman Empire with the crowning of Charlemagne in 800) and social historians identifying non-political phenomena (such as climate change and population migration) as being dividing moments between eras. Intellectual and cultural historians look at completely different events (such as the development of a new way of writing called Carolingian minuscule in the late eighth century or the invention of the printing press around 1450) as significant moments of transformation. Two general events in western Europe, however, are largely accepted as watershed moments in the development of medieval society: the Viking invasions, which began around 700 and continued nearly to the millennium, and the Black Death, a worldwide pandemic that combined three different forms of the plague bacillus in one deadly event, which spread throughout the Mediterranean and Europe beginning in 1347. Between 700 and 1347 western Europe experienced radical changes in population, political and legal structures, economic systems, and culture. These inevitably led to changes in family structure, the status of women and children, and the roles that family members played. Therefore, this 550-year period will be emphasized in both this and later chapters, although the earlier and later periods will be covered as well, if more briefly.

It is difficult to provide a general overview of family over such a long period of time and over such a wide geographical area. Nevertheless, it is possible to discuss the medieval family in general terms in the early, central, and late medieval eras based on certain specific issues that can be highlighted: traditional and legal definitions of family, roles family members played, and how generations within families are defined. It is important to bear in mind, however, that the reality of medieval family life in western Europe was much more complex and varied than the descriptions offered here: they should serve as a starting point for further exploration.

The Early Middle Ages: Period of Germanic Migration and Dominance

As mentioned in the previous chapter and above, the Roman Empire in the west was replaced, beginning around the year 450, with a large number of Germanic kingdoms. Not all of these survived, but within 150 years, Western Europe had experienced a profound social, political, and cultural transformation. By 600, three Germanic kingdoms dominated continental western Europe: the Frankish Merovingian dynasty ruled Gaul and much of Germany between the Rhine and the Oder Rivers (a region called Frankia); Lombard kings ruled both northern and south-central Italy (the Lombard kingdoms and the principalities of Benevento and Salerno); and Visigoths ruled Spain. In Britain, seven individual Germanic Anglo-Saxon kingdoms competed for dominance in about two-thirds of the island, with the extreme west (Wales) and north (Scotland) being retained by native Celtic kings.

The social structure of these kingdoms combined traditional Germanic systems with the Roman structures the new rulers found in place. As each of the Germanic kings converted to Christianity, Roman ideas filtered into their culture: although all these people spoke Germanic dialects, on the Continent this often combined with the local Latin to form hybrid languages, such as French and Spanish. In those areas with less Roman influence, German dialects survived more completely: Anglo-Saxon England and Germany being the most significant examples. In areas where the Germanic population was very small in comparison to the native people over whom they ruled, such as in Italy, Latin remained the common language (hence the origins of Italian). Written literature, as opposed to oral literature, was usually written in Latin (except in England, where there was a strong literary tradition in Anglo-Saxon, also known as Old English) and was controlled by church professionals. Although initially deliberately kept separated, the two populations—Roman and Germanic—also became more or less thoroughly blended by the end of the sixth century.

The invasion, conquest, and settlement of these Germanic groups in western Europe did alter the social, legal, and political systems of the region quite significantly, however, and one of the most obvious examples of these changes can be found in the early medieval family. The Roman system of the paterfamilias quickly disappeared, replaced by a no less patriarchal but structurally more fluid Germanic system. Germanic family structure combined both extended family and nuclear family elements. The center of the early medieval family was the husband/wife or father/mother team. Indeed, Germanic law (written, after 550, in Latin except in England) takes pains to define women's roles in the family far more explicitly than those of men, perhaps because their importance in the family unit seemed unusual to the Roman clerics who were writing down the laws under orders from the newly created kings.[1]

Germanic Law and the Early Medieval Family

As mentioned in chapter 1, the law codes of the early medieval Germanic kingdoms were very different from both Roman civil and modern legal texts. In most cases, and especially before the establishment of Charlemagne as king of the Franks in 768, it was not entirely clear how the laws that were written down were supposed to be enforced. As a result, many historians conclude that the written codes identify traditional ideals and relationships rather than create a useable legal system that offers a structure for actual dispute resolution. The Germanic groups had systems for assessing criminal activity and dispensing justice before these law codes were written down. They appear in the codes as a series of monetary payments that the guilty must pay to the victim or the victim's family based on a valuation called a *wergeld*—literally "man value"—in which human life was assessed a particular value based on sex, age, and social status. What does not appear in the codes, however, is an administrative structure designed to control lawlessness and oversee dispute resolution, which took longer to develop.

Family issues occupy a relatively small part of these law codes, and usually focus on issues of marriage, inheritance, and widowhood. Connected to these issues is that of the legal status of women, which had an effect on their position in the family. Marriage in Germanic law was minimally regulated. The main issue in the law codes had to do with the financial arrangements connected to marriage. Unlike in Roman law, where the dowry brought by the wife to the husband was the most important financial arrangement under law, Germanic marriage law stipulated that prospective husbands had to pay a bride price to the bride and her family and a second gift, called a morning gift (in Old English and Old German this was called a *morgengab*) directly to the bride the day after the wedding. Most law codes do not identify anything the bride might bring to the marriage except for her clothing and some household goods.

Marriages were relatively easy to dissolve under Germanic law, and more informal relationships, such as keeping a woman as a concubine, were also considered acceptable under law. Early medieval Christians were generally barred from practicing polygamy—the marriage of several women to one man or vice versa—but it is clear from non-legal sources that medieval Germanic kings were not strictly monogamous, either. Charlemagne, for instance, had a succession of wives and concubines throughout his life, many of whom overlapped in time, much to the dismay of the religious leaders in Gaul.

While married life is scarcely mentioned in Germanic law codes, the identification of people who can rightfully inherit property plays an important role in all the codes. Among all Germanic legal systems, the standard is that all male children inherit equal portions of the family's estate, and that female children inherit as well, although usually not as much as their brothers. The only exceptions to this are the laws of the Salian Franks, which bar females from inheriting land, and the law codes of the Celtic kingdoms of Wales and Ireland, which bar females from inheriting at all with the exception of a small dowry of moveable property (that is, property other than land). Many law codes, including those of the

Irish and the Welsh, include male cousins and paternal uncles as potential heirs. This extreme level of division that is possible in the distribution of a family's property must have been very stressful for families. Indeed, the potential for conflict was tremendous: it became a prominent feature of historical sources describing early medieval royal families, which spent a significant amount of time and energy trying to wipe out family members (including brothers) in order to amass a greater share of the family's estates.

The roles and status of wives and widows in early medieval Germanic law is an important component for many scholars who study the history of women in the medieval world. Women in Germanic culture were, like those in Roman culture, limited in their independence. The Germanic codes identify personhood, especially for women, by the term *mund* (Latinized in the law codes as *mundium*), which means literally "hand" or, figuratively, "protection." The term *mund* refers specifically to a woman's legal status as an autonomous person able to conduct business, buy and sell land, and operate independent of male control. It also at times referred to the king's responsibility to provide protection for all his subjects. Women and girls in Germanic culture never gained control of their own individual *mund*. That is, they were unable to gain legal autonomy at any time in their lives. Before marriage, a girl's *mund* was held by her father or closest male relative. Once married, he bride's husband controlled her *mund*. If widowed, the widow's *mund* was controlled either by her male next-of-kin, usually her son, or by the king.

The law codes of the Germanic kingdoms define female status by the concept of *mund*, but it is not at all clear how this affected women's actual lives. Even though a Germanic woman was unable in most cases to control her own *mund*, she still had a certain level of control over her financial wealth, especially as a widow. Germanic widows gained access to their morning gift and a portion of their husbands' estates—usually a quarter to a third. Often this dower depended on the widow agreeing not to remarry. In addition, widows sometimes could act as guardians of their children, which meant that in any public transactions, the holder of the widow's *mund* must have acted for her, but she was making the decisions.

Thus, Germanic law codes either presented elements of the traditional culture that were well known norms, or they introduced somewhat artificial formulas for defining interpersonal relationships that could not be enforced. When looking at the early medieval family, however, the law codes tend to concentrate on social and cultural issues familiar to all.

The Preservation of Roman Culture and the Christianization of the Germanic Kingdoms

After the Germanic invasions, vestiges of Roman culture did remain, although these were confined to central Italy, especially the city of Rome and its surrounding province, and portions of North Africa and southern Spain that were left relatively untouched by the Vandal and Visigothic conquests. These last two areas would ultimately be caught up in the seventh- and eighth-century waves of the Islamic conquest and become the Islamic states of the Almohads and al-Andalus in the eighth century, but until that time, the inhabitants retained significant cultural connections to Rome.

As the last official representative of Roman culture, the bishop of Rome, known as "Papa"—that is, Pope—from the reign of Gregory I (r. 590–604), became the most powerful religious figure in the west. Because of missionary activity and papal pressure, the kings of the Germanic groups began to convert to Christianity, although most Germanic groups adhered to a form, called Arian Christianity, that the papacy considered heretical.[2] One reason why the Merovingian Franks became dominant in Europe was because they converted to Roman Christianity and won the support of the papacy against the Arian Christian Visigoths, Burgundians, and Lombards.

Christianity proved to be the mechanism by which Roman ideas were conveyed to the Germanic kingdoms. The Roman culture that spread, however, was filtered through a Christian lens. This would have an effect on the transmission of Roman culture and the Latin language in the medieval period. This is discussed in greater detail in chapter 9. The connection between Roman culture and Christianity was less fixed in Italy, however. There, Roman traditions persisted, sometimes with a Germanic overlay. The remembrance of Rome's glories led to the development of unique political and social institutions in Italy: the city-state and the commune. It also lead to a preservation of Roman legal ideals, which in turn led to Italy, especially those areas less influenced by Lombard laws and culture, having significantly different legal systems than those of northern Europe. With respect to the family, for instance, Italian city-states emphasized Roman legal conventions, such as the dowry the bride's family supplied, over Germanic conventions, such as the bride price and morning gift.

The Division of Labor and the Status of Men and Women in Early Medieval Families

Adult males in early medieval families were expected to spend a great deal of their time away from the family unit, participating in warfare and raiding, in farming and herding, or in court administration and attendance. Early medieval sources depict adult men as very active, and often surrounded by other men—the warband in the case of the king or chieftain—not by women. In the history of early Anglo-Saxon England written by the Venerable Bede, for example, kings such as Ethelbert of Kent and Oswald of Northumbria debated the merits of Christianity or the proper date of Easter in a court containing nothing but men. In the *Life of the Emperor Charlemagne* written by his court historian Einhard, the emperor's many wives are relegated to the background and his public roles as king, warrior, and emperor are emphasized. In the *Life of King Alfred* written by the historian Asser, Alfred's children are scarcely mentioned and his wife's name does not even appear. The sources for early medieval history therefore emphasize the public and active roles of men. This obscures in many ways the private roles of men as husbands and fathers.

If early medieval sources emphasize the public activity of males, they also emphasize the private activity of females. Adult women, especially wives, ran the household: they oversaw not only the cooking, manufacturing, cleaning, child care, and accounts, but also much of the agriculture as well. Wives were considered the keepers of the keys, a distinction that persists throughout the medieval period, and that made them the people in charge within the house itself. In addition, women were in charge of entertaining guests: they welcomed travelers to their tables, they had the right to deny people entrance to their houses, and their hospitality reflected on the status of the family. Thus, although subordinate under law to their husbands, early medieval Germanic wives had significant rights and privileges as members of the family and some are depicted as powerful entities in the family's political fortunes as well. Indeed, when considering the elite levels of early medieval society, it can be difficult to separate the family unit from the political unit. The royal court was more or less the household of the royal family, whose familial and social roles were identical (or nearly so) to their political roles.

Perhaps the best illustration of these particular obligations of the wife in early medieval Germanic culture can be found in the Anglo-Saxon epic poem, *Beowulf.* When Beowulf arrives at the court of Hrothgar, king of the Danes, Hrothgar's wife, Wealhtheow, welcomes him in a formal show of hospitality: she presents him with a cup of mead and thanks him for coming to their aid. Wealhtheow is clearly responsible for the manner in which both residents of and guests to Hrothgar's hall are treated. In addition, she provides Beowulf with both gifts and praise, as well as valuable advice, all of which is depicted as occurring in public and in the great hall, the political as well as social center of the kingdom.[3] This is typical of depictions of royal women in Germanic literature before the millennium, suggesting an important political and social role for queens and princesses.

Early medieval elite women were also in charge of education and religion in the family. Indeed, some historians have speculated that more lay women were literate (i.e., they could read Latin) than lay men in the early Middle Ages. Although men were in charge of educating the boys in the family in arms, trades, and agriculture, women apparently oversaw all other forms of education, including book-learning. Mothers are sometimes mentioned as being the ones who hired tutors for their children and they were very important in encouraging the religious education of their families. Women often seem to have acted as the driving force behind a family's conversion to Christianity, and aristocratic and royal women formed powerful alliances with leaders of the church in their regions. Women also seem to have been more interested in guiding their children into religious professions—priest, monk, nun—than were men. These issues are discussed in more detail in chapter 9.

As is typical of the entire medieval period, the only literary examples of the activities of men and women in early medieval families come from the aristocracy. Two significant sources from the period are the late sixth-century text *The History of the Franks* by Gregory of Tours, which relates the triumph of the Merovingian Dynasty in the first few generations of their dominance in Gaul, and the late seventh- to early eighth-century text *The Ecclesiastical History of England* by Bede, which relates the history of the Anglo-Saxon kingdoms and the impact of Christianity on them from the sixth to the end of the seventh centuries. Both historians focus on the conversion of kings to Christianity. In the case of Gregory, he emphasizes that Clovis, the first Merovingian king, experienced a miraculous conversion, but only after considerably prodding by his wife, Clothild. In the case of Bede, the conversion of Ethelbert of Kent, whose wife Bertha, was a Christian Merovingian princess, occurred because of the intervention of Pope Gregory I—and considerable prodding by his wife. The depictions of these monarchs are important not only because of their transformations as Christians, but also because both historians seem to suggest that the intimacy married couples experience could have led to elite wives having had a certain amount of influence over their royal husbands.[4]

Women could also influence their husbands negatively, or could be placed in positions where their lack of status had to be overcome in order for them to make a positive contribution to the family. One important element of Germanic life was the feud: the seemingly perpetual warfare between competitors in the society. Women in feuding families could act as peacemakers or as provokers, and early medieval sources seem to emphasize that both men and women could have significant effects on the success of the family. Gregory of Tours, for example, accuses Queens Brunhild and Fredegund of perpetuating a feud between Clovis's sons, who were fighting over the boundaries between the territories they had inherited after his death. A queen-turned-saint, the Englishwoman Balthild, who became the wife of King Clovis II in the seventh century, is depicted in her official biography as both an exemplary patron of the church and as a peacemaker between her three sons, who inherited different portions of the Frankish kingdom. Thus, husbands and wives could operate as partners for good or ill in early medieval society.[5]

Family Membership in Early Medieval Germanic Culture

The people who comprised the early medieval family were similar to those in earlier more purely Germanic systems: people well beyond the nuclear family unit could be considered fully fledged family members.

Indeed, since early medieval inheritance practices emphasized the ability of all people in the family unit to be potential heirs, brothers, sons, male cousins, uncles, and even half-siblings and the illegitimate sons of a family's head were part of the larger family unit. Moreover, women and girls were not exempt from this system, since they could usually inherit property as well. Thus, the family was very broadly conceived, a situation that could lead to considerable upheaval when family members competed for scarce resources. The tales of murder and mayhem in the *History of the Franks* of Gregory of Tours that were perpetrated by royal brothers and cousins as they jockeyed for position in the increasingly divided Merovingian kingdom of Gaul, and the wars between the grandsons of Charlemagne over their divided empire, are both examples from the most elite social level. The law of fully partible inheritance might indeed have encouraged similar behavior on a smaller scale among less exalted families. Nevertheless, it seems that most living environments included only the more contained nuclear family of husband, wife, and children, although kin who shared family property probably lived near each other. In large families and among the noble class more communal arrangements might have been typical, since such families had more varied duties and obligations to perform. These living arrangements were probably more likely to encourage cooperation in families rather than conflict.

Another issue, especially with respect to noble families and the royal household, is the apparent prevalence of adult unattached males in the household: the so-called warband of the lord, chieftain, or king. Certainly some members of the warband were the lord's own sons, brothers, and cousins, but many were not related to their lord at all. Nevertheless, they were considered part of the family unit, in that the lord's wife welcomed them into her household, took care of them, and in a sense treated them like members of the family. Although there are few examples of such warbands outside of fiction (such as epic poetry), there are indications that royal households of the Germanic kingdoms and at least some of the wealthier and more powerful nobility maintained such groups of unmarried men. Indeed, members of the warband acted not only as the private guard of the king or lord, but also as his administrators. Count Roland, the hero of the tenth-century epic *The Song of Roland*, was in a position of military authority as leader of the rear guard in part because he was a member of Emperor Charlemagne's extended family. Queens also had warbands, as Gregory of Tours demonstrates when he discusses the ways in which Queen Fredegund controlled her male retainers, so it is likely that the men in the group answered to both the male and the female heads of the household.

Children and Childhood in the Early Middle Ages

The definition of children in early medieval families is both complex and not always explicitly stated. It is fairly clear that the period of childhood was much shorter then than it is now: children were expected to behave like adults as early as age 14, even though the legal age of adulthood was usually between 18 and 21 for both boys and girls under Germanic law. In addition, families could include a large number of children who were not necessarily closely related. Children in a given family could include not only the legitimate progeny of one set of parents, but also cousins, step-siblings, and children that the male of the household had had with previous wives, concubines, or mistresses. Therefore, a child could be raised in a household with many children, not all of them full siblings. What is more, wives could be expected to raise the children of their husband's other sexual unions. As can be imagined, this could lead to considerable family tension and competition. Once a child reached the age where his or her schooling would begin, private tutors or parents acted as teachers. It is not clear whether children were fostered in households other than those into which they were born (as occurred later in the medieval period), but there is literary evidence that suggests that male children were separated for a time from their families, especially among the upper class. Childhood for peasants was probably even shorter than it was for elites, although there are virtually no sources available to describe the experiences of peasants in the early Middle Ages aside from some legal sources relating to peasants working on imperial land in the Carolingian era. These sources do not discuss family issues at all.

Unlike the sources for the later period of the central or High Middle Ages, there are few sources available that describe children's experiences specifically. Legal texts mention them only in the context of their ability to inherit from their parents or, if they are orphaned, to whom the right of guardianship belongs. Nevertheless, it is likely that children's experiences during the medieval period did not change significantly over time, and so these will be discussed in the context of medieval culture in general in chapter 8.

The Family in the Central Middle Ages: Diversity and Change

As hard as it is to describe the family in the early Middle Ages, it is even harder to present a single picture of family life in the central Middle Ages. One reason is that, with the development of the Holy Roman Empire in 800, the Viking invasions and disruptions that followed soon after, and the localized and decentralized political and economic systems that appeared at the millennium, regional variations on family structures abounded. Another reason is that other parts of Europe, such as Scandinavia and areas to the east of the Oder, that were not part of the European cultural region before 1000, were incorporated into the existing territories, leading to even more variety in family structures. In addition, changes in both secular and church law in many areas of Europe altered the relationships of family members to each other, but the changes that exist on paper were not seen instantly on the ground: indeed, it took centuries for systems such as primogeniture (inheritance by the eldest son) to take hold, and there were always deviations from the legal ideal. Lastly, historians have much more information on medieval families after 800 than they do for the earlier period, and more information means more complexity in the analysis of structures and systems such as families.

What can be said with some certainty about families in the central Middle Ages is that they tended to be more nuclear in organization than during the earlier period, with fewer instances of broadly extended family units. That said, this is certainly not a hard-and-fast rule, since Scandinavia retained much of traditional Germanic family structure well into the fourteenth century. Peasant and urban working families were probably less formally separated by generations than were the wealthier aristocrats and merchants. Nevertheless, according to legal definitions of the family, which appear in greater numbers after 1000 than before, families are conceived as husband, wife, and progeny, with the wife being both a part of the family and an outsider. Indeed, the medieval definition of an orphan was a child whose father had died—the continued survival of the mother had no bearing on the legal definition.

The lifestyles of the different social classes differed more dramatically in this period of population growth and material prosperity. There was a greater division between rich and poor and this played out not only in the physical environment (castles, manors, and mansions for the wealthy, and mud huts and hovels for the poor) but also in the composition of the household, the closeness of the family unit, and the roles of family members. All of these will be discussed in greater detail in the topical chapters of section 2.

Medieval Law and the Medieval Family in the Central and Later Middle Ages

Perhaps most important to this general introduction is the fact that the legal definitions of family became far more complex in this period than they were before this time. The more informal and ad hoc relationships that were acceptable under Germanic custom, such as concubinage arrangements, were no longer considered legally binding in most of Western Europe and the children of those unions were not considered legitimate and could not inherit property from their fathers. The western church emphasized the permanence of marriage arrangements, which made the ritualized process of betrothal and marriage much more important. Public celebrations of marriage, usually in front of the parish church rather than inside it, in order to maximize the number of potential witnesses, became not only more common but also more necessary for the establishment of legitimate marriages. To make matters more confusing, the secular legal systems and the canon law of the Church of Rome frequently differed in their laws of marriage, and the conflicts that arose could be burdensome to families—or convenient, if partners whose marriage had been conducted in opposition to canon law wanted to dissolve that marriage.

Secular legal systems defined marriage as an alliance between two families, not a relationship limited to the bride and groom. Legal marriage under these systems was arranged by the families in question, involved some kind of financial transaction, and usually required evidence that the marriage had been consummated. In areas where Germanic law was more influential than Roman law, such as England, Germany, and Scandinavia, the financial element involved the groom granting his new bride a portion of his property: this is called the dower or the morning gift (and it persists in the modern marriage ceremony when the groom promises to "endow" his bride with "all [his] worldly goods"). Even though the bride's family was also expected to make a financial gift to the marriage, it was usually considerably less than that of the dower and it was not required for a legal marriage to be made. In areas where Roman law persisted, such as Italy, Spain, and southern France, the financial obligation was in the other direction: brides brought a dowry with them to the marriage. Although the husband was expected to provide his new bride with a small marriage donation or marriage gift, it was not necessary in order for a legal marriage to occur and was usually a fraction of the bride's dowry. Common law dower, such as existed in medieval England after the Norman Conquest of 1066, was defined as a standard percentage of the husband's landed and moveable property; dowry rules, on the other hand, were much more fluid. The result was a huge inflation in dowries, especially in Italy in the thirteenth and fourteenth centuries. This cost could be exorbitant for families with many daughters. Both church and lay authorities tried to put limits on the amount of the dowry demanded by potential husbands, but, despite their best efforts, the cost of dowries continued to climb until catastrophic events such as the Black Death of 1347 to 1350 put a brake on them.

As in the early Middle Ages, secular marriage in the central Middle Ages was a pragmatic institution that focused more on social and family issues than on love, companionship, or religious motivations. As a result, even if the marriage had been consummated, secular forms of marriage were not difficult to dissolve, especially when the couple failed to produce male children. Although the wife usually lost access to her children if her marriage was dissolved, she did get to keep the property she brought to the marriage and often a portion of the husband's contribution. Secular marriages were also often endogamous: they formed connections within families and communities rather than between unrelated people or strangers. It was not uncommon for close cousins to marry, and there are a few examples of royal sons marrying their step-mothers after their fathers died, and of men marrying their step-daughters.

The Roman Church's laws concerning marriage took a long time to develop, but by 1225 they were more or less fully formed and they were in fundamental (and deliberate) opposition to the secular laws of marriage found in Western Europe at the time. Where secular marriage was designed to be flexible, versatile, and endogamous, Christian marriage was inflexible, permanent, and exogamous (marriage outside the family unit). The church considered a marriage lawful on the basis of the free consent of the two people entering into the marriage, not on the arrangements of the families involved. If two adults consented to marry and they were not already married to other people, then the marriage was considered to have occurred even if it was never consummated, even if no financial transactions occurred, and even if the consent took place without any witnesses. What is more, Christian marriage was permanent: marriage was supposed to be the layperson's equivalent of a priest taking clerical orders and was included in church doctrine as one of the seven sacraments (baptism, confession, contrition, Eucharist, ordination, marriage, and extreme unction or last rites). The church did not make marriage an easy institution to maintain, however, because even though consent was the most important element to a legal Christian marriage, canon lawyers also added many other requirements for creating an approved Christian union. The potential spouses were not permitted to be related to each other, except in the most distant ways. Early church law forbade marriages within seven degrees of consanguinity (blood relationship), which meant that a couple who shared a great-great-great-great grandparent could not marry. This stipulation was moderated to four degrees of consanguinity in 1215, since the seven degrees was completely impossible to uphold by that time. Blood kin were not the only people a person could not marry, however. Godparents and their families and step-kin were also forbidden as marriage partners. Thus, the church restricted tremendously the possible marriage partners for medieval people. How successful was this policy of extreme exogamy? It is likely that the church knew that their laws would be impossible for laypeople to follow completely, but church authorities might have considered even this fact to be advantageous: couples who were unable to follow the rules could receive a dispensation to marry from their bishop or the pope, and the monetary fees involved could be a significant source of income for the church. The church's marriage laws were also useful for controlling the lay population, especially kings who had few enough appropriate marriage partners as it was, let alone finding one to whom they were not related.

Church law even defined legitimacy of children differently from secular law. In many regions of western Europe, such as England, children who were born out of wedlock but whose parents then married could be legitimated and considered heirs at common law. Church law considered any children born into illegally constructed marriages to be illegitimate forever, even if the parents subsequently married with the church's permission.

This circumstance had important political as well as familial ramifications. In the late fourteenth century, the illegitimate children of John of Gaunt, son of King Edward III and the Duke of Lancaster, were unable to make claims to the throne of England even after John married their mother, Katherine Swinford (his fourth wife and longtime mistress). The ambiguity of the law, however, required Duke John to take a formal oath that his young family would be barred from succession: it was not a given that they could not lay claim to the throne. The Beaufort family retained important connections to the royal government—and the Tudor dynasty that eventually usurped the throne derived on the maternal side from the Beauforts—but no Beaufort male ever laid legitimate claim to the throne. Yet, if English Common Law had been able to supersede church law, his children's offspring would have had a legitimate claim to the English throne after the death of John of Gaunt's great-grandson, King Henry VI.

The competition between the laws of the secular kingdoms of western Europe and the laws of the church was never resolved. Indeed, modern American traditions of marrying in a religious ceremony, which often takes precedence over the processing of a marriage license produced by the state government, reflects the longstanding tension between the religious and the secular systems: although most people consider their religious ceremony as the formation of their lawful marriage, in fact their signatures on the marriage license, the signature and seal of the witness/notary public/town clerk, and the fee paid in order to receive the license to marry are what constitute a legal marriage in the United States. In medieval western Europe a lot of negotiation between the parties interested in marrying, between their families, between the local clergy, and between the secular authorities tended to occur in order to minimize the conflicts and make the system more workable. Nevertheless, both the civil and the church courts of law saw a tremendous amount of litigation about marriage conflicts occur, especially after the mid-thirteenth century.

The Medieval Family and Socio-Economic Change from the Early to the Later Middle Ages

Certain social and economic developments that began during the Carolingian period and continued thereafter altered the experiences of the medieval family of all social classes, although whether these were perceived as changes by medieval people themselves is probably debatable. In particular, the transformation of the lower classes in most of western Europe from a combination of slaves and free peasants to a somewhat more uniform population of semi-free serfs altered the ways in which families were constituted and limited certain opportunities for personal development within the family.

It is hard to pin down exactly when the process whereby the free peasant proprietor, who lived on his small personal holding with his family, and the chattel-slave, who lived on an owner's estate, both were transformed into serfs living on a lord's manor and working a lord's demesne (the land the lord retained for his own use and income) in exchange for land and a dwelling occurred. Many historians believe that this process began at the end of the Merovingian era in areas that had been originally Roman, but that the Viking invasions accelerated this process significantly. Other historians see this process as being more artificially imposed during the Carolingian era and as accompanying a political and military system known as feudalism. Still other historians dispute that an identifiable process occurred and claim that it was an ad hoc and unsystematic evolution of the relationship between peasant laborers and aristocratic landowners.[6]

Nevertheless, however the process of transformation occurred, historians identify a real difference in status between peasant laborers in the early Middle Ages and their status by the millennium. In the earlier period, slavery was still relatively widespread, since both Romans and Germanic tribes used slaves for different kinds of labor. In the late Roman Empire, plantation style farming on huge state-owned farms called *latifundia* (singular is *latifundium*) fed the populations of Rome and Constantinople. These *latifundia* were worked almost entirely by slaves. Germanic groups dwelling in the Roman Empire adopted the terminology of the Romans in that they called their aristocratic landed holdings *fundia* (singular, *fundium*), but these were usually worked by a combination of slaves and day laborers called *colonii*. Other Germanic peasants worked their own plots of land alongside the larger aristocratic *fundia.* Both slaves and free peasants also worked mills, manufactured tools and weapons, and acted as domestic servants.

By the millennium, personal chattel slavery had largely disappeared in western Europe (although it still existed in the Mediterranean), replaced by a system in which the laborers were personally free, but were tied to an aristocrat's landed estate and could not leave it to pursue opportunities elsewhere. These semi-free peasants did not own their dwellings or the land they tilled for their own use: these were given to them by their lord in exchange for their labor and certain monetary services. This system, referred to as serfdom or villeinage, was a relatively efficient way of maximizing production at a time when land was plentiful, but labor was not. The system was not rigid, however: many parts of western Europe—especially those where colonization was being encouraged—had both serfs and free peasants in their populations. Moreover, when the population began to rise, reaching unprecedented levels in the thirteenth century, and land became increasingly scarce, peasant labor services began to be transformed into rents and other kinds of economic exchanges. These different forms of economic transactions freed serfs from the limitations of villeinage. They could leave the lord's estate, bequeath property to their children, and pursue different kinds of employment in different places.

Still, for at least three hundred years most peasants in western Europe experienced some form of villeinage, so it is possible to make some general observations about how this legal category affected the medieval peasant family.

One significant effect of serfdom was that it limited the people peasants could marry. Serfs had to gain permission from their lords in order to marry at all. If the happy couple lived on the same manor, this was not usually a problem, although they had to negotiate for a place to live on the manor and could not marry without paying for the lord's permission. The situation could get very complicated if the potential spouses came from different manors and had different lords. In order to gain permission to marry, the couple had to compensate the lord who would lose the labor services of the peasant who would be moving to the other manor. Although this was usually the potential bride, this was not always the case: daughters could inherit family holdings, so the serf making the move could easily be the potential groom.

Couples who tried to avoid securing the lord's permission and who formed informal unions got into even bigger trouble than those who went through the traditional channels. They and their families could, at worst, lose their holdings and, at best, had to pay a fine called a *merchet,* which was a kind of tax on illicit sexual activity. The *merchet* could be much more expensive than the marriage fine, although some historians suspect that this kind of sex-tax might have been imposed on all married couples regardless of whether they had the lord's permission to marry or not.[7]

The result of this situation was that peasant marriage tended to be extremely endogamous—marriages occurred between neighbors within the same manor or nearby adjoining manors, not between people who came from other parts of the region. As mentioned above, this kind of marriage strategy could run afoul of the church's restrictions on marrying kin, step-kin, or god-kin. As a result, the parish priest could also gain some income from the fines married couples had to pay in order to get around those restrictions.

The limitation on potential marriage partners also limited the numbers of people who could marry at all. Historians have demonstrated that peasants married at significantly later ages than aristocrats. Whereas members of the nobility usually married between age 14 and age 20, peasants probably married in their mid- to late twenties. It is likely that new families could not form until the parents of the potential couple were either dead or old enough to retire, so that they could turn over their land and dwelling to the new couple. It is also possible that some peasant men and women could not marry at all because they had no means of independent support, especially if they were members of large families with lots of children. Examination of manorial records in England, however, suggests that peasant families were never very large: infant mortality was extremely high and the later age at marriage also limited the fertility of wives.[8] Finally, until the mid-thirteenth century, there was a common perception that there was plenty of land to go around, so building the population of manors seems to have been more important to lords than retaining demesne lands in their own hands.

Feudalism and the Medieval Aristocratic Family

The aristocracy, after the millennium, might also have experienced changes in their marriage strategies, not just because of church restrictions on whom they could marry. Some historians identify the socio-political and military system popularly known as feudalism as influencing the formation of marriage among the knightly and noble classes. Other historians see feudalism as having much less influence, but nonetheless do see some changes resulting in the period between 1000 and 1300 that might have something to do with changes in social, political, and military systems.

Feudalism (not to be confused with manorialism, with which it is often incorrectly combined) in its simplest form creates a relationship between a member of the knightly class and an aristocratic landowner, or lord. The knight pledges to provide military and administrative services to the lord and the lord grants the knight a fief—usually land (a manor)—and protection. Feudalism probably evolved from a combination of the Germanic and early medieval warband, which involved groups of unrelated men pledging loyalty to a chieftain who gave them treasure as well as allowed them to live in his house, and the Roman system of clientage, in which men gained elite and influential men as patrons in exchange for their political support. It was a very complicated system—not the neat pyramid that often serves as a graphic model of it—and exhibited tremendous variety from region to region in Western Europe and the areas westerners conquered, such as the Crusader States and the Latin Kingdom of Jerusalem.

The relationship between the development of feudalism and changes in aristocratic marriage patterns and the formation of the aristocratic family is very complex and much debated. Some historians, such as Georges Duby, see the combination of feudalism, changes in inheritance patterns, and the influence of church laws concerning marriage as fundamentally altering aristocratic marriage and notions of the family. For them, this triple threat resulted in marriage becoming fully exogamous (going outside known social and kinship networks) and limited to the eldest son, who would inherit everything in a system known as *primogeniture* (that is, the eldest son is the heir), and one or two daughters. The remaining children would be dedicated either to the church, as priests, monks, and nuns, or would become eternal bachelors: unmarried men attached to a noble household who had little chance of acquiring a fief unless they were lucky enough to marry a wealthy heiress or widow.[9]

Other historians, such as Theodore Rivers, Amy Livingstone, Kimberley Lo Prete, and this author, see the situation unfolding as far more subtle and less absolute.[10] Although primogeniture did alter the amount of land each child in the family received, this view suggests that all the children nonetheless were invested in the family fortunes either directly through inheritance, or indirectly through family associations. Although aristocratic families did tend to have a lot of children, there does not seem to be any evidence suggesting that only the first few to survive to adulthood were married off and that the remainder were relegated to careers in the church, lives as mercenaries, or sitting by the fire as perpetual maiden aunts. Families employed many different parental strategies for ensuring the wellbeing of their children, including marriage, dedication to the church, and professional employment. Moreover, other members of the family were included in these patronage networks, such as cousins, nieces, and nephews. Children were highly valued and their futures seem to have been the topic of considerable discussion and planning. There is little evidence of children being thrown out of their houses and left to make their own way in the world once they reached adulthood. Indeed, even when the family was not able to offer their younger children any significant material benefits, they took great pains to ensure their establishment in other households or professions, as will be discussed in greater detail in chapters 7 and 8.

Feudalism did affect family organization and formation in important ways, however. Firstly, the relationship between a knight (also known as a vassal) and a lord was reciprocal and had political as well as socioeconomic importance. Networks of knightly and noble families developed as a result of these relationships, ones that could often determine whom one married, where one lived, and what one's profession would be. Secondly, children were shared among the families in these feudal networks, through a tradition of fosterage, in which boys and, sometimes, girls would be exchanged to be raised. This was seen as a civilizing feature of a child's education, not as a way to discard un-needed or superfluous children. Thirdly, since the eldest son (if there was one) did inherit the bulk of the family property—at least the property passed down from his father—this meant that his younger brothers were subordinate to him to some extent, although essential to the maintenance of the family fortunes. Thus, a certain pecking order could develop that could have emotional consequences as children grew up.

Medieval Italy: A Hybrid Legal and Social System

When discussing medieval western Europe, it can be virtually impossible to include Italy in generalizations about legal and social systems. Italy itself was a complex collection of independent city-states, provinces, and kingdoms, each with a unique institutions and certainly with no unified legal system. In southern Italy and Sicily, Normans conquered the Lombard duchy of Salerno and the Byzantine province of Sicily. They established there a kingdom notable for its lack of continuity: the Norman kingdom of Sicily was the most culturally diverse region of the medieval world. In the central and northern regions, where independent city-states developed, each city developed its own legal systems, influenced by both Roman and Lombard law, with different definitions of family and unity. In the regions north of Rome, the laws of the city-states were similar to each other, but not identical.

Italian marriage law, then, experienced a deep north-south divide. In the Norman south, dower was more important than dowry. In the medieval city-states, dowry became more important. Italy did not become completely feudalized or manorialized, as the northern portions of the continent did. As a result, older Roman traditions persisted in some places. Slavery was somewhat more common in Italy than elsewhere in Europe, for example. Peasants were more likely to own their land. Aristocrats were more likely to live in cities, in urban townhouses, than being isolated in castles in the countryside.

As a result of these differences, family structures could be different in Italy as well. There seems to have been a more segregated social system between male and female spheres of activity. Daughters tend to be under-counted in public records, which has led some historians to speculate that the practice of female infanticide (the killing of female babies) might have been practiced at times. On the other hand, girls of the urbanized elite were more likely to have some level of formal education, through a tutor, than girls elsewhere, in the early medieval period in particular. Family strategies in Italy, however, were more or less identical to those of their northern neighbors.

Cities, Law, and the Medieval Family

Early medieval western Europe had few cities, especially in the north, but by the millennium, urban centers were growing in both size and number, as well as in political and economic importance. Unlike modern-day cities, medieval towns were largely independent of the county or regional authority, often held royal charters granting them independence, and frequently maintained their own legal codes unique to each urban area. Urban families were organized for different economic purposes than were peasant or aristocratic families, so even though they often shared values, they sometimes looked different.

Medieval urban families were more or less nuclear in organization. Even when these nuclear families maintained their own households, however, they maintained important linkages to other families, both blood relations and unrelated but economically linked associates. By the thirteenth century, the basis of urban organization was the guild: associations based upon specific professional, trade, or manufacturing professions that operated as the bases for political, social, economic, and educational structures. For example, in Florence the Lana guild oversaw trade in wool, educated youngsters as apprentices, patronized churches, and engaged in political governance. The center of medieval London's political and legal world was its Guildhall, which to this day houses the offices of the mayor and council of the city.

Guilds were in complete control of the day-to-day lives of their members. They authorized workshops, decided which members could marry, determined the training curriculum of apprentices, and established prices for goods that were manufactured or traded by guild members. Perhaps the most important guild provisions for the medieval urban family were the prohibitions against apprentices and journeymen being able to marry, and the pressure often wielded by guild governors on masters to marry only women from fellow guild families. Like the marriages of both peasants and nobles, this stricture against marrying outside the guild made it difficult to abide by church laws against marrying cousins, step-kin, and god-kin. The regulation of guild marriages was very important nonetheless to the survival of the guild and its monopoly.

Since the apprentices assigned to guild masters lived in the masters' households, family systems also included children not related by blood to the nuclear family. Women—especially wives of masters—therefore oversaw the maintenance of a complex family unit, especially when the family's own biological children were sent to other households to be educated and trained. This seems to have been viewed as a way to acculturate children and a means by which guild masters could enhance their political and social networks. As a result, an entire body of urban laws grew to manage these associations, including regulations about the treatment of apprentices, attempts to protect women and girls from sexual exploitation, and strategies for maintaining workshops following the death of the master. All of these issues will be discussed in greater detail in chapter 10.

Conclusion

Although it is clear that changes in law throughout western Europe during the Middle Ages influenced developments in the structures of and relationships within medieval families, laws were only one part of the process. For one thing, peasant families, living in isolated villages with little access to the makers of law and legal theory, probably were little affected by these changes, except perhaps over the very long term. Aristocratic and merchant families were more immediately affected by changes in political and legal structures, and they were far more intimately involved in making those changes themselves. As a result, they resisted changes that could adversely affect the ways in which they operated.

The long transformation of the Roman Empire in the west into the feudal kingdoms that were fully established by the year 1100 certainly prompted profound changes in family organization and structure. The influence of Christianity on pre-Christian Germanic traditions, changes in economic focus, and the development of a unique hybrid culture all contributed elements to medieval family life in western Europe. In the early Middle Ages, the newly formed Germanic kingdoms experienced a great deal of tension between long-standing traditions and the efforts of church leaders to Christianize and Romanize their cultures. Forms of marriage that had been flexible, fluid, and useful to the Germanic population, while elite families jockeyed for position and the peasantry tried to adjust to changes in governance and administration, came under attack by religious professionals who were determined to mold this vibrant but un-Roman, and therefore somewhat alien, culture into a more Christian ideal. They were only partially successful.

Disruptions from invasion and internal conflict between 800 and 1000 led to changes in social organization. Manorialism developed as an economic system that both exploited peasant labor and defended the peasant class from attack by grouping families into village communities under the lord of the manor's protection. Feudalism developed as a political and military system that reflected both the fragmented nature of royal authority and the need for systems of patronage and alliance that could be preserved through formal relationships between lords and vassals. In these changing times, family structures changed as well. The church's demands that medieval people conform to the laws against consanguineous marriages began to affect the kinds of marriage alliances people formed. Feudal relationships fostered different kinds of marriage alliances, ones that could operate as linkages between lords and vassals, but also between vassals themselves. Peasants tied to the land as manorial serfs found their marriage choices limited by the requirement they secure the lord's permission, on the one hand, but perhaps improved, on the other hand, because of the increased level of security they experienced.

After the millennium, the relative stability of European life until the massive upheaval of the Black Death 350 years later, led to a similar stability in marriage and family life. Regional variations occurred, especially in parts of Europe, such as Italy, where cities began to grow and urban elites took over positions of authority from the rural aristocracy. The nobility of high medieval Europe became in a sense more cosmopolitan, especially as they often had to seek appropriate marriage partners from far away. A noble family in England probably lived very similarly to its counterpart in France, Germany, northern Spain, or Sicily. In the same way, a member of the urban elite might feel at home as easily in Bruges or Ghent as in Florence or Siena. Peasant lifestyles, which were far less affected by political upheavals or changes in legal systems, were probably virtually identical to those of hundreds of years before. For everyone, however, family life centered on the cooperation and partnership of all its members: that requirement would never change.

Notes

1. Various law codes of the early medieval Germanic kingdoms have been edited and translated, available both in print and in *The Internet Medieval Sourcebook.* See http://www.fordham.edu/halsall/sbook-law.html.

2. Arian Christianity modeled the Trinity as a pyramid: the Son and Holy Spirit are subordinate to the Father. Nicene Christianity, which became the position of the Roman church, proposes an un-model of the Trinity: three in one, co-eternal, and of the same essence.

3. *Beowulf* is available in numerous translations in print and online. See *Beowulf,* trans. Francis Gummere at the *Internet Medieval Sourcebook,* http://www.fordham.edu/halsall/basis/beowulf.html, and the translation by David Breeden at "Lone Star," http://www.lone-star.net/literature/beowulf/index.html.

4. The standard texts for Gregory and Bede are: Gregory of Tours, *The History of the Franks,* trans. Lewis Thorpe (Baltimore: Penguin Books, 1974); and Bede, *The Ecclesiastical History of the English People,* trans. Leo Sherley-Price (Baltimore: Penguin Books, Rev. Ed. 1991), but they are also available online: "Medieval Sourcebook: Gregory of Tours (539–594): History of the Franks: Books I–X," http://www.fordham.edu/halsall/basis/gregory-hist.html; "Medieval Sourcebook: Bede (673–735): Ecclesiastical History of the English Nation: Book I," http://www.fordham.edu/halsall/basis/bede-book1.html, with the remaining four books of the text following and linked to the first book's page.

5. Early medieval queens and their families are the subjects of several essays in Derek Baker, ed., *Medieval Women* (Oxford: Basil Blackwell, 1978). See, especially, Joan Nicholson, "*Feminae gloriosae:* Women in the Age of Bede" (pp. 15–30); Janet L. Nelson, "Queens as Jezebels: The Careers of Brunhild and Balthild in Merovingian History" (pp. 31–78); and Pauline Stafford, "Sons and Mothers: Family Politics in the Early Middle Ages" (pp. 79–100).

6. These debates continue, but starting points for these discussions are Henri Pirenne, *Mohammed and Charlemagne* (New York: Dover Publications, 2001), Marc Bloch, *Feudal Society,* 2 vols (Chicago: University of Chicago Press, 1964), and J. Horace Round, *Feudal England: Historical Studies on the XIth and XIIth centuries* (London: S. Sonnenschein, 1909).

7. See, for example, Eleanor Searle, "Seigneurial Control of Women's Marriage: The Antecedents and Function of *Merchet* in England," *Past & Present,* no. 82 (1979): 3–43 and the debate in *Past & Present,* no. 99 (1996): 123–160.

8. See, for example, Zvi Razi, *Life, Marriage, and Death in a Medieval Parish: Economy, Society, and Demography in Halesown, 1270–1400* (New York: Cambridge University Press, 1980).

9. See, especially, Georges Duby, *Medieval Marriage: Two Models from Twelfth-century France,* trans. Elborg Forster (Baltimore: The Johns Hopkins University Press, 1978) and Duby, *The Knight, the Lady, and the Priest: The Making of Modern Marriage in Medieval France,* trans. Barbara Bray (New York: Pantheon Books, 1983).

10. See, for example, Theodore John Rivers, ed., *Aristocratic Women in Medieval France* (Philadelphia: University of Pennsylvania Press, 1999) and Linda E. Mitchell, ed. *Women in Medieval Western European Culture* (New York: Garland Press, 1999).

3

The Family in the Byzantine East

Introduction: From Roman to Byzantine

Although the Enlightenment historian Edward Gibbon saw the western Roman Empire as "falling" at the death of the last western Roman emperor, Romulus Augustulus, in 483, he considered the empire to have continued in the east until 1453, when the capital of the eastern Roman Empire, Constantinople, fell to the Ottoman Turks. Western medieval historians often overlook the eastern empire—indeed, until quite recently, most American students were taught that the Roman Empire ceased to exist when the western half divided into Germanic kingdoms after 500—but the culture of the Late Roman Empire did indeed continue to develop in the east, from modern-day Croatia to the border between Afghanistan and Turkey, in the medieval Middle East, and in southeastern Europe, as far north as Bulgaria, Romania, and Hungary. Nevertheless, historians consider the abandoning of the city of Rome and the consolidation of power around Greece and the imperial city of Constantinople to have signaled a profound cultural change: the evolution of the so-called Byzantine Empire (Constantinople was originally called Byzantium).

When the Romans gained control over the Hellenistic kingdoms in the eastern Mediterranean in the 150 years between the end of the Third Macedonian War and the victory of Augustus over Marc Anthony and Cleopatra at Actium (14 B.C.E.), they ruled them more or less indirectly as client states rather than as imperial acquisitions. This changed dramatically once Augustus gained control of the *imperium*—the sign of his personal authority outside the boundaries of Rome itself. The entire Mediterranean world became part of the immense Empire, governed directly by Roman appointees and defended by Roman soldiers. Municipal centers run by professional administrators and the Roman army were established throughout the eastern Mediterranean. Many of these were originally Hellenistic cities—Alexandria, Antioch, and so on. Some were more remote Hellenistic outposts guarding the border of the newly expanded empire—Thessalonike (the northernmost city of Greece), Dura Europus (in modern-day Iraq), and the cities of Pontus (the northern shores of the Black Sea), Armenia, and Afghanistan (east of modern-day Turkey). The small provincial but ancient city of Byzantion (Byzantium in Latin) was one of those outposts until the fourth century C.E. By that time the importance of the eastern half of the empire had grown to such an extent that the emperor of the newly unified empire, Constantine, made the decision to transform the little city that guarded the entrance into the Black Sea from the Aegean into a new Rome, which he renamed after himself: the city of Constantine, *Constantinopolis* in Greek, and *Constantinople* in Latin.

Constantinople was intended to be equal to Rome in importance and the principle city of the eastern empire. It took hundreds of years for the city to achieve these goals, not because the efforts of emperors to make the city primary were deficient, but because the loss of Rome to Germanic conquerors, and of Antioch (in Syria) and Alexandria (in Egypt) to Muslim conquerors—the three most wealthy and powerful cities of the empire—made Constantinople the only imperial center to be retained by the eastern so-called Roman authorities. The first of these cities to be separated from the empire was Rome, which came to be governed by its bishop (the so-called pope) in the sixth century. Although Rome remained nominally connected to the imperial center of the Roman Empire after the rest of central and northern Italy had been taken over by the Lombards in 600, it broke away completely with the creation of the Frankish king Charlemagne as Christian Emperor of the West in 800.

Between 500 and 800, Constantinople and the eastern Roman Empire underwent radical changes in culture, population, and geographical extent. Although the eastern half of the empire was ruled separately from the western half beginning in the late fourth century, it was still connected to Rome linguistically and culturally. The official language of the Roman administration was Latin, even though the majority of the population in the east were native speakers of Greek and a number of different Semitic dialects (such as Coptic, Syriac, and Hebrew). A separate Senate was established in Constantinople by Constantine, made up of Roman families who emigrated to the new imperial city. Eventually, quite a few Roman families, as well as prominent groups from other major imperial cities, moved to Constantinople so that its elite class—the Patricians—soon rivaled that in the ancient city of Rome itself.

Constantine's sons and grandsons continued to focus on the eastern half of the empire, even to the point of separating the empire into two halves for administrative purposes. By the third quarter of the fourth century, however, Constantine's dynasty was defunct, replaced by a far more energetic dynasty begun by Emperor Theodosius I (r. 379–395) that survived until 450. The Theodosian dynasty is notable for its energy in retaining control over the entire empire and holding off the Germanic advance into the western Mediterranean by a combination of military brilliance and canny diplomacy. This unity was shattered soon after the death of Theodosius II in 450: between 450 and 500 the western empire ceased to exist. It was divided eventually by its Germanic conquerors into small independent kingdoms, each headed by a Germanic dynasty (this is discussed in chapter 2). Rome still retained a loose connection to the emperor in Constantinople, but Gaul, Britain, and Spain were lost to Roman dominance forever.

Historians consider the transitional period between late Roman and Byzantine to have occurred during the sixth-century reign of the Emperor Justinian (r. 527–565) and his co-ruler, Empress Theodora. Justinian was born and raised in the easternmost outpost of the western empire, the Balkans region between Italy and Hungary. Although he spoke Latin, his entire military and political career was based in the Greek-speaking Eastern Empire, where he succeeded his uncle, Justin, to the imperial throne of Constantinople. The western Empire had long before broken up into separate Germanic kingdoms, with North Africa ruled by Vandals, and Ostrogoths led by King Theodoric in Italy. Justinian was not interested in recovering the majority of western territory, but he wanted to control the Mediterranean, so he pursued a re-conquest of both North Africa and Italy. The former was accomplished within five years, and the region was ruled from Carthage until the Muslim conquests of the next century. Italy, however, was a much harder nut to crack: the destruction of the Ostrogothic kingdom took 20 years and much of Italy was ultimately abandoned by the eastern emperor, including the city of Rome. Despite his best efforts, Justinian was able to retain only the southernmost portion of Italy (Calabria and Abruzzi), Sicily, and the eastern city of Ravenna as imperial territory. Ravenna itself, and with it, all of Italy north of the city of Taranto, was more or less lost a mere six years later with the successful conquest of the Lombards, who ruled as kings in the north and as dukes and princes in the regions between Rome and Calabria.

By 600, the eastern Roman Empire was a very different place than when Constantine celebrated the founding of his imperial city. Large portions of the southern Mediterranean territory had been conquered by a newly resurgent Sassanid Persian empire; the cities of Antioch, Alexandria, and Jerusalem were in Persian hands, although Christianity was tolerated in those regions. The eastern Empire was ruled by Greek-speaking emperors living in the Greek city of Constantinople. The imperial administration was also conducted in Greek and the culture of the administration was increasingly influenced by Persian culture. Eunuchs (castrated males) ran the administration and even oversaw the army. Emperors demanded that all supplicants perform obeisance, called prostration, and they characterized themselves as semi-divine representatives of God on earth. The Senate, even in its impotent imperial form, ceased to exist entirely, and the Emperor ruled over both the church and the state. Although the Persian conquerors were eventually routed and the cities in the southern Mediterranean recovered by the Emperor Heraclitus (r. 610–641), Slavic and Hunnic invasions into the northern portions of the empire and the Muslim conquest of the southern Mediterranean ultimately shrank the borders of the Byzantine Empire to Greece, the Greek islands, and western Anatolia, with independent Christian kingdoms in Armenia and Pontus. This Byzantine Empire would continue to exist, sometimes shrinking, sometimes growing, until 1453.

Religion in the Byzantine Empire

The Emperor Constantine I (r. 306–337) is best known for an act that initially had very few repercussions: the legalization of Christianity in the Edict of Milan in 313. Constantine himself could be called at best only a nominal Christian, although his mother Helen was a devout believer and he allowed all his children to be baptized in their youth. Constantine himself was baptized only on his deathbed. Even though he promoted Christianity, had significant connections to professionals in the church, and presided over the first ecumenical council of the universal (in Greek, *katholicos*, hence the term "Catholic") Church at Nicaea, it is likely that his religious zeal was considerably less evident than the picture presented of him by the fourth-century historian of the church, Eusebius of Caesarea.

Constantine might have been the first emperor to legalize and promote Christianity, but the traditional religious centers of Antioch and Alexandria and the secondary centers of Rome and Jerusalem were far more important to the development of the church than the patriarchate diocese (major bishops are known as Patriarchs in the Orthodox Church) established in his namesake city. Nevertheless, Christianity was promoted in Constantinople and the traditional Roman imperial cult was minimized. This led Emperor Theodosius I ultimately to make Christianity the only legally sanctioned religion in the empire in 395.

Christianity was fundamentally a Greek-speaking religion from its very beginning. The original biblical texts were written in Greek, the religion originated in the Greek-speaking cities of the southern Mediterranean, and the structures of the church were invented there as well. The church of Rome and the use of Latin were both afterthoughts in the religion for centuries. Indeed, only with the final separation of the eastern and western empires did the Roman church come to attain a separate and independent existence. The dominance of the Greek language in Christianity in its first three centuries might have contributed to the ultimate dominance of Greek as the language of the Byzantine Empire.

Christianity developed differently in the eastern Roman and Byzantine Empires than it did in the West. Since the sacred texts were written in the vernacular language of most of the inhabitants—Greek—anyone who had achieved basic literacy could read them. In the west, Latin-speakers did not have access to an accurate translation of the Bible until St. Jerome's *Vulgate,* or the Authorized (by the Bishop of Rome) Version, was completed in 405. By this time, literacy in Latin was confined to the Mediterranean region. Within a hundred years, the Germanic invasion and settlement from Roman Britain to Spain would succeed in replacing Latin with Germanic-Latin hybrids that would eventually develop into the Romance languages of Spanish, Italian, and French and the Germanic languages of Old English, Dutch, Flemish, and German. Latin became a professional language used by the clergy and legal professionals and not by the common people. Thus, most people in western Europe, unlike Byzantine Christians, were unable to understand even the prayers they were taught to recite.

The eastern Roman Empire and its successor, the Byzantine Empire, were also more urbanized and more densely populated than the western provinces. Christianity originated in an urban setting and thrived in the eastern and southern cities. As a result, the Byzantine church was far more intellectually focused, with almost all the great theologians of the religion coming from Byzantine cities: Gregory of Nazianus, Athanasius of Alexandria, St. John Chrysostom, and Origen being only a few who influenced the development of Christian theology enormously.

Byzantine Christianity was also somewhat more authoritarian and imperial than Roman Christianity, which was at least at first a more flexible system because of the need to Christianize and incorporate so many groups with few ties to Rome and Roman culture. The Patriarch of Constantinople was in theory the head of the Byzantine Church, but it became more or less a branch of the imperial government from the days of Constantine to the end of the Byzantine period. The emperors acted as patrons of the church and the elaborate decoration of Christian churches and the growth of equally elaborate ritual in the Byzantine liturgy came to mimic the grandiose decoration and elaborate pomp of the Byzantine imperial court.

Individual Christians were more intimately involved in the theological disputes that rocked the early centuries of Byzantine Christianity. Arguments about the nature of Christ and the Trinity became the stuff of marketplace debates. This had an impact on family life since theological conflicts could tear family unity apart. When Iconoclasm (literally, the destruction of religious images) was promoted as orthodox doctrine in the east in the eighth and ninth centuries, the controversy not only drove the eastern and western churches apart, but also affected families profoundly. Most rural Byzantine Christians were devoted to the idea of the sanctity of icons, but the more educated urban population—and people who had come into contact with Islam, which was highly critical of the use of images in Christian worship—rejected them. The ultimate failure of Iconoclasm as a religious doctrine, while it reunited families separated by their allegiance to or rejection of icons, did not help the conflict between Christian authorities in Rome and Constantinople. Ultimately, the religious controversies of Byzantine Christianity were resolved in ways that further separated the east from the west.

Sources for the History of the Byzantine Family

Historians actually know very little about the organization of Byzantine families below the level of the high aristocracy, although information about the urban elite family is growing. One problem is the survival—or lack of survival—of Byzantine records and texts. The many invasions, conquests, and internal conflicts that occurred in Byzantine territory between 500 and 1500 (including the Crusades) resulted in the wholesale destruction of much of its material culture. The libraries of Alexandria and Constantinople were destroyed several times, and the archives in Antioch, Damascus in Syria, and Baghdad (the last two centers of Muslim cultural production) also burned a number of times. The long Ottoman occupation of Greece and the Balkans as well as of Mesopotamia, which ended in Greece in the 1820s and elsewhere only in the twentieth century, resulted in the disappearance and destruction of administrative, legal, and literary records from the Byzantine period. In addition, the relatively recent breakup of the Ottoman Empire and the lack of interest in Byzantine social history until very recently both have worked against attempts to recover the records of medieval Byzantine families. The loss of these irretrievable artifacts from a culture that was profoundly literate and that relied fundamentally on written records hampers our understanding of many aspects of Byzantine culture and society. Most of the records that do exist today come from the religious culture or from the imperial administration, preserved at times through its adoption by the Ottomans after 1453. There is not a lot about common people or common family issues in these kinds of records.

Historians of the last twenty years have begun to fill in the blanks in the social history of the Byzantine Empire but their revelations are based on sources that do not necessarily present a view of daily reality. Rather, social historians have been basing their conclusions on sermons by important Byzantine theologians, histories of the imperial families written by court historians, and legal treatises interpreting Byzantine law. While all of these sources are valuable, they rarely give the reader a picture of the way people lived in the Byzantine Empire; instead they provide information on the ways in which authorities thought Byzantine people ought to behave. There is also a tremendous amount of material available about the families of imperial dynasties that has been mined effectively. Unfortunately, the emperor's family bore little resemblance to that of the common peasant farmer or urban laborer. Byzantine art is probably the most well-documented aspect of the culture of the empire, but since the overwhelming majority of Byzantine images are religious in nature, this also works against understanding the family: the Holy Family is scarcely an appropriate model, especially given the sacred nature of Byzantine iconography. Nevertheless, certain elements of the Byzantine family can be discussed in some detail, especially when legal and religious issues are included.

Byzantine Legal Culture and the Byzantine Family

Unlike the western European Germanic kingdoms, the Byzantine Empire was thoroughly imbued with both ancient pre-Christian and Christian culture. The Byzantine Empire's legal system dated back to the original Roman Laws of the Twelve Tables and continued through every imperial reign's additions and alterations. In addition, the intersections between religion and politics were also embedded into the legal system so that it became difficult to separate canon (i.e., religious) from civil law in the way they were separated in the west. When the emperor Justinian commissioned the collection and codification of all Roman law into one massive encyclopedic source, this was the first time in over a thousand years of Roman legal practice that such a task had been attempted. This is fortunate for the historian of family life, because without the *Corpus Iuris Civilis*—the *Body of Roman Civil Law*—we would have little substantive information on the ideals of family land and the way those ideals changed over time.

If you were to look up the words "marriage" and "family" in a modern translation of the Byzantine-era *Corpus iuris civilis,* you would discover that Byzantine jurists were still debating the power of the paterfamilias over adult children, over marriage, and over the Byzantine family.[1] Nevertheless, the Roman notion of the paterfamilias had been abandoned, replaced by a more Greek paternal system in which daughters remained under the authority of their male relatives but sons were emancipated (given their freedom to act independently) at the age of majority. The family, too, was constructed more along traditional Greek lines than Roman ones: nuclear families, even though they acknowledged a relationship to more extended kin were the norm rather than the extended family groups found in traditional Roman and Germanic practice. Thus, although the basic outlines of the Byzantine family remained largely untouched by this massive legal system, the issues surrounding betrothal and marriage, inheritance, and legitimacy or illegitimacy certainly were affected significantly by the body of Byzantine law that developed from the Roman period until the end of the Byzantine Empire.

Marriage in Byzantine society was a highly formalized system with legal foundations in both Roman and Greek law. Marriages were arranged by either the parents of the potential couple, the parents of the bride-to-be and the groom-to-be (if he was already an adult), or some combination of these people along with a professional matchmaker. A marriage contract was negotiated, which included stipulations as to the dowry of the bride, the marriage gift the groom intended to give to his bride, the portions of the family property that would be granted to the surviving spouse, and identifications of guardians for the children should the husband die before his wife and the wife not automatically get guardianship. These arrangements were often made in writing and followed the legal practice set out in the Byzantine civil code known as the Eclogues, which stipulated that three witnesses were required for the marriage contract to be considered valid.

One of the eclogues of eighth-century Emperor Leo III, dated 726, provides an example of how marriage in early medieval Byzantine culture ought to proceed. The law states that the "years of discretion" (that is, the age of adulthood for the purpose of marriage) for men is 15 and for women is 13. This was seen as the minimum age of marriage at the time, although this changed fairly dramatically as the centuries progressed. Consent of both parties and of the parents was required: "both being desirous and having obtained the consent of their parents, shall be contracted." The contract was to be in writing, made before "three credible witnesses according to the new decrees auspiciously prescribed by us [by Leo]." Elaborate arrangements regarding property are to be written into the contract. Finally, if the husband dies before his wife, and there are children, "the wife being their mother, she shall control her marriage portion and all her husband's property as becomes the head of the family and household."[2]

The legal contract was the culmination of marriage negotiations and was probably more important than the ceremony itself, although among people of lower socio-economic status, the celebration of a marriage and its contractual arrangements could easily have occurred more or less at the same time. Once contracted, the marriage was considered more or less permanent, although divorce was not unheard-of in the Byzantine period. Indeed, it is possible that divorce became more easy to accomplish over the years, with the imperial family in particular being able to manipulate their marriage strategies in order to try to guarantee the production of a male heir. This activity was probably condemned strongly by the religious authorities at all times, so the option of divorce was likely to have been less available to couples belonging to social levels below the imperial family.

Byzantine law, like western Christian canon law, eventually developed strict regulations about marrying close kin. Before the eleventh century, endogamy—the marriage of people related to each other—was common, especially among the aristocracy. This form of marriage was also very common not only in the ancient world and the Roman Empire, but among all the medieval cultures, especially in the early Middle Ages. The preservation of family property when legal systems mandated its division among various heirs usually spurred people to practice endogamy. Marriage between cousins and even uncles and nieces guaranteed that the bulk of the property would remain undivided. Beginning in the eleventh century, however, the Byzantine church began to expand the condemnation of marriage between close kin to a larger number of relations, much as had occurred in the west at an earlier time. Like western European society, this push against what were termed consanguineous marriages (that is, marriage between people who share blood ties) was resisted strenuously by the aristocracy and imperial families in particular. According to the historian Angeliki Laiou, the process of enforcing church rules against consanguineous marriages took more than two hundred years to succeed.[3]

Once the marriage had taken place, Byzantine law also regulated the lives of family members to some degree. Roman law had been wary of the idea of spouses being able to give each other gifts; this was not so much the case in Byzantine law, but marital property still fundamentally belonged to the paterfamilias. The husband, nevertheless, was required to keep his wife's dowry intact; he was also supposed to ensure that the widow's portion represented a full quarter of the estate, should he die before her. Women whose property had been lost or frittered away by their husbands had few recourses while they were married, however. They were not able to sue their husbands in court, for instance. If widowed, though, women could seek recovery of their property from their late husband's family. How effective this might have been, on the other hand, is unknown: if the family happened to be impoverished by bad business deals or financial mismanagement, recovering even a quarter of the estate must have been nearly impossible.

The laws regarding inheritance and guardianship of minor children were quite complicated as well. Byzantine Greeks followed Roman law in encouraging the writing of wills that specifically delineated bequests to specific people. Unlike Roman law, however, wives could make wills without requiring the permission of their husbands. This was because Byzantine law gave women more or less full control of their dowries, even though they probably could not exercise that control while their husbands were alive, except in the writing of their wills. Once widowed, however, a woman gained control of at least a quarter of her husband's estate as well as of her dowry. If the couple had had children who were still minors at the time of their father's death, then the widow usually became the guardian over both her children and the entirety of the estate. If a woman died before her husband, then he was obligated to fulfill the bequests in her will, or to disperse her dowry to her next of kin if there were no children. He was, however, able to retain a quarter of anything she brought to the marriage.

Byzantine law also followed late Roman imperial law in that all children in a family could expect to inherit something from their parents, but the bulk of the estate still would go to the eldest son or, in the absence of sons, daughter. Daughters received dowries from the parents' property, but this likely represented only a small part of the estate if they had brothers. Illegitimate children were expressly forbidden from inheriting property, but it is not clear how significant this legal prohibition was. The presence of illegitimate children must have been fairly common in Byzantine society, but there are few sources that even mention them. In addition, the Roman laws of adoption, which made it possible to adopt a child as one's heir, could have worked against the stigma of illegitimacy.

The Structure of the Byzantine Family

At the center of the Byzantine family was the father. He did not have the kind of absolute authority over the other members of the household that the early Roman paterfamilias enjoyed, but paternal authority was comprehensive: the father ruled the household. The wife of the male head of household was also an important figure in the family, but one with significantly less public power and virtually no public persona. As in the ancient world, wives oversaw the maintenance of the house, a task which could include the requirement to be able to read at the very least. Wives had no legal personality in that they could not engage in business, buy or sell land independently, or invest family funds without their husbands acting for them. Nevertheless, some women did engage in business, although they were not members of the elite, and imperial women had many more opportunities for wielding political influence than women of other social classes. According to religious sources, such as theologians' treatises on the ideal wife, elite wives were supposed to be physically restricted as well and discouraged from being seen in public. When they did go out, they were expected to be veiled more or less from head to toe (possibly one of the origins of the Muslim burka, as well) and accompanied by a man. Women of less exalted status did not have the luxury of maintaining this façade of respectable womanly behavior, however, and they might have suffered a loss of status and respect as a result. On the other hand, sources for the imperial family, where women played significant political roles, rarely describe empresses and other imperial women as being confined to women's quarters, or *gynekaia,* or of being completely veiled.

Different political situations might have affected the segregation and isolation of women in Byzantine culture. When the Fourth Crusade of 1204 resulted in the conquest of Constantinople and the rest of Greece by western European crusaders from France and Italy, western customs, which advocated less restrictive practices for women, might have moderated the stricter practices of previous decades. In addition, by mining different kinds of sources—not just the religious tracts that proclaim the ideals the religious community hoped to encourage among the lay population—historians have recently produced a somewhat different picture of the lives especially of women in the Byzantine world. In these newer views, Byzantine women were more visible in the public venues of the marketplace and the dining room and might even have abandoned their veils when among people with whom they were related even in public.[4]

Families were often extended, especially in the countryside. Multiple generations likely lived together and sustained the family both economically and socially. This is still the case today in Greece; historians suspect that the social structure of the modern-day countryside might not be all that different from that of the medieval past. Although the nuclear family was probably more the norm in urban areas, where cramped houses restricted the number of people who could be comfortably maintained, rural communities probably relied heavily on extended family for both livelihood and maintenance.

The ages at marriage of Byzantine brides and grooms probably depended on social status even though the legal ages at marriage would have been theoretically the same no matter what social level the potential couple enjoyed. Elites probably married earlier and people of lower social status might have had to delay marriage for economic reasons—a pattern that exists in the west for the same period, thus making it possible that this occurred in the east as well. As mentioned earlier, eighth-century laws regulating marriage suggested that the minimum age should be 13 for girls and 15 for boys; by the twelfth century this had changed only a little: among elites, the age considered ideal for marriage for women was 12 to 15 and for men around 20. Nevertheless, the relative ages of husbands and wives could be extreme. For example, Emperor Andronicus I Komnenos (r. 1183–1185) was 65 when he married Princess Agnes of France, who had just turned 12. Although chroniclers such as Nicetas Choniates ridiculed the emperor for this marriage, extreme differences in age were not all that unusual among Byzantine elites, especially when widowers remarried. Men persisted in preferring adolescent virgins as their brides.[5] This radical division in age must have made communication and companionship difficult. Since marriages among elites were usually arranged with the help of professional matchmakers, it was likely that the newlyweds were more or less strangers, so developing a relationship in which both parties were equal was probably impossible to achieve except in very unusual cases.

Girls married in their mid-teens were expected to produce large families. Since infant mortality rates were quite high throughout the medieval world, this did not necessarily mean that families ultimately were very

large, but certainly most women must have experienced multiple pregnancies starting at a very young age. Children in Byzantine families were
raised largely by their mothers, at least until about the age of 12, when
girls would be prepared for marriage and boys would begin their public
education. The female rooms in the home were also the nursery and the
workroom for the female members of the household. There is little material evidence that discusses the issue of blended families, half-siblings, or
step-siblings except with regard to the imperial family, where competition among potential heirs could be fierce. Women whose husbands died
were actively discouraged from remarrying by the religious culture, as
were men whose wives had died, but the social and economic realities
of the Byzantine world probably made remarriage an attractive prospect
for both widows and widowers. Therefore, it is possible that households
could contain a fair number of half-siblings. Evidence as to how they
interacted, however, is lacking.

Stories about the imperial family suggest that the extreme age difference that often occurred between husbands and wives could mean that
mothers related more to their children than to their children's fathers.
Indeed, the eldest child could easily have been closer in age to his or her
mother than the mother to the child's father. In histories of the emperors,
this situation sometimes played out as competition between the Dowager
Empress and her young emperor son. In other circumstances, this could
have encouraged cooperation between mother and son, perhaps even
against the emperor-husband-father.

The Byzantine imperial dynasty of the Komnenoi can provide an
example of the ways in which the imperial family could operate both
as an efficient and cooperative unit and as a backbiting and competi-
tive power struggle. When Alexios II Komnenos (r. 1081–1118) became
emperor, it was the result of a combined effort of both his natal family,
including his formidable mother, Anna Dalassena, and that of his wife,
Irene Doukaina, a member of the powerful Doukas family. Alexios's long
reign was marked by significant political and military upheaval, evidenced by his probably inadvertent initiating of the First Crusade. He was
devoted to his mother, whom he crowned as *Augusta* rather than his wife,
a move that did not endear him to her or to her Doukas relations. Anna
Dalassena was, however, a supremely competent politician who juggled
both acting as regent when Alexios was away from Constantinople and
as grandmother to Alexios's children, in particular his talented daughter,
Anna. Court intrigues between Irene Doukaina and her mother-in-law
led to further intrigues against Alexios's chosen successor, his son John II
Komnenos, creating more instability at the end of the reign.

Anna Komnene, Alexios's eldest daughter, became the court historian
of her father's reign. She was raised by her grandmother, Anna Dalassena,
and her description of her grandmother suggests that the elder Anna was
a truly remarkable woman.

One might perhaps . . . blame my father's decision to entrust imperial government to the gyneceum [the women's quarters in the house]. But once you understood the ability of this woman, her excellence, her good sense, and her remarkable capacity for hard work, you would turn from criticism to admiration. For my grandmother really had the gift of conducting the affairs of state. She knew so well how to organize and administer that she was capable of governing not only the Roman Empire but also every other kingdom.[6]

Anna's admiration for her grandmother and father, however, did not stop her from plotting with her mother to remove her own brother from the imperial throne and replace him with her own husband, Nikephoros Bryennios. Thus, the Komnenoi, although they were a tight-knit family who had to depend on each other in order to succeed, still fell apart when competition and conflict pulled the individual family members apart.

Conclusion

The historical sources for the Byzantine Empire focus virtually all attention on the highest levels of society: the imperial dynasties and the aristocracy. This makes uncovering the typical Byzantine family very difficult, indeed. Nevertheless, certain general conclusions can be made. Byzantine ideals about marriage and family, based on legal and religious sources, expected individuals to be married quite young, especially women, and to be married only once. Families were expected to be large and husbands and wives were supposed to come from different lineages. Extended family relationships were ideally encouraged with respect to cooperation among family members, but discouraged with respect to intermarriage between them.

The reality of Byzantine experience seems to have been far from the ideal, especially if one looks primarily at the ways in which the imperial family operated. Marriage between close kin, although condemned by the church, was vital to the maintenance of family property, as well as of its political power and authority. The age difference between husbands and wives could be enormous, especially when men remarried two or three times. Extended family relationships could be fraught with strife as siblings and cousins competed, sometimes violently, for political and economic advantage. The intrigues of the Byzantine imperial court encouraged all of the elites to behave like the imperial family. The possibility of supplanting the emperor and replacing one dynasty with another was very real.

Below the level of the aristocracy, the view of the Byzantine family becomes very hazy, indeed. The kinds of sources available to historians of western Europe simply do not exist for the Byzantine east. As a result, a picture of the common Byzantine family must remain speculative. Historians assume that peasant family structures that existed in Greece during and immediately after the Ottoman period (from 1453 to Greek independence in 1832) probably resembled those that existed in the Byzantine period. Early modern Greek peasant families lived in large extended family systems in order to maximize their economic viability. There is some evidence that medieval peasant families in the Byzantine Empire could be tied to the land, much like western peasants were, especially if they lived on and worked on aristocratic estates. This situation probably did not alter the fundamental reality that all peasant families faced: that survival depended on cooperation on both a family and a community level.

Since peasant culture tends to be both conservative and fairly similar from place to place, the experiences of medieval peasants in the west, which are better documented, might also be able to inform the picture of the Byzantine peasant. If that is the case, then Byzantine peasant families, like their western counterparts, probably married at somewhat older ages than did members of the upper classes. They probably had fewer children both because of decreased fertility and high infant and child mortality. Finally, they probably shared living space with multiple generations if grandparents were lucky enough to survive, but were more likely to live with siblings and their spouses and children in order to prevent precious land from being divided.

The family life of non-elites in Byzantine cities is equally difficult to uncover. It is likely that the wealthiest members of the urban middle class mimicked the elites in their marriage patterns, living arrangements, and production of children. Poorer urban families were more likely to resemble rural families in their structure and survival strategies. One difference is the likelihood that urban families tended to be nuclear, since living space was quite limited and cramped and this would have discouraged multiple generations from living together.

Despite the lack of sources, it can be stated that Byzantine families, like families throughout the rest of the medieval world, operated as intimate partnerships, Their very survival depended on cooperation. This could be a difficult task for young or newly married couples to accomplish, since if they were not related to each other by blood, they were probably strangers at the time of their wedding. Nevertheless, successful families learned how to work together and prosper.

Notes

    1. The standard text in English is S.P. Scott, ed. and trans. *The Civil Law Including The Twelve Tables, The Institutes of Gaius, The Rules of Ulpian, The Opinions of Paulus, The Enactments of Justinian, and The Constitutions of Leo: in Seventeen Volumes* (Cincinnati: The Central Trust Company Publishers, 1932; Reprint, New York: AMS Press, 1973).

    2. E. Freshfield, trans., *A Manual of Roman Law: The 'Ecloga'* (Cambridge, 1926), 72–74 and reprinted in Deno John Geanokoplos, *Byzantium: Church, Society,*

and Civilization Seen Through Contemporary Eyes (Chicago: University of Chicago Press, 1984), 266–267. It is also found at the *Internet Medieval Sourcebook,* http:// www.fordham.edu/halsall/source/byz-marr726.html.

3. Angeliki E. Laiou, *Mariage, amour et parenté à Byzance aux XIe-XIIIe siècles* (Paris: De Boccard, 1992), 21.

4. This is discussed by Alexander P. Kazhdan, "Women at Home," *Dumbarton Oaks Papers* 52 (1998): 147.

5. Laiou, *Mariage, amour et parenté,* 96–97.

6. Anna Comnena, *Alexiad,* "Anna Comnena Commenting on Her Grandmother," in *Women in World History Curriculum,* http://www.womeninworldhistory. com/dalassena.html. Although the modern spelling of Greek names in the Roman alphabet uses spelling that more accurately reflects the original Greek, many texts still use a Latinized form of Greek names. Thus, Komnene becomes Comnena in some texts.

4

The Family in the Islamic World

The Arabs who occupied the enormous Arabian Peninsula between the Mediterranean Sea and the Persian Gulf had done so for millennia. They were the Semitic neighbors of the ancient peoples of Mesopotamia (the area between the Tigris and Euphrates rivers—now Iraq and the Persian Gulf nations) and were related to the Hebrews, Syrians, Phoenicians, and Babylonians who succeeded the ancient Sumerians and Akkadians in the region. Some Semitic communities were absorbed into the Hellenistic and Roman empires but the Bedouin culture—nomadic tribal communities who operated the caravan trades across the desert between the Jordan River and the Tigris—was never conquered by either Alexander the Great or Augustus. As a result, the Bedouins did not absorb either Greco-Roman polytheism or Judeo-Christian monotheism in significant ways, despite living side by side with these two religious systems that dominated the Mediterranean region. Indeed, the animist and tribal-based religious system that had long been part of Arab culture persisted well after Christianity came to rule over all other religious systems in the eastern half of the Roman Empire.

In the seventh century, when the prophet Muhammad, at age 40, began to believe that God was speaking to him, Arab Bedouin culture was changing rapidly. The formerly migratory Bedouin were becoming acclimated to urban life once the cities of Mecca and Medina (both now in modern-day Saudi Arabia) became centers of the caravan trade. Both were international cities with substantial Christian and Jewish populations who established trading posts there to bring goods from the Persian Gulf and India into the Byzantine and North African Christian empires and kingdoms. Muhammad was profoundly influenced by both Judaism and Christianity: although he had probably never read the Bible, his visions incorporated biblical imagery and stories and these were compiled after his death into the collection of prophetic visions known as the Quran. In addition, Arab culture's centuries-long contact with Roman, Hellenistic, and Greek civilization had imbued those geographical areas where most of the contact occurred with a hybrid culture that incorporated elements from all of the dominant societies in the Mediterranean, Arabian, and Mesopotamian regions.

After Muhammad's death, his successors (called caliphs, that is, literally successors of the prophet) embarked on a rapid military expansion and conquest of the southern portions of the Byzantine Empire. By the year 750, the Islamic world encompassed the entire southern Mediterranean, portions of the Iberian peninsula (modern-day Spain), the Arabian peninsula, Mesopotamia, most of the Persian Empire (including modern-day Iran, Afghanistan, and parts of central Asia), and nearly the whole of North Africa. This does not mean that all of the people living in those regions (most of whom were Christians) converted to Islam. Indeed, at first only people of Arab descent were considered appropriate candidates to convert to Islam. As a result, Muslim rulers governed over overwhelmingly non-Muslim populations and local customs and traditions entered into Islamic religious and social culture as a direct result. When the first dynasty of caliphs, the Umayyads, established their political center at Damascus, in Syria, they created an international and cosmopolitan center of Mediterranean culture that incorporated everything from Greek, Roman, and Byzantine law, philosophy, and science to Judaic and Christian theology into an Islamic-focused civilization. They also established a separate caliphate in Cordoba, Spain, in the process of conquering the Iberian peninsula, which became the Islamic state of al-Andalus. The Umayyads were followed, around 750, by a second caliphate, the Abbasids, who moved their capital from Damascus (which remained the most important intellectual center of the Islamic world) to a new city, Baghdad, in the ancient center of Semitic civilization, Mesopotamia (modern-day Iraq), in order to reflect the growing importance of Iranian/Persian culture to the development of Islam. The period between 800 and 1000 was a high point in Islamic intellectual culture. The court of the most famous Abbasid caliph, Haroun al-Rashid, was the most brilliant in the medieval world, outclassing both the Byzantine imperial court of its day and that of the Carolingian emperors in the west. After the reign of Haroun, however, the Abbasid caliphate went into a slow decline. Although the caliphs continued to sit on the throne in Baghdad until 1258, when a descendent of Ghenghis Khan, Hulagu Khan, sacked Baghdad, governance of their empire had been assumed by Turkish amirs, the Mamluks, who had been introduced into the Arab world soon after they converted to Islam. Around 1000, other Turkic groups, such as the Seljuks, also invaded the Abbasid Empire, and established themselves as sultans of largely independent states throughout Anatolia (modern-day Turkey) as well as a substantial portion of Persia and into central Asia. They transformed the ruling class, which had been ethnically Arab and Semite, into a predominantly Turkish one. Further Seljuk incursions in the eleventh century resulted in a series of Turkish-dominated Islamic states that stretched from Palestine in the west to Persia and Afghanistan in the east, nearly to their border with medieval India. Although the Seljuks acknowledged the hegemony of the Abbasid caliph in Baghdad, in fact the caliphs were mere puppets, never to hold the actual reins of power again.

Thus, the Islamic world in the Middle Ages was phenomenally diverse, encompassing a multitude of ethnic, cultural, and religious identities. The progression of the religion, after its first flowering among ethnic Arabs, was relatively slow, however. Areas that had close associations with the Byzantine Empire, such as Anatolia and northern Syria, retained Greek Orthodox Christianity as their dominant religion for many decades. Christians and Jews mixed with Muslim converts throughout the Islamic world. When the western Crusades launched western European-style kingdoms and principalities in the midst of the Islamic Middle East, Catholic Christians were included in the mix of religions and cultures. Even though the crusades ultimately failed to establish a permanent western-style state in the Holy Land, the presence of the Crusaders for two hundred years probably delayed the complete Islamicization of the southern and eastern Mediterranean region. Although most of the populations eventually converted to Islam, this process took hundreds of years.

The Religion of Islam

The Arabic word *Islam* means "submission to God," and a *Muslim* is "someone who submits." As Muhammad seems to have conceived it, Islam is an outwardly simple faith. It is strictly monotheistic and believers are required to adhere only to five basic precepts, called The Five Pillars of Faith: to believe that "there is no god except God and Muhammad is his Prophet;" to pray five times a day; to tithe 10 percent of one's annual income for the maintenance of the poor and needy; to fast during the holy month of Ramadan; and to make a pilgrimage (*Hajj* in Arabic) to Mecca to worship at the *Kaaba* at least once in the believer's lifetime. In reality, however, Islam is a more complex system that involves both universal elements derived from the religion's sacred texts, the Quran and the Hadith (a collection of sayings and statements/interpretations of the Prophet, his family, and his successors), and cultural elements from the regions where Islam spread.

Islam, in the years following Muhammad's death, became an all-encompassing way of life, in the same way that Judaism and Christianity incorporated their own specific religious perspectives into every aspect of the life of the community of believers. Islamic law, known as *sharia*, regulated the lives of Muslims, known as the *umma*, the community of believers. Just as Judaic and Christian laws include extensive definitions of and regulations for family, so do Islamic laws, many of which owe a debt to the legal systems of the Hebrew Holy Scriptures found in the books of Leviticus and Deuteronomy.

The Status of Women and the Structure of the Family

Although modern-day Muslim culture is often viewed in the west as socially backward, especially with respect to the status of women, most historians believe that Muhammad was in fact determined to modernize (at least from a seventh-century perspective) Arab culture, to improve the status of women, and to pull the Arabian peninsula's population into the larger Mediterranean cosmopolitan community. Although this seems to have been the case with respect to the Bedouin culture that dominated the deserts of the central Arabian peninsula, some historians are re-evaluating the impact of Muhammad's agenda on the urban centers of Mecca and Medina, where Bedouin traditions had been supplanted by social systems influenced more by Byzantine culture and by the frontier nature of the new and burgeoning urban landscape.

According to the traditional view, women in Bedouin and Arab culture were legal non-persons who were considered the absolute property of their fathers. Fathers could demand that girl babies be killed outright; they also sold their daughters to other men as wives and sexual partners. Daughters had no rights of inheritance and lived at the whim of their male relations. Muhammad declared that women could be full-fledged members of the Islamic community, the *umma*. He mandated, according to the Quran, that women could own property, could inherit land from their fathers, and could not be sold in marriage. He also is said to have declared that girl babies could not be killed on the command of their fathers.

While it is likely that Bedouin culture did treat females as wholly inferior to males in most cases, historians have begun to question the characterization of pre-Islamic Arab culture as totally backward. For instance, elements of Muhammad's own biography contradict the traditional view. His first wife, Khadija, was a wealthy widow who was running a business in Mecca when she hired Muhammad as her overseer. She was considerably older than he when she proposed that they marry. Khadija was very active in the spread of Islam: she was one of the first converts to the new religion. Moreover, although Muhammad permitted polygyny (one man married to several women) and eventually married 11 women, he did not do so until after Khadija died. Clearly, some women in pre-Islamic Arabia exercised considerable personal autonomy.

In addition, there were fairly significant populations of Jews and Christians living in Arabia and Syria at the time of Muhammad's expansion of Islam. These became targets for proselytizing and it is possible that the status of women in these communities declined when their families converted to Islam. Certainly they were owners of property, were able to inherit property from their parents, and were active in their communities before the coming of Islam.

Finally, the much-debated issue of the confinement, segregation, and veiling of women in Islam is a subject of significant controversy. There is some evidence that aristocratic women throughout the Mediterranean and even the medieval west did cover their heads and possibly their faces, too, when they appeared in public. This was a holdover from ancient Greek and Roman practice, possibly emphasized by St. Paul when he stipulated that women must cover their heads in church "on account of the angels."[1] There is also evidence that many women were not veiled, especially those who worked in public. The wives of Muhammad, with the possible exception of 'Aisha, his favorite, did not apparently wear veils of any kind. Veils could be thought of as actually alluring in Byzantine culture, since they were usually transparent. Therefore, it is not clear in any way where the practice of veiling in various degrees, from simply covering the head to the full burka, came from in Islam. These practices are likely to have been cultural overlays with little to do with Quranic texts or Hadith interpretations of them.[2]

The status of women before and after the establishment of Islam is this still a matter of debate. What is relatively clear, however, is that the religion absorbed many different cultural perspectives from its inception and long after. This might be particularly true in the case of family structures. The polygyny that was apparently common to Bedouin society met the strict monogamy of Byzantine Christian culture in all the regions conquered by the armies of Islam. The result was probably a hybrid of both traditions.

Indeed, the influence of Byzantine culture on Islam was significant once the successors to Muhammad (the caliphs) began to expand Arab influence into the southern Mediterranean portions of the Byzantine Empire and ultimately conquered the empire of the Sassanid Persians, the Byzantine states of Syria and Egypt, large portions of Byzantine Anatolia, North Africa, and Spain. Since the Muslim population in those conquered territories was miniscule in comparison to the Christian populations, at least for the first few hundred or so years of Islam's existence, and since *shari'a* was specific only to Muslims, many different legal traditions co-existed in areas of Islamic political dominance. Nevertheless, family traditions intermingled and altered the social landscape for Muslims and non-Muslims alike in those areas. Islam was a flexible and adaptable system throughout the Middle Ages and some historians have viewed it in many ways as more enlightened than either Christianity or Judaism during that period.

Certainly the legal definition of family was more broadly conceived than the more rigid systems present in Western Europe and the Byzantine Empire. Many different gradations of family organization, ranging from permanent monogamous families to polygamy and even temporary arrangements usually considered illicit in Christian culture, were accepted in Muslim culture. Like Christian and Roman culture, the power of the patriarch was emphasized in Islam. Women, children, and slaves were all subject to the authority of the male head. He arranged—and could some-times dissolve—marriages for his children, could favor younger sons with impunity, and had virtually autocratic powers within the family confines. He could also decide which children born into the family were to be raised by the family. Even though infanticide was forbidden, fathers had to formally acknowledge every child (a system similar to that of Rome) and anecdotal evidence suggests that newborns were sometimes abandoned or exposed on the patriarch's order. The patriarch was also, however, required to educate his male children (literacy in Arabic was a requirement for all male Muslims) and to ensure that his daughters married men appropriate to their social station. The husband of more than one wife was also required to give all his wives sexual access and was not permitted to favor one wife over another. This was very important to the status of wives in the aristocratic Muslim family, since women's status in general was based more upon their childbearing capacities than any other criterion. A wife who was sexually neglected could demand access to her husband, or even demand a divorce on the basis that he was depriving her of status in the household.

Although sources emphasize the two-generation household—one man, his wife or wives, and their children—as the norm, it is likely that different household arrangements were common, with multiple genera-tions living under one roof. Sources concerning the Jewish community in medieval Egypt, for example, suggest that not only three-generation households were common, but also extended households in which broth-ers lived together with their parents, wives, and children. Since this arrangement was not automatic or traditional among Jews, it is probable that the Muslim household in Egypt originated this system and that it was adopted by their Jewish neighbors.

Children and the Extended Medieval Muslim Family

With such a strongly patriarchal system, it is not surprising that chil-dren were fundamentally associated with their fathers' lineages. Given the traditions of tribal organization that formed the basis of Arab culture long before Muhammad, children were not necessarily associated only with their biological fathers, however. Extended kinship among males operated both as social networks and as political connections. For exam-ple, the great Kurdish general Salah ad-Din (aka Saladin), who conquered

Fatimid Egypt in the twelfth century and negotiated with the English king Richard I during the Third Crusade, was raised by his uncle, Shirkuh, and succeeded him as sultan in Egypt. The courts of the different caliphate dynasties, centered first in Damascus and then in Baghdad, abounded with extended family networks, and heirs were not necessarily eldest sons at any time and in any family. Indeed, there were instances in which daughters apparently succeeded their fathers as rulers, and women in the families of the caliphs were powerful and influential not only as patrons of culture but also as political and even military leaders.

Thus children were raised in large extended kinship environments where legitimate and natural, full and half-siblings intermingled freely. The ideal was that the sexes, however, did not intermingle after puberty. Girls in wealthy families were confined to the women's quarters. The so-called harem of western imagination was very different in reality: the women's quarters were anything but dens of inquity and decadence. Women in harems had virtually no contact with adult men other than their husbands. Although they were permitted to be seen by male members of their families, such interactions were discouraged. In the wealthiest households, eunuchs might have guarded the harem, but the sexuality of the women was strictly controlled. Children were also housed in the harem, but boys were probably removed once they were old enough to recognize sexual difference. There is also evidence of a significant level of competition between wives in the harem, not only for attention from their husband, but also for the ambitions of their children. Since the eldest son was not automatically preferred over younger sons, wives competed to raise their own status by promoting the interests of their own children. In families below the social level of the wealthy aristocracy, in contrast, the strict segregation of the sexes was undoubtedly far less complete and women were visible in the very public environments of the marketplace, the urban streets, and the rural farm.

Marriage and Divorce in Medieval Muslim Law

Muhammad did not only provide the religious foundation for Islam, he also provided new structures for Arab Bedouin culture that were at times in direct conflict with the cultural traditions he had experienced growing up. Although polygamy is approved under Muslim law, men are limited in both the number of wives they might have (four is generally considered to be the maximum allowed) and in the ways in which these multiple marriages ought to be organized. All the wives had to be treated equally, a conception that was left deliberately vague in the legal literature and therefore permitted a variety of experiences for women engaged in polygamous relationships. This provision could—and did—encourage monogamy simply on the basis of economic realities. In addition, men could have a relatively limitless number of other sexual encounters, including concubines resident in the household (usually slaves or of lower social status than wives) and more casual alliances, considered temporary marriages that could last only a matter of days. On the other hand, control of their sexual urges was considered to be an admirable trait for all men to have and indiscriminate sexual activity was frowned upon.

Legal marriages were conducted under strict guidelines as formal contracts. Three elements were essential in the formation of a valid marriage (even the so-called temporary marriages required these): the consent of both parties, a contract specifying the marriage gift or dowry the husband was providing the wife (this is called dower in western societies, in contrast to dowry, which is defined in the west as the property the wife's family provides the bride), and the presence of at least two witnesses. Indeed, consent and the provision of a dowry were considered the most important elements and without them, a marriage was not valid.[3] Women were permitted to demand additional contractual agreements during marriage negotiations, such as a stipulation that the husband not practice polygamy, that the level of the bride's maintenance be included in the contract, and even that the bride be able to divorce her husband under certain specified circumstances. Whether women who were able to include these kinds of demands actually succeeded in having them enforced is not clear. Islamic law relied heavily on the adjudication of trained judges called *qadis*, who had the power to invalidate contracts or to reinterpret their provisions. Moreover, the legal texts, coming as they do out of the religious books of the Quran and Hadith were open to significant interpretation and different regions of the Islamic world interpreted them in different ways.

Although there was no fixed age of adulthood under Islamic law, puberty—considered to be around age 12 for boys and 9 for girls—was considered the age of independent consent, if not independence. In general minors could not be forced into marriages, although parents or guardians could arrange marriages for them, and it was considered illegal to consummate a marriage with a minor until she (or he) had attained puberty. Once a child who had been married before puberty reached that stage, she or he could renounce the marriage as long as it had not been consummated. Even though these protections were placed into the legal system, it seems fairly clear from literary evidence that parents—especially wealthy ones—arranged marriages for their children long before they reached the age of puberty. Nevertheless, as will be discussed below, this law did make it possible for young women forced into marriages to obtain redress.

Since the Muslim conquerors of the Byzantine Middle East, North Africa, and Spain were ruling over largely non-Muslim populations for at least the first hundred years or more, Islamic law also had to address the issue of mixed marriages. This was not as much an issue in other medieval communities, since western Europe and the Byzantine Empire were both overwhelmingly Christian, and Jews living in either the Christian or the Muslim regions maintained strict regulations against intermarriage. Perhaps predictably, Islamic law permitted Muslim men to marry non-Muslim women, as long as they were either Christian or Jewish (that is, *dhimmis,* or "People of the Book"), and the children were raised to be Muslims. Women, on the other hand, were not permitted to marry outside their faith. Muslims were completely barred from marrying Zoroastrians and Hindus, even though they, too, were considered "People of the Book," because their religions were based upon written texts. It is possible that the closer connections of Islam to Christianity and Judaism were important to this legal decision.

Marriage in the Islamic world is considered a contractual arrangement, rather than a religious obligation, so there are far fewer burdens placed upon married couples who want to dissolve their marriages than occurred in either medieval Christianity or Judaism. Most westerners know about the formula of the husband declaring "I divorce you" three times in succession as a way to end a marriage, but in fact that was only one of—and the most drastic of—the measures that married couples could take to end their union. Texts in both the Quran and the Hadith literature state that a couple can divorce and remarry each other twice, but that the third time they divorce the resurrection of the union cannot occur until the divorced wife remarries again and her new husband either divorces her or dies. The legal system developed in the Middle Ages created mechanisms by which this rule could be maintained. The easiest kind of divorce to un-make involved a husband divorcing his wife with a formal contract and then the couple waiting for three months before either reconciling or completing the divorce procedure. Another form occurred in which the husband declared the marriage dissolved once a month for three successive months. This was seen as a more permanent form of divorce, one that was harder to back out of. The third, and most final form, was the well-known system of the husband declaring in front of witnesses "I divorce you!" three times. In all three forms of divorce, the wife retained the dowry her husband had given her, although this, too, could be negotiated if the dowry amount was a source of family strife. Once divorced, husbands could remarry other women immediately, but the ex-wife was required to wait at least three months, during which time her ex-husband was required to pay for her upkeep. This waiting period was designed to ensure that the divorcée was not pregnant at the time of the divorce. A similar arrangement was also made should a wife outlive her husband: although she could remain in her husband's house and retain the maintenance she had received during the marriage for a year, widows were also permitted to remarry once it was guaranteed they were not pregnant—in this case after 4 months and 10 days.[4] Divorced wives usually received their dowries back if they were not considered at fault, and they did not suffer any specific legal loss of status, although their children were separated from them. Nevertheless, there was some stigma attached to being divorced, especially for women and especially if fertility was the issue, since this would mean it was unlikely that the divorcée could remarry. Single women were viewed with considerable suspicion in Islamic culture (as they were in Mediterranean Christian and Jewish culture as well) and the requirement that they remain under the perpetual authority of some male or suffer a loss of respectability meant that widows and divorcées who could not remarry could find themselves in very risky circumstances.

Even though marriage was not considered a specifically religious act, as it was in western Christianity, it was still nonetheless overseen by traditional Islamic law. The *qadi* (a judge in a *sharia* court) was given responsibility for adjudicating disputes between married couples, for determining whether a divorce could be obtained and which of the parties would have to pay the expenses, and for deciding on cases of abandonment and legitimacy of children. Although virtually none of these kinds of cases are preserved in documentary sources, one that came from late medieval Egypt that was discussed by the chronicler Nur al-Din 'Ali ibn Da'ud al-Jawhari al-Sayrafi formed the basis for an analysis of marriage and divorce law and procedure by the historian Carl Petry. In this particular case a young woman who was forced into marriage before she had reached the legal age of adulthood, and whose marriage was both abusive and illegal, was permitted to divorce her husband and seek a new husband as if she were a respectable virgin. Her husband and his associates, however, were not punished particularly rigorously for their actions.[5] This one case—and there are so few examples that this must suffice—suggests that, much like other medieval legal systems, *sharia* presents an ideal that is not played out in reality. The cultural norms of the dominance of men, the perceived inferiority of women, and the power of patriarchs to rule their households were ultimately more significant in people's daily lives than were the legal and philosophical texts that form the basis of the intellectual community.

Representations of marriage in literary texts are also somewhat unreliable as road maps to the realities of Muslim family life. The literary texts available to the modern reader are either religious or epic and many are legendary in character. In these texts, women are often depicted as being wily and powerful, in competition with husbands, sons, and stepchildren. They are seen as sources of both nurture and disruption and marriage is depicted both romantically (as in the famous stories in the *Thousand and One Nights*) or as politically significant (as in the Persian *Book of Kings*).[6] There are no convenient contemporary depictions of peasant marriages, as exist in some later medieval western literature such as *The Dream of Piers Plowman*. While it can be assumed that Muslim marriages were not all that different in quality from those in contemporary Judaic and Byzantine culture, with the exception of the presence of polygamy in Islam, there is little evidence available either to confirm or deny this assumption. Certainly the family needed to operate as a partnership to assure the survival of all its members. Husbands and wives were committed to rearing children, caring for the elderly, and supporting the family's economic viability. In literature, marriages are often depicted as being loving, even passionate, and husbands and wives are described as equal partners in the family dynamic. Legal texts, most of them dealing with failed marriages of couples seeking divorces, provide a less cheerful picture, one in which abuse of wives and abandonment of financial responsibilities figure prominently. The *suras* (the individual chapters of the Quran) and Hadith readings relating to marriage and the family present yet another perspective. Muhammad seemed intent upon describing the responsibilities of women in the family as clearly as possible and these goals were emphasized in later writings of his successors. Although extensive, these readings are still not reliable indicators of the actual state of affairs. They do, however, outline the concerns of the early leaders in Islam, and therefore might reflect the state of marriage at the time Islam was developed.

Children, Legitimacy, and Illegitimacy

Children from marriages or formal concubinage arrangements are considered legitimate under *shari'a,* so the wealthiest Muslim families tended to be enormous, with dozens of children. Other Muslim families, however, resembled in both size and organization other Semitic and non-Semitic families in the Mediterranean region, with both nuclear and extended families existing side by side, as long-standing cultural traditions were maintained. In these families, it was probably more typical for the number of children to be somewhat limited by both financial level and the high rate of infant and child mortality.

The issue of legitimacy was very important to medieval Muslim society because both boys and girls could inherit family property, and eldest sons were not as privileged in their position as they were in western Christian and Judaic culture. The law stated that girls inherited one-half of the property inherited by boys, but that stricture was apparently often overlooked, with girls receiving considerably less than half of what their brothers inherited. Only children born within an approved legal relationship could be considered legitimate, although some Muslim groups were willing to consider children born at least six months after the marriage ceremony to be legitimate.[7] Children could also be brought into a family by a form of adoption known as acknowledgement of parenthood, although if there were already children in the family unit, such adoptees could not inherit family property.[8]

The propagation of children was considered one of the most important duties of Muslim couples. It is likely that the mortality rate among

Muslims was more or less identical to that of other medieval people—that is, very high indeed, especially among young children and babies—so fertility was emphasized. While the wealthy Muslim family probably contained many children, particularly those in which polygamy was practiced, poorer Muslim households must have experienced the same barriers to childbirth experienced elsewhere in the medieval world. Poor diets and hard work could cause women to be infertile. Between this reality and the high rate of infant mortality, the average medieval Muslim family could have been quite small.

Depictions of Marriage and Women in the Hadith Literature

Unlike medieval Christian culture, where sources describing the day-to-day realities of married life and the family exist in some quantity, pre-modern Islamic culture has few equivalent sources. Family life was considered extremely private; it was considered shameful for a man even to mention his wife or wives to another man in public. Romanticized stories of life in the royal or aristocratic harem are as unreliable as depictions of aristocratic marriage in western courtly love literature. Although some legal texts have been discussed by historians of medieval Islam, those that might describe real relationships between husbands and wives are very rare. As a result, the main sources for discussions of marriage and family come from religious texts, the Quran and the Hadith literature. These texts represent attitudes of the leaders of the religious community and present the ideals and cultural norms of the Islamic system. As such, they are valuable in identifying dominant attitudes about the family, but it is difficult to uncover the reality hidden by these idealized views.

Book 62 of the Hadith text *Sahih Bukhari* focuses on comments about marriage, family, and women made by Muhammad, his wife Aisha, the first caliphs who followed Muhammad, their families, and some of the Prophet's more influential followers. The texts describe ideal marriages, outline whom men can and cannot marry, identify reasons and procedures for divorce, and provide glimpses of cultural attitudes toward women. Central to this collection of readings is the primacy of marriage in Muslim culture. Unlike medieval Christianity, which tended to view marriage as a necessary evil that controlled the sinful sexual urges of human beings, but was not nearly as sanctified as a state of celibacy, Islam considered marriage essential for everyone in the culture: "O young people! Whoever among you can marry, should marry, because it helps him . . . guard his modesty [prevents him from engaging in illegal sexual activity]."[9] Several verses in this book go so far as to permit penniless men to marry as long as they are devout and have memorized their *Quran suras* (the chapters of the Quran): "I marry her to you for what you know of the Quran [as her dowry]."[10] Men who cannot engage in permanent unions are permitted a form of marriage known as *muta*—a legal union that lasts for three days—although the text presents contradictions in this instance, since Ali (and therefore the Shiite form of Islam that considers him to be their founder) is claimed to have outlawed *muta* marriages.[11] Reactions on marriage also appears in this volume, especially prohibitions against marrying step-siblings, foster siblings (those who shared the breast milk of a wet nurse), and the daughters, mothers, or aunts of wives.[12]

Scenarios of irregular or illegal marriages connect in the Hadith readings to discussions of divorce, the proper behavior of wives, and the proper treatment of wives by husbands. What is significant in this context is the tone of the Hadith texts when discussing women. Although several statements are attributed to Aisha, Muhammad's favorite wife, and frequent mention is made of some of his other wives, the general impression of these readings is largely negative with respect to women. Marriage might be a necessary component to full membership in the Muslim community, the *umma*, but women are presented ambivalently. When discussing children, girls are mentioned only in the context of wealthy heiresses whose guardians covet their property. Wives are to be treated honorably, but they are not granted opportunities for independence. Women who speak to the Prophet are considered shameful by his followers. Finally, in one series of statements, Muhammad claims to have seen in a vision that most of the inhabitants of Paradise are male, while most of those consigned to the "Fire" (i.e., hell) are female.[13]

Although there certainly are many negative statements about women to be found in the *Hadith* texts, there are also texts that command men to protect women, that prohibit the exploitation of orphaned heiresses by guardians, and that extol the virtues of religious women who, according to the Prophet, make better wives than do rich or influential women.[14] This ambiguity with respect to women certainly must have had some effect on the cultural attitudes about women in Muslim society, but whether it seriously affected real women in the same way is difficult to determine. Certainly the day-to-day activities of medieval Muslims had to lead to the kind of pragmatic partnerships that married couples in the other medieval cultures usually experienced, where the legal and religious texts also exhibit a profound ambivalence, even a hostility, toward women. The ambivalence toward women did, however, affect their capacity to inherit property and affected even the law of consent required for a valid marriage: a woman's silence constituted consent.[15]

Conclusion

Like the late Roman Empire, the Byzantine Empire, and the medieval West, medieval Muslim culture had rich legal and cultural traditions that shaped the ways in which families were organized, the position of women in the family, definitions of legitimacy, and notions of extended family. These traditions were not confined to the Arabian Peninsula.

Instead, Muslim culture drew from a wide array of influences—Roman, Byzantine, Jewish, and Christian—that reflect the kinds of transformations experienced by the peoples of the Mediterranean world from the mid-sixth century on. For the Muslim population, which until the later Middle Ages was spread somewhat thinly through the largely Christian world, such influences made it possible to coexist with the people they conquered. Even the veiling of women, a subject of so much controversy today, was not unique to Islam: all medieval cultures practiced a form of veiling of women in public and those who could not be veiled because of their work or lifestyle were considered less than respectable.

One of the strengths of Islam lay in its flexibility and willingness to adopt from and adapt to the cultures they conquered. It thus makes it possible to discuss Muslim families not as systems unique to a rigid and segregated system, but as embodying many of the characteristics of family life throughout the medieval world.

Notes

1. This is a little understood statement that probably refers to the episode in Genesis 6: 1–4 just before the Noah story: "The sons of the gods saw that the daughters of men were beautiful; so they took for themselves such women as they chose . . . In those days, when the sons of the gods had intercourse with the daughters of men and got children by them, the Nephilim [or giants] were on earth. They were the heroes of old, men of renown." *The New Jerusalem Bible* (New York: Doubleday, 1999), 6–7.

2. Eleanor A. Doumato outlines the arguments for all of the above issues very nicely in "Hearing Other Voices: Christian Women and the Coming of Islam" *International Journal of Middle East Studies* 23, no. 2 (1991): 177–199. They are also discussed at length by Leila Ahmed, *Women and Gender in Islam: Historical Roots of a Modern Debate* (New Haven: Yale University Press, 1992), especially 9–124.

3. A good comparative study of the so-called classical and modern approaches to Muslim family law is Fazlur Rahman, "A Survey of Modernization of Muslim Family Law," *International Journal of Middle East Studies* 11, no. 4 (1980): 451–465.

4. This is discussed by Rahman; see, especially, 454–462.

5. Carl F. Petry, "Conjugal Rights versus Class Prerogatives: A Divorce Case in Mamluk Cairo," in *Women in the Medieval Islamic World*, ed. Gavin R. G. Hambly (New York: St. Martin's Press, 1998), 227–240.

6. See, for example, Remke Kruk, "The Bold and the Beautiful: Women and 'Fitna' in the *Sirat Dhat al-Himma': The Story of Nura*", 99–116, and Geoffrey Lewis, "Heroines and Others in the Heroic Age of the Turks," 147–160 in Hambly, *Women in the Medieval Islamic World*.

7. Rahman, "Survey," 462.

8. Rahman, "Survey," 462.

9. *Translation of Sahih Bukhari, Book 62* in *USC/MSA Compendium of Muslim Texts*, http://www.usc.edu/dept/MSA/fundamentals/hadithsunnah/bukhari/062.sbt.html, Volume 7, Book 62, Number 4.

10. Book 62, Number 58, et passim.

11. See, especially, Book 62, Numbers 51, 52, 130.
12. See, for example, Book 62, Numbers 35, 36, 37, 38, 39, 41.
13. Book 62, Numbers 24, 48, 124, 125, 126.
14. See Book 62, Number 27, et passim.
15. Book 62, Numbers 67, 8.

5

The Jewish Family in the Middle Ages

After the destruction of the Second Temple in 70 C.E. and following the last major revolt of the Jews in Roman Judea in the early second century, this ancient people, already well integrated into the Hellenistic and Roman Mediterranean world, spread even further. By the end of the Roman Empire in the West, Jewish quarters had emerged in all the major Mediterranean urban centers, from Rome to Ravenna to Constantinople, Antioch, Alexandria, and Carthage. In time, Jews settled throughout Western Europe as well as the Mediterranean, mostly in urban centers as these developed. The largest Jewish populations remained in Muslim-dominated areas such as the Iberian peninsula, in the region of al-Andalus, and Egypt. These form the origins of the Sephardic Jewish community. Northern Europe had few Jewish communities until after 800, when Charlemagne encouraged Jewish settlement in the growing towns along the Rhine, especially Mainz, Cologne, and Metz. In the thirteenth century, many of the Rhineland Jews formed communities called at the time the Pietists, which eventually became the source for Hasidic Judaism. England received an influx of Jewish settlers only after 1066, when they came in the wake of the Norman conquest—William the Conqueror actually relocated Jewish families from Normandy to England—where they settled in the cities of London, York, Norwich, and Lincoln. Once the Byzantine Empire's urban centers had shrunk to only Constantinople and cities on the Greek mainland such as Athens and Thessalonike, its Jewish population also shrank, since the Byzantine cities conquered by the Muslims, such as Alexandria and Antioch, had retained larger Jewish settlements than the Christian cities of the northern Mediterranean shore. The modern phenomenon of substantial populations of Jews living in Bohemia (the modern Czech Republic), Poland, Ukraine, and Belarus began in the later Middle Ages, when Jews fled Western Europe and England because of expulsions and persecutions, and were encouraged by the Holy Roman Emperors as well as native princes, such as the kings of Poland, to settle in the more sparsely populated areas of eastern Europe. These communities formed the basis of the Ashkenazic Jewish community.

Jewish traders formed the basis for the international carrying trades, especially between the Mediterranean and the Germanic kingdoms in Gaul and Spain. As Christian regions, these early medieval kingdoms were unable to encourage the development of urban trade among their own peoples in large part because of the western church's laws against the practice of usury, defined at the time as the lending of money at any interest. Since the church considered trade to be a form of money lending, the leaders also considered those engaged in investment and trade to be usurers, hence the need to engage Jewish traders in the West. In the Byzantine East, the laws against usury were much more relaxed, probably because international trade had taken place for millennia in that region and Christian traders were not about to give up lucrative businesses to Jewish traders from Antioch or Alexandria. Jews were responsible for a great deal of the luxury trades, but they also engaged in other kinds of work, such as tanning leather, that Byzantine Christians considered to be impure.

Eventually, when western laws relaxed strictures against Christians engaging in trade, Jews were pushed more and more into the business of money lending, especially in Western Europe. Jewish bankers provided a vital service to Christian kings and nobles, bishops, and even popes who relied on loans to fund everything from building projects to wars, including the Crusades. At the same time, the Jews were vilified by these same groups as exploiting the Christians by providing the very services that kept Christian institutions operating. Jews had very few options in Christian Europe when it came to ways of making a living, and virtually all options open to them could also be used by Christian authorities for propaganda against them.

Jewish populations in Western Europe were officially under the official protection of local bishops or of kings and feudal lords, depending on the region. This protection was sometimes actual, such as when bishops in cities along the Rhine tried to protect Jews from being massacred by mobs headed to the Holy Land after the preaching of the First Crusade in 1095. More often however, the protected status of Jews was a euphemism for the authorities' exploitation of the Jewish community's financial resources. As William Chester Jordan describes,

The twelfth century . . . saw the formulation of a theory that being a Jew was a legal status in and of itself in feudal law; and increasingly the essence of that status for every Jew came to be his susceptibility to arbitrary taxation by the lord who exercised criminal justice over him . . . Contributions to the lord's coffers were the price for these forums for adjudication. An obvious way for a lord to get at the (perceived) wealth of the Jews in moneylending was by taxing their outstanding loans.[1]

Indeed, medieval kings and feudal barons who wielded this authority had to temper their voraciousness delicately because, if they impoverished the Jewish community, this convenient source of income would disappear. So they encouraged Jewish money lending, even against the protests of the religious authorities, and took legal steps to ensure that borrowers did not default on their debts.

At times, royal greed exceeded royal good sense. The French king Philip Augustus (r. 1180–1223), for instance, permitted a raid on Jewish synagogues in the royal domain in 1180 in which all the moveable items sacred to the Jewish community were confiscated. He then extorted the payment of a ransom for their return that amounted to "one and one-half times what Philip's government might expect in normal predictable revenue in an entire year."[2] The English king Edward I (r. 1272–1307) and his wife, Eleanor of Castile, engaged in such wholesale exploitation of the Jews in England that, when Edward expelled the Jews from England in 1290, he "was hardly depriving himself of a substantial source of future revenue," since he had already confiscated virtually all their wealth.[3] Indeed, by the end of the thirteenth century, the papacy had liberalized its laws on money lending even further and Christian banks were becoming more significant in the business of managing the financial needs of kings, princes, and popes. This rendered the Jewish communities more or less superfluous in places like England, where they were both a tiny portion of the population and almost entirely engaged in banking, so Edward did not think twice about expelling them from the country.

Jews settled in cities and engaged in trade because both Christian and Muslim laws forbade them from owning land in many regions. These regulations were often overlooked, especially in the Middle East, in areas where Christian monarchs encouraged immigration and settlement such as central Europe, and in the major cities where significant international trade occurred. Laws in Christian regions also often forbade Jews from intermingling with the majority population, which encouraged the establishment of closely linked enclaves of Jewish settlement. Even so, Jewish families in some areas lived in more loosely organized communities and Christians also lived alongside and within Jewish neighborhoods. Jewish religious requirements that Jews live near the community's synagogue, because they were forbidden to ride on the Sabbath, encouraged the development of Jewish neighborhoods even when there were no laws restricting their living arrangements. Fears of violence, which tended to occur with more frequency after the First Crusade, also encouraged Jewish families to cluster together into enclaves that were more easily protected from Christian incursion. Although initially segregated by choice, Jews eventually were physically barred from living in areas of Christian settlement by being pushed into gated portions of the city. The most famous enclosure of this type would eventually be an area of sixteenth-century Venice called The Ghetto (the Venetian spelling of the Italian word *getto,* meaning a jet or spray and referring to the foundries that were common in the area), a term that changed in meaning to become associated with any segregated section of a city, but especially one in which Jews were housed. The ghettos of Christian cities were teeming with life and people, but they were deliberately removed from the main Christian population centers. The ghetto of Rome, for example, took up a number of streets behind the Theater of Marcellus, an area that lay outside the *abitato* (the region of greatest population) of the medieval city.

The Jews of medieval Europe were not merely ghettoized, however. Eventually, particularly in areas where royal control of the Jewish population exhibited significant material exploitation, such as England and France, Jews were expelled from the kingdoms altogether. The most famous expulsion occurred in 1492 Spain and all its subject territories, including Sicily and Sardinia, when both Jews and Muslims were forced to leave following Ferdinand and Isabella's unification of the Spanish kingdoms of Leon-Castile and Aragon with al-Andalus and the Kingdom of the Two Sicilies. Jews in other kingdoms, however, suffered expulsion centuries before this particular example. They were forced out of the area of the Crimea (the north coast of the Black Sea) as early as 1015, from a number of different German provinces beginning in the twelfth century, from England in 1290 (they did not return to England and Wales until the seventeenth century), France in 1306 (they were permitted to return in small numbers about a decade later but under highly restrictive circumstances), from numerous places in central Europe in the fourteenth century, and from Austria, Lithuania, Provence (a largely independent region of southern France), and Portugal by the end of the fifteenth century. Most of the Jewish communities in these areas had migrated by 1500 either to areas of the southern Mediterranean controlled by the Ottoman Empire or to Poland, which had a more liberal policy regarding the Jews until the seventeenth century.[4] By that time, the Jews remaining in Europe (with the exception of Poland) were completely segregated from the Christian population. Although the ghettoization of the European Jews occurred only at the end of the Middle Ages, when anti-Semitism was growing along with the Catholic Church's concerns over the Protestant reformation movement and the failure of the Crusades, the Jewish communities had to be careful to tread lightly in the Christian cities of Europe throughout the period: persecution and violence against them were common occurrences.

In areas under Islamic rule, the relationship between Jewish residents and the Muslim government and population was somewhat different.

For one thing, Jews were not the only religious group with second-class status: Christians living in Muslim-dominated areas were more or less treated the same as the Jewish communities. Secondly, the restrictions on Jews (and Christians) in Muslim lands were largely politically and economically motivated, rather than part of the religious doctrine. Whereas Christians rationalized the persecution and limitation of Jews on the basis that "Jews killed Christ," Muslims lumped them together with Christians and (to some extent) Zoroastrians as peoples of the book, or *dhimmis* who were not privileged to be full-fledged members of the political community. This did not prevent individual Jews from attaining significant status, such as the philosopher Moses Maimonides, who was prominent in Fatimid Egypt in the twelfth century, an area that experienced a significantly more liberal attitude toward Jews and Christians until the conquests of Salah ad-Din in the twelfth century.

Jews were not only able to move around more freely in lands under Islamic rule, they were also able to engage in a wider variety of professions. The emphasis on international trade that existed in Europe in the early Middle Ages, therefore, did not change significantly among Jewish communities in the Middle East. Indeed, their vast international networks grew in the High Middle Ages, with permanent trading posts appearing as far away as India in order to make the long-distance trade in spices and luxury goods more efficient (this is discussed in greater detail in chapter 10).

The fundamental basis for the international trade relationships developed by Jewish communities in the Middle Ages was the family: business simply could not be conducted without one. Jews engaged in the carrying trades relied on family members setting up offices in all the major Mediterranean cities. Jewish bankers, goldsmiths, silversmiths, and jewelers created dynasties in their businesses because they were barred from the guild system that regulated Christian trade and manufacture. Casual travelers, such as the Jewish trader Benjamin of Tudela, who wrote a memoir of his travels throughout twelfth-century Europe and the Mediterranean, relied on family members in far flung cities to give them a bed and a good meal when on the road. Even teachers and rabbis tended to come from families that had developed traditions of producing intellectuals, teachers, and rabbis.

Jews occupied a liminal space in the medieval world. They were a necessary part of every culture and society, but were at best considered second-class non-citizens, and at worst actively persecuted and their destruction rationalized on the basis of religious fanaticism. This made the preservation of families and culture exceedingly difficult and, if it were not for the occasional Christian monarch and the relative tolerance of the early Muslim caliphs of al-Andalus (if not the later Almohad dynasty) and Fatimid Egypt, Judaism might have disappeared entirely. Indeed, the culture and history of the Jewish medieval population was substantially preserved by the family traditions practiced by the Jews of the diaspora (the dispersal of the Jews outside Palestine and Roman Judea).

Family Structure, Judaic Law, and the Legal Systems of the Medieval World

Jews throughout the medieval world were subject both to their own law and to the laws of the land where they lived. Royal courts were set up to adjudicate cases between Jews and Christians, such as the English Court of the Exchequer of the Jews, but the Jewish community was permitted to regulate itself, for the most part. Jewish law was based upon both the sacred texts of the Jews—the Holy Scriptures (what Christians call the Old Testament)—and on interpretations of those texts found in a number of rabbinic volumes, among them Mishnah and Talmud. The Hebrew Scriptures contain many laws regulating marriage, inheritance, and definitions of legitimacy. Not all of these were appropriate to the circumstances in which Jews found themselves in the medieval world. For example, Jews living in Christian Europe and the Byzantine Empire were monogamous—one wife to a man—because Christian law forbade polygamy, even though there is no biblical law specifically prohibiting it. Jews living in Muslim lands, on the other hand, followed Muslim practice and did practice polygamy if a particular man was wealthy enough to be able to afford more than one wife. Since Jews were usually not permitted to own land, the western feudal laws of primogeniture (inheritance by the eldest son) were not relevant. Therefore, as long as Judaic law did not contradict the laws of the region in which they lived, it was considered to stand. In the Byzantine Empire, the continuation of Roman law, which regulated the Jews living in the Roman Empire (especially after the conversion of the emperor Constantine), continued to be active, at least with respect to Jewish-Christian interactions. Many of these laws were protective of Jewish rights to property, but also emphasized their subordination to Christians. As a result, Jews could be significantly disadvantaged not only to interact on an equal basis with Christians, but also to control their own property and to preserve it from government interference. Nevertheless, in internal matters at least, Jews were allowed to regulate themselves. Jews in the Muslim Mediterranean world were far more thoroughly integrated into the community, especially in Muslim Spain and Fatimid Egypt. Indeed, one of the richest series of sources available for the lives of Jews in the Middle Ages comes from the storage warehouse of Cairo's synagogue, a structure called the Cairo *geniza* (a term that designates a sacred space where used or damaged torah scrolls were housed, since they were not permitted to be destroyed, and that also housed the private papers of members of the community). These *geniza* records are invaluable for historians to reconstruct the lives of everyday Jews living in Muslim Egypt and they also provide interesting insights into the international networks Jewish traders maintained in order to preserve their society.[5] Because in the Christian world marriage was subject to canon law, and in the Muslim world it was based upon Islamic law, or *sharia*, Jewish marriage was regulated by the communities themselves, in large part according to traditional interpretations of biblical law, but also influenced significantly by the laws of the regions in which they lived.

Marriages according to Judaic law were supposed to be endogamous: that is, Jews were supposed to marry within their communities, even within their own families. Indeed, the marriage of first cousins was seen as advantageous among many Jewish groups and was encouraged in certain circumstances when the family's property was in danger of being divided through inheritance. Although marriage between generations within a family (such as an uncle and his niece) was relatively rare, it was also not forbidden, a situation that would have appalled a Christian living under his own system. In Muslim parts of the medieval world, however, the marrying of very close kin occurred regularly among both Muslims and Jews. Where Jews were allowed to own land, the need to maintain the integrity of family holdings encouraged the marriage of cousins. In addition, traditional systems, such as that of levirate marriage, under which a man marries his brother's widow in order to impregnate her so that the dead man will have an heir, continued to exist at least as a possibility, even though this marriage system was usually forbidden under both Christian and Muslim law.

In portions of Europe where Germanic and canon law influenced Judaic practice, such as the Rhineland region, Jews were more likely to practice exogamy, marriage to someone not closely related. The reasons for this difference lie in changing inheritance laws and less emphasis on maintaining family property within the family, since most of the property under consideration was moveable and not based on land ownership.[6] This stress on marriage outside the family was also no doubt influenced by Christian practice, since canon law had very strict laws against consanguinity, the marriage of close kin. Jews would have made an effort to conform to the prevailing norms of the dominant culture in order to avoid conflict. Additionally, the smallness of the Jewish communities in the west might have encouraged marriages that extended networks of kinship and friendship farther afield. The information on marriage practices among Jews in the Byzantine Empire is so sparse that it is difficult to say whether their marriage patterns resembled those of the Christian west or the Islamic Mediterranean. It is far more likely, however, that Jews living in the Byzantine Empire were much more Mediterranean and Middle Eastern in their cultural focus, so they were more likely to practice the more traditional endogamy found there than the exogamy of the Rhineland Jewry. If evidence from after the Ottoman Conquest of the Byzantine Empire in the 1450s has any validity for the period just before that time, then it is entirely possible that Jews in Byzantine Constantinople or Thessalonike lived quite similarly to Jews in Islamic Cairo, Antioch, or Alexandria. In other words, they married close kin and engaged in long distance trade rather than money lending.

Unlike both Christianity and Islam, Judaism requires in theory that the prospective bride and groom arrange their own marriages, either personally or through a third party, who could be a parent. Daughters still considered minors (that is, under twelve and a half years of age) could have marriages arranged by their fathers, but such arrangements could be nullified once the daughter reached her majority if she refused to consummate the marriage. In reality, parents, sometimes assisted by professional matchmakers, were significantly involved in marriage arrangements. The "Fiddler on the Roof" image of the professional matchmaker actually has its origins in the Middle Ages, in part because communities of Jews were so scattered that professional matchmakers were to some extent needed to locate appropriate marriage partners. Early marriages for both members of the couple were common, since the minimum legal age of marriage was 12 years for girls and 13 for boys. Studies show that children as young as nine were married and that marriage soon after reaching the minimum age was common.[7] One rationale was that Jews living in hostile territory were in fear of death on a daily basis, so having children was of vital interest to the community, and the younger a girl married, the more likely it was that she would have more children. Children who were married at such young ages did not always live together, however, until they were older. Young men might be sent to school for further study, which usually was completed at around age 18, or the children might remain at the homes of their birth parents for a few years until they were mature enough to enter into a sexual relationship.

Unlike Christianity, divorce was possible, but, unlike in Islam, not always and everywhere easy to obtain. In areas such as Fatimid Egypt (about which there is a great deal of information, perhaps skewing our picture of Jews living in Muslim lands), divorce was both an easy and relatively neutral process, with neither party being penalized for dissolving the marriage. In Christian regions, the Christian hostility towards divorce made the system more difficult. One significant prohibition was that of marrying outside the religion. Unlike in Islam, where a Muslim man could marry a Christian or Jewish woman as long as the children were raised Muslim, Jewish men and women were not permitted to marry anyone who was not Jewish. Since Christian countries reacted violently toward women or men who might desire to convert to Judaism—it was illegal in all Christian countries to do so and the convert was considered a heretic who could be tried before the Holy Inquisition—this was probably a matter of community safety in addition to a religious obligation.

Divorce was overseen by Judaic law no matter where the community might be living. As in Islam, only men could initiate the legal proceedings for divorce, but a woman could demand that her husband divorce her for specific reasons, such as adultery or abandonment. It seems that rabbis in Europe were more reluctant to allow divorces that women might have initiated, perhaps because of the influence from the dominant culture, which was suspicious of women's motives for wanting their marriages dissolved.[8] In the Islamic world, divorces seem to have been fairly frequent and rabbis might even compel a man to divorce his wife if she petitioned the rabbi and presented compelling reasons for wanting the divorce. Sometimes men who were going to be away for long periods of time performed a ceremony of provisional divorce in case they died and their widows were unable to establish the fact of their deaths. This is discussed in greater detail in chapter 7.

One of the more unusual aspects of modern-day Judaism is that Jewishness is passed from the maternal line rather than the paternal. This is sometimes explained by the statement that it is pretty easy to identify your mother (unless you are adopted), but you can never be quite sure if your father is really your father. This was particularly true in the centuries before the invention of DNA testing. Medieval Judaism, which was for the most part a highly patriarchal culture, recognized that the survival of their communities depended on a specific definition of what constituted Jewishness. Thus, even if a Jewish woman were kidnapped and forced to convert to Christianity (events such as this did occur, especially during the Crusades era), her community of origin would still consider her children to be Jewish.

The Jewish family, by both law and custom, was profoundly patriarchal just like those of their Christian and Muslim neighbors. At the same time, Jewish men were warned against becoming tyrants in their household and marriage was conceived as a partnership between husband and wife. Each could demand that the other behave respectfully and lovingly. Children were very highly valued and the birth of both boys and girls was celebrated.

Unlike Roman law, the Jewish patriarch did not have absolute power over his family, but there was generally a clear division of labor between male and female spheres of activity. This line could blur, however, as the need arose, with women assuming public and business responsibilities sometimes in parallel to their husbands, sometimes as replacements for them. Indeed, legally mandated roles for husband and wife were far more focused on religious or ritual issues than on practical day-to-day ones.

The legal requirements for a valid marriage included both the standard of consent and the monetary transaction of the dowry. In Western European communities this dowry could be quite substantial, although it rarely included land. The dowry was also officially the property of the wife and she could complain to the authorities—usually the rabbi—if it was being used improperly by her husband. Dowries were also important to Jewish marriage in the Islamic Middle East, where elaborate marriage contracts have survived in large numbers. Dowries conferred a certain amount of independence on wives: they gained bargaining power by reason of their personal financial stake in the marriage.

Although the legal definition of family might suggest that the two-generation nuclear family was the ideal, in fact, Jewish households often comprised extended family units. In Egypt, it was not unusual for brothers and their families to live in the same house, along with the paternal parents. Relationships between adult brothers and sisters could also be close and widowed sisters might be welcomed into the household.[9] Evidence of similar extended family relationships is lacking for Jews in Europe, where nuclear family units was more the norm. It was typical, however, for brothers to be partners in business.

Status within the family was regulated to some extent by Judaic law, with the eldest boy and girl being given a higher status than their younger siblings. S. D. Goitein mentions that the rest of the siblings were expected to kiss the hand of the eldest brother, and that Jewish parents—like their Muslim counterparts—referred to themselves as the parents of their firstborn son.[10] In medieval Europe, Jewish families were likely to have been structurally indistinguishable from their Christian neighbors, as were Jewish and Muslim families in the east. Elder sons were expected to go into the family business, and children were expected to demonstrate marked respect for their parents. Indeed, the status of the mother in Jewish families might have been higher than it was in Muslim or Christian ones.

Women and Children in Medieval Jewish Culture

The preservation of Judaism as a religion required the perpetuation of Jewish families. Children were therefore vitally important in ways that neither Christian nor Muslim families experienced. Every Jewish community, especially those in Europe, teetered between stability and extermination. Indeed, the propagation of children was considered a religious imperative and all Jews were expected to marry and produce progeny. As in all other cultures of the time, boys were preferred over girls, but unlike Christian and especially Muslim cultures, girls and women were not as restricted in their activities. Although unable to attend formal yeshiva schools, which taught boys to read and write Hebrew, Arabic, and, eventually, Yiddish, girls were taught by tutors and in the home and were expected to achieve basic literacy. Women could engage in trade, could invest in businesses, and could work in public spaces without stigma. Married women in Europe were free to run businesses, including money lending, without the interference of their husbands and they had legal autonomy in all aspects of their business. Although a little later than the medieval period, the memoirs of Glückel of Hameln, a Jewish woman living in Germany in the seventeenth century who raised a large family on her own after her first husband's death and the financial bankruptcy and death of her second husband, suggest that Jewish women were far more visible within their communities than were Christian and Muslim women of the time. Glückel had to raise 12 children on her own, which she did by engaging in business in one of the largest commercial centers of early modern Europe. Unfortunately, no equivalent source exists to illuminate the lives of Jewish women living a few hundred years earlier.[11]

The status of women in Jewish families depended to some extent on where they lived. Although the position of wives under Judaic law presents them as subordinate to their husbands, but with significant status within the domestic household, women in Muslim-dominated settings were probably somewhat more confined than their co-religionists in Europe. Their status everywhere was enhanced by motherhood, but they could expect the biblical precept to "honor thy father *and* mother" to act as part of the family's governing principle.

The education of boys and girls was extensive and especially gifted boys were encouraged to continue their education to become teachers, rabbis, and intellectuals. In Muslim Spain, Jewish administrators and philosophers were responsible in many cases for the day-to-day running of the caliphate. Boys in particular were taught to read and write Hebrew, Arabic, Latin, sometimes Greek, and the local vernacular language. Eventually, central and eastern European Jews developed their own vernacular language, known as Yiddish, that was written using the Hebrew alphabet, but which was founded on a combination of Hebrew, German, and Slavic dialects. Not only was this the common language of nearly all European Jews, but it also became a significant literary language in its own right. This meant that girls whose education in Hebrew might have been lacking could still read and understand the tenets of their faith in order to impart them to their own children. Indeed, references to discussions of scripture among men and women, and to the wives of rabbis teaching other women in their communities, suggest that the Judaic emphasis on education was not confined to males. Boys were sent away to school to pursue their studies, but usually remained close to home for the first few years of their education. Those destined to follow their fathers in trade or industry left formal school once they had attained basic literacy to continue their training in the family business. Girls were taught on much the same level, but as they were married at such young ages, their training in household responsibilities replaced the higher learning expected of the boys.

Inheritance, Legitimacy, and Illegitimacy

Since children were highly valued in medieval Jewish culture, the laws restricting illegitimate children from inheriting were moderated in parts of Europe. In Muslim Spain, for instance, illegitimate children could be included among their father's heirs and dowries could be provided for

daughters born out of wedlock, although such children were not considered to be the "real children of the father."[12] Indeed, legitimacy issues that
weighed so heavily among Christian populations, where primogeniture
was the norm and wealthy elites had huge landed estates to distribute, did
not matter as much among Jewish communities. Since most Jews owned
no land, and the biblical laws of inheritance stipulated that all children
would partake of the parents' estates in varying degrees, the distribution
of property was somewhat easier to manage among Jewish families. The
eldest son received twice the amount of his younger brothers and girls all
received a tenth of the family's estates as dowries.

There is some debate as to the size of Jewish families in the Middle
Ages. According to historians who focus on Jewish families in western
Europe, such as Kenneth Stowe, Jewish families were quite small, most
of them having only one or two children who survived childhood. Large
families were apparently rare in those regions. In Fatimid Cairo, on the
other hand, the *geniza* documents record much larger families, with 8 or 10
children being common enough not to cause comment. These issues will
be discussed at greater length in the chapters on marriage and children,
chapters 7 and 8, but family size certainly had an effect on inheritance patterns, since the more children who survived meant the more fragmented
estates could become. There is some evidence of competition between
brothers in business, but on the whole the political and social situation in
which Jews found themselves in the Middle Ages probably encouraged
cooperation within the community rather than the competition that might
call the attention of the Christian or Muslim authorities to them.

Conclusion

Jews in the Middle Ages were a tiny population in comparison to those
of the dominant cultures in which they made their home, but their importance to medieval culture was immense. From the Roman period, Jewish
families and their migrations from one region to another brought different cultural elements to the far reaches of the medieval world. Indeed,
the intellectual culture of medieval western Christianity, the so-called
Scholastic system, would never have acquired the vitally significant texts
of Aristotelian philosophy without the efforts of Jewish translators who
worked in Muslim Spain. Jewish traders and bankers provided Christians
and Muslims alike with goods, such as spices, that enlivened daily life,
and the financial means to develop a money economy. Jewish families
operated as virtual businesses, with all members dedicated to the success
and prosperity of the kinship unit, whether nuclear or extended.

The importance of Jews in the maintenance of medieval Christian society might in fact have contributed to the hostility Christians exhibited
against their Jewish neighbors. Christians were utterly dependent upon
the willingness of Jews to lend them money, to do jobs considered unclean

by Christians (such as tanning leather), and to provide them literally with the spices of life. This dependence bred resentment, especially among the common people. This, coupled with popular preachers who ranted against Jews as so-called Christ killers and who accused Jewish communities of everything from poisoning the public wells to murdering Christian babies, led to Jews being savagely attacked at certain critical times. Kings, barons, and bishops were wholly dependent for centuries on Jewish willingness to be their bankers. This dependence bred a cynical attitude of exploitative indifference in which Jews suffered because they were successful at the professions they were pushed into assuming. Exploited, attacked, and always designated as second-class, Jews nonetheless survived and contributed to their civilization.

Notes

1. William Chester Jordan, *The French Monarchy and the Jews: From Philip Augustus to the Last Capetians* (Philadelphia: University of Pennsylvania Press, 1989), 29.

2. Jordan, *The French Monarchy,* 30–31.

3. Michael Prestwich, *Edward I* (Berkeley: University of California Press, 1988), 345. Prestwich discusses this situation at some length. See 344–346.

4. For a useful map and timeline tracing the expulsions of the Jews from European kingdoms and regions, go to *A Teacher's Guide to the Holocaust,* "Map of Jewish Expulsions and Resettlement Areas in Europe," http://fcit.usf.edu/HOLOCAUST/gallery/expuls.htm.

5. These are compiled and analyzed by S. D. Goitein in a multivolume work that is abridged as *A Mediterranean Society: An Abridgment in One Volume,* ed. Jacob Lassner (Berkeley: University of California Press, 1999).

6. Kenneth R. Stow has explored the differences between customs in Europe and those elsewhere. See, especially, Stow, "The Jewish Family in the Rhineland in the High Middle Ages: Form and Function," *The American Historical Review* 92, no. 5 (1987): 1085–1110; and Stow, *Alienated Minority: The Jews of Medieval Latin Europe,* (Cambridge, MA: Harvard University Press, 1992), Chapter 9: The Family, 196–209.

7. See Stow and Norman Roth, *Daily Life of the Jews in the Middle Ages* (Westport, CT: Greenwood Press, 2005), especially 43–72.

8. This is discussed briefly by Alexandra Rothstein, "Gender and Feminism: Medieval Jewish Attitudes Toward Women," on *MyJewishLearning.com,* http://www.myjewishlearning.com/ideas_belief/genderfeminism/Fem_Traditional_TO/Fem_Medieval.htm.

9. See S. D. Goitein, *A Mediterranean Society,* 337–342.

10. Goitein, *A Mediterranean Society,* 340.

11. *The Memoirs of Glückel of Hameln,* tr. Marvin Lowenthal (New York: Schocken Books, Inc, 1977).

12. Roth, *Daily Life of Jews in the Middle Ages,* 54–55.

II

THE ENVIRONMENT OF THE FAMILY IN THE MIDDLE AGES

Medieval families did not exist in a vacuum. Everything from the physical environment in which they dwelled to the ways in which the idea of family was used as a rhetorical device by the political culture affected the medieval family's existence and modes of operation. The chapters in this section each focus on a specific topic that affected family life in the Middle Ages. These topics are discussed in a comparative context, as they affected family life in the four medieval cultures—western Christian, Byzantine, Islamic, and Jewish—under observation. Thus, the reader will be able to gain greater insight into specific elements of family life and experience; this insight will enhance the general knowledge acquired through reading the chapters in section 1. As in the previous chapters, historical context has been added when appropriate to help the reader understand how a particular topic interacted with historical issues that affected it.

6

The Physical Environment of the Medieval Family

Like families from all other historical eras and geographical regions, the living arrangements of medieval families depended significantly on socio-economic factors and, perhaps somewhat less significantly, on geography and location. Wealthy families lived in far more luxurious and spacious surroundings than did poor ones; rural families experienced different stresses in their environments than did urban ones. For all parts of the medieval world, it is easier to recreate the physical environments of wealthy and ruling families than those of poor families because the remains of medieval aristocratic and noble life have survived in much larger amounts: wealthy people throughout the medieval world built in stone and brick, not mud and thatch. Castles, palaces, and monasteries were far more likely to survive than the huts of medieval peasants or the tents of Bedouin caravan leaders. Nevertheless, certain kinds of sources reveal a great deal about the lives of medieval peasants, especially those in Europe, where the survival of records having to do with the poor has been far more successful.

Sources for Identifying the Physical Environment

The survival of medieval castles, manors, and townhouses makes it relatively easy to recreate the lives of the wealthiest 10 percent of the population of medieval Europe. The preservation of buildings is less common in the Byzantine east and still less in the Muslim Middle East of today, but archaeologists find it easier to locate and excavate stone buildings than wooden ones. As a result, modern-day historians have a great deal of information available to them about the physical environment of this small but influential population. Documentary sources, ranging from deeds outlining transfers of land and other property, wills, letters, even building plans also survive, although the documentary record is richer in some places than in others. In Britain, for example, a tremendous number of documents from the Middle Ages have survived, especially from 1200 to the present day. In Central Europe, Germany, and Eastern Europe—not to mention Byzantine Greece, Turkey, and the Muslim-dominated Middle East and North Africa—collections of documents are much less plentiful. Sometimes document collections were destroyed in modern times, such as occurred in Dublin in 1922 and Naples in 1945. Sometimes unusual document collections come to light, as occurred in Cairo in 1896 with the discovery of the Cairo synagogue's *geniza.*

New technologies and techniques in archaeology have also expanded the historian's understanding of the physical environment of the medieval family. Aerial photographs taken by reconnaissance planes during World War II revealed the outlines of early medieval arable fields underneath the later medieval and modern outlines. Identification of wood fragments in the ground have revealed the posts used to erect peasant houses in the English and French countryside. Excavations in European cities to build skyscrapers have uncovered medieval walls, houses, cemeteries, wells, and manufacturing centers. All of these have helped to expand our understanding of the ways in which medieval families lived and worked, and new discoveries are changing that picture every day.

The Environments of the Wealthy in the Medieval World

The common perception of today's students of medieval history is often a combination of King Arthur and *Monty Python and the Holy Grail.* Knights and ladies live in luxurious castles where servants silently cater to their every whim. Peasants live in tidy hovels where cool cider is always available to every passing knight errant. Even King Alfred the Great is instructed in oatcake-making by the elderly peasant woman who allows him to hide from the Viking marauders in a famous (although apocryphal) tale told often in both folklore and history books. Unfortunately, medieval life was not nearly so clean, tidy, and ordered.

Although only perhaps 10 percent of the population of the medieval world could in any way be considered wealthy—or even comfortable—and those 10 percent also comprised the politically enfranchised class, they loom large in modern imaginations because of the things they have left behind. Castles, cathedrals, monasteries, guildhalls, townhouses, palaces: all of these survive in very large numbers. It is hard to travel anywhere in Europe, the Middle East, or North Africa and not come across some physical evidence of medieval wealth and influence. What is surprising is how many structures were built for the comfort and care of so few people. In Wales and the Welsh March (the borderlands between England and Wales) castles dot the landscape every 6 to 10 miles, with almost as many monasteries in between, where the children of wealthy families were educated and occasionally housed, and into which young men and women entered as professional religious.

The development of the castle as both residence and fortification, however, took hundreds of years, reaching its greatest extent by the end of the thirteenth century. In the early Middle Ages, aristocrats throughout western Europe lived in large barn-like wooden buildings called longhouses. These were the center of noble life: a chieftain and his family lived in their longhouse, as did the war band (the young unmarried men attached to the household as the warriors of the chieftain's private army) and the servants. All activities engaged in by the early medieval aristocracy occurred in and around the longhouse, from sleeping and eating, to training, fighting, manufacturing, and agriculture. These structures were usually defended by wooden barriers, similar to stockade fencing, made of split tree trunks and woven battens, and were usually built on high land or even (especially by the Vikings) in the middle of ponds or lakes with causeway bridges built that could be broken up to secure the longhouses and other dwellings.

Life in and around the longhouse was focused on communal activities. Because the main source of heat was usually a central hearth that vented through a hole in the thatched roof, subdividing the longhouse into small rooms was not practical. As a result, everyone lived and worked in the same large open space. A partition might be erected to give the chieftain and his wife some privacy, but the modern notion of "a room of one's own" was not an issue in the Middle Ages. Indeed, there is some evidence to suggest that early medieval aristocrats brought their most valuable animals into the longhouse to protect them in the long cold winters and in times of war.

Because of the danger of fire in structures built of wood and thatch with open hearths at their center, kitchens tended to be located away from the main building. This minimized the danger of a kitchen fire spreading to the main structure and also kept the nasty smells, that came from slaughtering animals to be cooked and the garbage heaps of kitchen waste, away from the chieftain and his clan. Unfortunately, it also meant that food prepared in the kitchen had to be carried through the open air to the longhouse to be consumed. This system would continue until the development of chimney and flue technology in the twelfth century made it possible to locate kitchens closer to the buildings where the food was eaten.

In early medieval Gaul, the Merovingian elites were likely to have maintained a kind of hybrid dwelling that the historian Gregory of Tours referred to as a villa. These were, like longhouses, made of wood with outbuildings that contained space for livestock as well as amenities for the noble family. They were sometimes surrounded by fortifications, sometimes not.[1]

Sanitation facilities were minimal at best, especially in the early Middle Ages in western and northern Europe. Latrines were usually dug in the farthest corner of the fortified compound, often dangerously near the main water supply. Chamber pots might be employed by the women in the household, but the men were far more likely to use the corners of buildings as their privies. Until the development of the garderobe (to be discussed below), life in a medieval nobleman's house must have been overpoweringly smelly.

The furnishings of early medieval houses—even the wealthiest—were also minimal: tables that could be broken down and stacked against a wall, backless chairs that folded and could be stored in a cupboard, benches, straw-filled mattresses, and a bed only for the heads of the household. These items were made of wood, so very few survive, but those examples we do have suggest that they were built for comfort and durability rather than for aesthetic reasons. Tapestries or other kinds of woven hangings might have adorned the walls to keep out drafts as much as for their pleasing appearance. Woven mats made of rushes and other grasses were laid on the floors, in large part to pick up debris, mud, and fleas dropped on the floor by the inhabitants.

The prominence of Constantinople throughout the medieval world meant that its palaces—especially the Great Palace of Constantinople, built in the sixth century, and the Blachernae palace just outside the city built by emperor Alexios Komnenos around 1080—were considered the exemplar for all opulent structures that followed for several hundred years. Imperial palaces in the Byzantine world were, indeed, opulent, as were those of the caliphs in Damascus and Baghdad and of more local Muslim leaders in other parts of the Middle East. Examples such as the palace of Hir Al-Gharbi built in the late seventh century by caliph Hisham Ibn-Abdul Malik as a hunting lodge in the Homs region of Syria had amenities such as running water and interior gardens that Byzantine palaces also had, but that western elite structures would not match for centuries. Recent excavations in Lebanon of the Umayyad palace complexes at Anjar have unearthed a structure that might have looked at home in Europe four hundred years later: a large rectangular space enclosed by walls, with each wall containing a gate, defensive towers, and machicolations (openings in the upper walls through which defenders could pour nasty things on invaders).[2] The Umayyads were also responsible for building as many as five palaces in Jerusalem after their conquest in the late seventh century.[3] Until the later eighth century, such structures, built in stone and lavishly decorated, existed in the west only in the context of churches. Probably the most notable secular building of the early Middle Ages in the west was the palace of Emperor Charlemagne in Aachen. This was modeled on Byzantine examples and included a chapel (all that actually survives of the original structure) that contained mosaic decoration styled on Byzantine models in Lombard Italy.

The Development of the Castle in the Medieval West

With the coming of the Viking, Magyar (that is, Hungarian), and Muslim invaders into the western European world, it became increasingly necessary to erect fortifications to protect both landed estates and towns and villages. The building of towers, which had dropped significantly after the end of Roman rule in the west, rose again. Fortifications were most typically made of wood—high stockade walls were common, much like those of the American West in the nineteenth century—and surrounded longhouses and other outbuildings as ways to deter invaders. Eventually, the longhouses were replaced in much of western Europe by artificial mounds called mottes, with large wooden towers called keeps or *donjons* erected on top. The motte and its keep, along with the flatter land below the motte, were then surrounded by a wooden wall, called a bailey. This motte-and-bailey castle became the standard model for noble and royal fortifications in Continental western Europe from the tenth century, eventually being built in stone and then becoming far more sophisticated in style as the centuries progressed.

The transition from building in wood to building in stone began around the year 1000. This was in part because deforestation made building massive walls of wood less viable, in part because medieval engineers recognized that stone, while far more expensive and difficult to use, was far more secure. The incorporation of local stone—both recycled from Roman structures (Roman brick is often found in castle walls) and quarried anew—required significantly more manpower and skill than the building of wooden structures. As a result, castle building became possible only for the wealthiest members of medieval society. This was also more or less the case in the Byzantine and Muslim worlds, but in both a significant portion of the population lived in towns and cities that were surrounded by massive walls, so a greater portion of the population might have benefited from the protection stone walls could afford than most people in the west before towns began to be fortified.

Several areas of Europe experienced a building boom of castles in stone beginning in the mid-eleventh century: France, the Rhine region of Germany, Britain, and southern Italy and Sicily, both of the latter areas after they were conquered by Norman nobles. The development of castles and a castle culture in England, Wales, and Ireland indeed clearly followed the Norman conquests of those lands and so can provide a useful example of the ways in which castles grew and developed. The Normans who followed their duke, William the Conqueror, to England felt the need to demonstrate their dominance in a region where they were a tiny minority and the building of massive stone keeps (and large cathedral churches as well) was one way to spread the message. William himself built some of the first all-stone castles, particularly in London (the White Tower) and Dover Castle. His followers did the same in the regions they controlled by feudal tenure, such as the area between Wales and England known as the Welsh March. By the middle of the twelfth century, stone castles were plentiful throughout the British Isles, significantly altering both the landscape and the settlement patterns of the resident population. In Sicily and Southern Italy, the members of the Hauteville family who conquered originally as representatives of the pope, and then took over the region as dukes, princes, and, eventually, kings, followed a similar pattern. They were even more foreign to the region than their counterparts in England, so the building of major fortifications that represented both the pinnacle of contemporary engineering and the power of the ruling dynasty became a common concern. In France and the Holy Roman Empire, where the government was far less centralized, building styles varied considerably according to local custom. Medieval central and northern Italy was far more urbanized than areas to the north, and castles were far less typical. Instead, noble families built tall, narrow towers—sometimes several at a time—in the middle of town that acted as both a residence for the family and as a defensive structure to protect them in the numerous feuds that tended to develop among noble Italian families. Indeed, the historical basis for Shakespeare's *Romeo and Juliet* was such a feud among the nobility of Verona in the thirteenth century.

Beeston Castle, Cheshire, England (13th century).

Although there were numerous variations in castle building, in size, style, methods of construction, and location, a number of generalities can be made. Stone castles in medieval Europe tended to be located on high ground—often near a river or other body of water that could be diverted to form a moat. They were encircled by massive walls interspersed by towers that were sometimes square, sometimes octagonal, and sometimes

View of San Gimignano, Italy. Photo Credit: Erich Lessing/Art Resource, NY.

round. The outer curtain wall contained a fortified gate called a barbican, and entrance to the castle was made over a bridge through this gate. Inside the walls was the outer bailey. This was an open area used by the soldiers of the garrison as a practice field, by merchants as a place to sell wares, by the lord of the castle as a place to hold judicial courts (which could be held outdoors in good weather or inside the main tower or barbican). Other buildings dotted the landscape of the outer bailey: kitchens, workshops, blacksmith's forge, and so on. If the castle was small, then this was the only bailey and the great barbican gate led directly to the bailey and inner keep. The keep was usually the largest structure inside the castle walls, often centrally located. It housed the family, contained the kitchens for the domestic center of the castle community, and also contained storerooms and holding cells in the basement. The French word for the keep is *donjon,* which is where the word "dungeon" comes from. This was not originally meant as a prison, but rather prisoners were kept temporarily in the basement storerooms of the keep before they came to trial.

The family apartments in the keep were usually found on the floors above the ground floor (what in America is called the second and third floors, but in Europe is called the first and second stories). In the Middle Ages, ground floor rooms were almost always used as public spaces and storage, with private domestic spaces on upper floors: it was not only safer, but cleaner and airier. In castles built before 1300, family spaces were usually large open rooms with hearths on opposite ends. Small subdivided rooms were rare until the thirteenth century because chimneys were not invented until the later twelfth century and were not in wide use until the thirteenth century. Thus, in order to stay warm, but not be choked with smoke from the fireplace, rooms had to be large. The lord and lady of the castle might have their own bedroom, but the rest of the household lived far more communally. The Great Hall was used as a dining room, entertainment center, and dormitory for members of the household. The few women who worked as servants in the household had separate quarters, usually on an upper floor. The lady of the castle might also lay claim to the sunniest part of the keep: a small room on a high floor that faced the southwest, known as a *solar.* These were sometimes located in the southwest tower instead of the keep. This was almost always the center of activity for the women of the household, who wove and sewed in the room. Recent archaeological excavations, especially of castles in England and Wales, have revealed that the women's quarters in High and late medieval castles were often deliberately placed as far away from the center of the formal, public, and ceremonial spaces of the castle, such as the barbican and great hall, as possible. Although some archaeologists have suggested that this might have resulted in rendering the women who lived in the castle—of which there were few in most castle communities regardless—virtually invisible, other archaeologists, among them Roberta Gilchrist, dispute that the de-centering of female spaces in castle architecture makes them invisible and suggests other possible reasons for the locating of women far into the interior of the castle environment. For example, it might have been easier to protect women in the castle from invaders if their spaces were surrounded by public spaces dominated by males such as the garrisoned troops. On the other hand, women's spaces sometimes were located in the tower farthest from the main gate, which meant that their space was vulnerable to invaders, but protected from the invasion of male residents of the castle, whose interest in the women housed there might not have been all that benevolent. Thus, the location of female spaces within the medieval castle was probably designed to keep women separated physically from men, in much the same way as the *gynekaea* (that is, the women's rooms) operated in Byzantine elite houses (to be discussed later in this chapter). This physical separation was not like that of the Islamic harem, however, in that the women of the household were not restricted from entering the public spaces when their duties required them to do so.[4]

In addition to the usual domestic arrangements of bedrooms, *solar*, female work spaces, and so on, the family's domestic spaces also included a chapel, although in very large and fancy castles chapels were often built as separate buildings from the keep. The chapel often had direct access to the women's private spaces, as well as a public entrance for the use of the rest of the family. Multiple chapels are known to have existed in some castles, especially those that maintained large garrisons, since the troops and household servants would have been expected to engage in religious services as well as the family. Medieval noble families always had a chaplain in attendance, who often doubled as a secretary. Thus, the family could hear mass every day without having to leave the castle to go to church.

Soldiers garrisoned in the castle were housed in the towers of the outer bailey's wall. They might also have a separate kitchen that catered to their needs and perhaps even a mess hall if the castle were particularly large. Servants' lodgings were scattered throughout the castle: in outbuildings in the bailey, in the Keep, and in the towers. In addition, there was probably a lot of movement in and out of the castle, because the very act of building a stone castle tended to bring settlers into the region, and towns often grew in the shadow of the castle wall. In times of strife or war, the town residents were welcomed within the walls, the portcullis was lowered, and the drawbridge raised, cutting everyone off from potential invaders.

In very large and elaborate castles, especially ones built over a long period of time, this simple wall-bailey-keep design could become quite complex, including the use of outer and inner baileys, outer and inner keeps, concentric walls, and multiple gates. Castles could become virtual towns in their own right. And the more elaborate the castles became, the greater the population needed to sustain them. This, in turn, encouraged the further growth of towns around a castle, through settlement from the surrounding countryside as well as emigration from farther away.

Only the wealthiest and most important nobles were usually permitted by the king to build castles. Ironically, the large number of castles that existed in the Middle Ages was not because of a large number of people building them, but because a relatively small number of people built more than one castle. Indeed, the members of the upper nobility usually built castles in every location where they held significant amounts of property. Between 1190 and 1245, the Marshal earls of Pembroke, for instance, controlled most of south and south-central Wales, including more than a dozen castles they either inherited or built themselves in an area roughly the size of Rhode Island. When the earldom of Pembroke was divided among multiple heirs in 1245, the heirs then set upon a frenzy of castle building and improvement that lasted another hundred years. According to the Web site "Castles of Wales," more than five hundred medieval castle sites have been identified in a land mass of around 8,000 square miles—that is, an area smaller than the state of New Jersey.[5]

The facilities in medieval castles could be primitive indeed: wealth and status did not necessarily mean that living arrangements were luxurious. Although the family's quarters could be relatively spacious, sometimes even containing windows with glass panes—a real luxury before

Kidwelly Castle, Wales (13th century).

1400—they were usually very simply furnished: a bed for the lord and lady, and perhaps their children still in the home; removable bedding for the rest of the family who had to bed down in the great hall, nursery, or women's quarters; large trestle tables that could be broken down and pushed against the wall; folding wooden chairs and benches; and large sarcophagus-shaped storage boxes called wardrobes or presses that held everything from clothes to books and kitchen utensils could be all the furniture contained in a keep. Portable pillows might soften the surface for an elderly behind, but upholstered furniture was unheard-of until the fifteenth century.

Indoor plumbing and easy access to hot water did not exist until well into the nineteenth century, so sanitary facilities in castles, especially those housing large populations, could be difficult. Wells were dug inside the castle walls so that the inhabitants had fresh water for drinking and cooking, but if the well was not deep enough, the water could be fouled by contamination from the moat. The moat at the best of times—when it comprised water from a stream or tidal river that could flush out the worst of the contamination by means of sluice gates and the rising and falling tides—was more or less an open sewer. The castle's inhabitants flung their waste into the moat; the latrines—called garderobes (from which we get the term wardrobe) throughout most of Europe—that were built into the main towers and the keep, drained directly into the moat, and animals that fell into the moat likely drowned and then decomposed. The smell of the moat—not to mention the garderobes themselves—must have been close to unbearable when the castle was fully occupied. Garderobes were most frequently located in the towers of the outer bailey, where the drains could be built directly over the moat. They were accessed through a long narrow passageway—which probably made the smell easier to manage—and often had two seats instead of just one. The idea of a wardrobe containing both a toilet and a clothes closet comes from the invention of the garderobe: medieval people sometimes kept their clothing in or nearby the garderobe because the smell deterred moths. Bathing facilities were also limited to portable tubs, housed usually in the kitchens where it was warmer, and small basins sometimes built directly into the walls of a room that would hold water for washing the face and hands. In some castles, these basins actually had drains that emptied into the moat, making it much easier to keep both one's person and one's sink clean. Medieval Christian people in western Europe, unlike Jews, Byzantine Christians, and Muslims, did not bathe their entire bodies all that often, since heating water for a tub, filling the tub, and draining it afterwards were labor intensive jobs. Nevertheless, they were not as filthy as modern-day people might think. The use of steam rooms and saunas occurred all over the medieval world—from Muslim Anatolia to pagan and Christian Scandinavia. In the Mediterranean, the tradition of cleaning the body with olive oil, which was then scraped off the body with a special tool, continued into the Middle Ages. In addition, bath houses were built in Mediterranean regions and in Jewish quarters that were frequented by members of the community from all economic and social levels. Medieval aristocrats in the west were particular about their appearance and it was considered very poor form to come to the dining table with dirty faces or hands. All medieval cultures made soap from the fat of animals and vegetables and tried, at least, to keep the clothes worn against the body (called linen because of the fiber used to make them) clean.

Heating large, drafty, stone structures was also a problem. For the wealthy, the hanging of tapestries and the use of wood-framed partitions and screens helped to dissipate the worst of the rising damp experienced in a stone structure. Until the invention of the chimney, however, fireplaces were not well vented, so the great hall, with roaring fires on both ends, was undoubtedly horridly smoky (there is evidence that many people suffered from respiratory ailments in the years before central heating), and small rooms could not be heated by using a fireplace or hearth at all. Instead, small iron baskets, called braziers, were used: these held sea coal (soft coal that appeared just below the surface of the earth in some parts of Europe) or charcoal, partially burned logs, and other materials that would burn more cleanly than untreated, unprocessed wood. Saplings could be soaked in oil for both light and heat, but they were dangerously flammable and so not used in open hearths and braziers. In the Muslim Middle East, tar pools of raw petroleum were tapped to provide fuel for lamps but the climate in most Mediterranean areas did not require additional heating for much of the year. The lack of wood in those areas, though, made heating even more difficult.

The invention of the chimney in the late twelfth century, and the development of new techniques for making clear window glass at the same time, changed the domestic spaces of the wealthy classes immeasurably. Chimneys—often built in much the same way as garderobe drains—pulled the smoke from the fire upward and away from the ceiling. The addition of air circulation in the fireplace also made the fire burn hotter and kept coals going longer. Fireplaces with chimneys could be engineered so that the heat was thrown outward, making the area around it warmer. Fireplaces also made it more sensible to partition large rooms into smaller spaces, because the heat could be used more efficiently: it is hard to heat a huge hall from a fireplace, no matter how large the hearth might be.

The size and number of windows also affected the efficiency of medieval heating systems. Most residential structures throughout the medieval world had windows that were covered by woven screens or shutters. These kept out birds and other critters who might come through the window, but offered little protection from the elements (unless the shutters were completely closed) and did not permit much light to enter. Thus, interior spaces must have been lit with torches and rush lights nearly all the time, especially in winter, when the weather would have encouraged the shuttering of the windows. Window glass was used in the west first in churches in the early Middle Ages and then in royal residences by around the year 1100. It was, however, rare in other structures until the fifteenth century because of the huge expense involved. Glass made it possible to cut larger window openings—as long as it was safe to do so—so that more natural light entered the interior. Rooms were instantly warmer than they had been with open windows because the glass protected inhabitants from outside temperatures and the vagaries of the weather.

The conveniences and amenities developed for western European castles—fireplaces with chimneys, glass-paned windows, garderobes, and eventually water-closets—trickled down to the houses of the knightly, gentry, and merchant classes by the end of the Middle Ages. As will be discussed in the next section, the vast majority of people living in medieval Europe were not to experience such luxuries for many years.

Members of the lesser nobility and of the knightly class did build spacious, gracious homes for themselves, but these were rarely fortified to the degree a castle was. These fortified manor houses could be quite large and elegant, but they differed from castles in that they did not house a substantial garrison; the outer walls of the house often served as the main

Picton Castle, Wales (14th century).

fortifications; and the main gate opened directly into a courtyard where the manor house stood. Outbuildings were fewer and the number of non-family members housed in the manor was relatively small. Occasionally the king would grant permission to crenellate a manor house, which meant that the owner could build a higher wall with a parapet that could be used by soldiers to protect the manor. This essentially turned a manor into something resembling a castle, but often the difference of degree in fortifications was significant.

Stokesay Manor is a good example of a later medieval fortified house. It was constructed of stone on the lower floors, and half-timber (wood, rubble, mortar, and stucco) on the upper floors. The outer walls of the buildings in the compound were also in use as fortifications, the gate does not include a barbican, and there are no towers aside from the crenellations on the manor house itself. The result was a manor house that was spacious and lightly defended, but because of its location was more protected from determined and large bands of marauders than usually existed on a local level. This became far more typical of aristocratic housing, especially after 1400, when many castles were converted to more luxurious mansions, complete with large glass windows (sometimes known as oriel windows), multiple fireplaces, elegant staircases, and

Acton Burnell Fortified Manor, Shropshire, England (13th century).

Stokesay Manor, Shropshire, England (14th century).

Chirk Castle, Wales (13th–14th century).

even water-closets, which had toilets that could be flushed with water, replacing the earlier garderobes.

Elite Houses in the Mediterranean World

The dwellings of elites in the western Mediterranean regions were often very different from those of northern Europe. In Christian Spain, southern France (what is now called the *Côte d'Azur*), Italy, and the western Balkans, feudalism was less thoroughly incorporated into elite culture, so one impetus for building castles was missing until the thirteenth and fourteenth centuries. In Italy, from Rome to Lake Como in the north, elites were less concerned with fortifying their rural villas and more concerned about building defensive structures in the crowded cities that were experiencing significant growth in both population and wealth by the second quarter of the thirteenth century. The Italian aristocrat built tall narrow defensive towers in these urban areas, sometimes linking them on upper floors by using bridges. Although far less spacious than a rural or even urban castle of northern Europe, these towers served similar purposes as means of defense of assets, administration, and also domesticity. Although most of these towers were pulled down by popular uprisings in the later thirteenth and fourteenth centuries, the skyline of the Tuscan hill town of San Gimignano can provide the modern viewer with a feel for what it must have been like to live in such a city. The multiple towers rise over the town in a tight cluster. Although these structures are only a small percentage of the many that must have existed in the Middle Ages, they can nonetheless provide a tiny window into medieval aristocratic life.[6]

The famous tower built on Tiber Island in Rome, right against the Fabricius Bridge, can provide a closer view of what tower dwelling might have been like in the Middle Ages. Originally built in the late tenth century by the Pierleoni family, it was eventually sold to the Caetani family in 1294, who used it as one base for their fortress. Several important events took place there, such as when Countess Matilda of Tuscany hid there with Pope Victor III in 1087. There is evidence that it was used occasionally as a dwelling, but its tiny windows, single garderobe that emptied directly into the river, and cramped quarters probably could not compare to the spacious palaces and other, more spacious, towers built in Trastevere and the Campo Marzio by Roman aristocratic families.[7]

Historians have much less information on the living arrangements of people living in the Byzantine Empire and the southern Mediterranean in the Middle Ages. While it is clear that rulers lived in imposing and lavishly appointed palaces, the domestic spaces of aristocrats, the wealthy urban dwellers, and especially the poor majority are less easily reconstructed. It is clear that members of the ruling class built fortified structures to live in, with walls and towers, that in some ways resemble medieval western castles. Indeed, some historians suggest that western castle building was influenced significantly by the experiences of crusaders going to the Holy Land in 1096: the massive walls of the cities of Constantinople and Antioch and the fortifications of the Turkish amirs were certainly imitated by the Knights Hospitaller when they expanded Krak des Chevaliers in Syria (which had originally been built by the Turks) and by King Edward I when he built Caernarvon Castle in the 1280s. When, in 1204, western European crusaders were diverted to conquer Constantinople, capital of the Christian Byzantine Empire, instead of Muslim Egypt, those westerners who settled in Greece and the Aegean islands built castles there modeled on the ones they built at home. Native residential spaces, even for the wealthy, must have been somewhat smaller than in the west, however, because the elite populations in the eastern Mediterranean tended to live in urban environments. Such structures have long since disappeared under the pavements of modern-day cities, making their recovery virtually impossible. Historians have tended to base their conclusions about such living arrangements on the assumption that housing styles today are very similar to those in the ancient world: most people live in multi-room structures built of brick and stucco. These buildings are usually two stories high, with an enclosed central courtyard. The main rooms that faced the street were used by the men in the family (the ancient Greek tradition of the *andron*—the man's room—seems to have persisted), with the kitchens and women's spaces located in the back of the house and the upper floor. Furnishings in these homes tended to be quite simple, although the use of luxury fabrics such as silk and silk-wool blends was probably common for the wealthy class and the moveable accoutrements, such as dishes, drinking vessels, religious artifacts, and so on, were probably of very high quality.

Recent archaeological findings have verified many historians' assumptions about Byzantine housing throughout the Mediterranean. Early Byzantine houses (that is, until about 700) for elites often took the form of a peristyle house: an extended house built around a central courtyard that was enclosed by a covered gallery called a peristyle, containing an elaborate dining room called a *triclinium* (this refers to the three couches that were built into the walls of the room), and of varying size depending on the location—urban or rural—and terrain. This style of house can be seen in Roman era remains and is a feature of elite houses from Pompeii to Syria. Many of the houses used by elites in the early Byzantine period indeed seem to have been built earlier and might have been used as dwellings long after the peristyle house had stopped being built.[8] Less wealthy early Byzantine families lived in smaller structures that, like peristyle houses, had central courtyards but were less elaborate. Rooms were partitioned in ways to make them more versatile.

In the later Byzantine period, although cities apparently contracted significantly in size, urban living retained its importance for the aristocracy. As in the early period, a central courtyard was an essential component to houses from all social levels, but second floors might also have added more space for the wealthy elites. Building materials might have actually been culled from ruins of earlier structures. Kitchens and sanitary facilities are hard to identify in such archaeological remains, but it is likely that much of that kind of activity occurred in the courtyard, where the heat from cooking fires would dissipate without overheating the domestic apartments.[9]

Members of the aristocracy who lived in the countryside throughout the Byzantine and Muslim empires seem to have continued this conservative approach to domestic spaces. The old Roman-era villa style of home seems to have persisted. This was comprised of a large and spacious house that sprawled over the landscape in order to benefit from both sun and shade, with outbuildings for the maintenance of agricultural labor and the storage of supplies and produce. Indeed, in the medieval Balkans (the region between Italy and Greece) and the kingdom of Hungary, the Roman *latifundium* remained as a common system for the exploitation of peasant labor and the production of cash crops such as grapes for wine and olives. These spacious settings for a wealthy lifestyle were probably little different from their Roman predecessors, although the absence of the so-called Roman Peace probably meant that they were fortified with at least a wall around the villa and outbuildings to protect both the inhabitants and the profits of the villa.

The conquest and settlement of western European crusaders into the Mediterranean world altered not only the political and social structures of the Byzantine Empire in particular, but also its architecture. The Europeans who conquered Constantinople in 1204 established feudal-style lordships in Greece and the Aegean islands that persisted for a century and even two centuries afterwards. They built western-style castles and usually avoided living in cities. Their building styles therefore influenced domestic architecture in the countryside, which had retained its Late Antique character for a long period of time, despite changes in agricultural production over the early Byzantine centuries.[10]

The interiors of the houses of wealthy Byzantine elites ranged widely from extreme luxury to surprising simplicity. Although most of the evidence is anecdotal, it would seem that the wealthiest homes enjoyed many luxuries, from frescoed and decorated walls to cushioned furniture, glass and metal utensils, and beds with elaborate draperies. Less extravagant houses of the wealthy classes just below the highest level might not have had such amenities. Bedding might have been laid on the permanent benches built into the walls of the dining room, or *triclinium,* and tables were likely to resemble those in western European keeps: wooden tops and trestle legs that could be folded and stored for convenience.[11]

One source of significant debate is whether Byzantine women were confined in women's quarters in the ways that ancient Greek and medieval

Muslim women were claimed to have been. There is no firm conclusion about this issue, because the literary statements about such confinement of especially elite women is not reinforced by the archaeological record and other kinds of sources, such as wills, that suggest there was no separation between men and women.[12]

The homes of wealthy Muslims resembled those of elite Byzantine Christians. They were usually made of stone and stucco, with plain fronts and opulent interiors, all focused on central interior courtyards. Unlike Byzantine homes, which tended to be somewhat Spartan in their furnishings, Muslim elites enjoyed handmade carpets on the floors, cushioned furniture, tiled and painted walls, and so on. Decoration included beautifully lettered Quranic inscriptions written in Arabic calligraphic script and other ornamental designs.[13]

Although Muslim leaders built fortresses and castles, these were more for defense and less like western castles, which were also residential in purpose. Still, fortifications such as the massive stone forts of Syria and the mud and clay brick castles of Iraq and Iran, of necessity housed many people, from military leaders and soldiers to common people who supplied the troops. In addition, Muslim rulers built palace-castles as retreats in the Jordan desert.

Domestic Arrangements in Cities in the Medieval West

The living situations of even wealthy people living in the small and cramped urban centers of medieval Europe were very different from those of the landed aristocracy. Members of the urban wealthy elite—the guild masters, wealthy merchants, and professionals such as lawyers and notaries—lived in houses that, by the standards of the urban landscape, were spacious and elegant but could not compete with the elaborate halls of the aristocrat's castle. Houses were multi-story, built of stone and stucco in the southern portion of the continent and usually of half-timber—a combination of exposed wood beams and stuccoed rubble—in the north, with small enclosed courtyards and gardens. The entire structure might be surrounded by a wall, but it is far more likely that the ground floor of the home was used for commercial purposes, as a shop or office, so walls surrounded the rear portions of the house and garden in order to provide some measure of privacy for the family. Family members lived in the upper stories of the urban home, with the ground floor and basement levels devoted to storage and commercial operations. Kitchens were often attached to the back end of the house, or in some cases separated entirely from the house itself, in order to protect it from fire: a constant problem in medieval cities. Servants and apprentices slept in the attics and shop floors. Staircases were often attached to the exterior of the houses, surrounded by flimsy walls, since it was easier to build them that way and it maximized the space inside the house.

The wealthiest members of the urban elite devoted their disposable wealth to the decoration of their homes rather than to creating huge palatial structures. The interiors of these houses were luxurious indeed, with the whitewashed walls hidden behind tapestries that began to be mass-produced in the thirteenth century, glass-paned windows, fireplaces with elaborate mantels, painted ceilings, and expensive furniture. Unfortunately, sanitary facilities in medieval cities were not comparable to those found in castles. Elites would usually have a latrine or outhouse in the back garden, but servants would have to make do with the public latrines found at the end of city streets, where the raw sewage flowed directly from the latrine into the teeming street.

One home design that became quite popular, especially in northern Europe and the British Isles, incorporated the air space available at the levels above the street in order to make the living spaces for wealthy families more spacious. The second and third floors of the houses (called the first and second stories in Europe) were extended outward beyond the foundation's footprint so that they overhung the street. These extensions were then braced from below by buttressing made of stone and wood. Although an effective method for gaining greater interior space, this design made the streets of medieval cities even darker and more grim. The overhangs often blocked almost all the sunlight getting to the streets, and the tendency to hurl the contents of chamber pots and rubbish bins from the upper story windows into the open sewer running down the middle of the street not only contributed to what must have been a horrible stench, but also endangered people walking on the sidewalks, who were only partially protected by the overhang (this is the origin of the tradition of ensuring that women walked on the inside of the sidewalk, with men walking on the outside, nearer the curb: that way, women's clothing did not get splashed!).

Since people tended to live and work in the same space, a great deal of the house could be devoted to economic interests. Even the upper floors of the house could be turned over to production and manufacture if the business required large machinery (such as a printing or bookbinding shop) or employed a large number of apprentices and journeymen. Businesses tended to be clustered in particular parts of the city, such as in medieval London, where printing, book production, and notarial services were clustered along Fleet Street and Chancery Lane on the western end of the city, which was also the center of lawyer training and support for the law courts. Butchers, fishmongers, and tanners, on the other hand, all lived along Cheapside, on the opposite end of the city. This meant that some parts of the city were truly unhealthy to live in, but even the most successful butcher in London could not move his business away from Cheapside because his business would collapse.

The living arrangements of the poor in medieval cities were grim indeed. Confined to slums in the worst parts of town—usually downriver from the elites' quarters so that even the water was fouled from the rubbish and sewage thrown into the river upstream—with inadequate light, sanitation, or housing, these parts of the medieval city were truly unspeakable. Attempts to clean up such city quarters were rare, and notoriously unsuccessful. The political leaders of London, for example, banned the dumping of sewage and garbage into the Thames, but they were completely unable to enforce these bans, which were renewed every decade to little effect. Sometimes the best thing to happen to a city slum was a massive fire, which destroyed everything and probably deodorized the quarter to some extent. The lifespan of the urban poor was woefully short, with disease and starvation far more common than health and success.

Urban Living in the Mediterranean World

No matter the cultural environment—Roman Christian, Muslim, or Byzantine Christian—the Mediterranean Sea and the long history of cities around it determined the shape and the living arrangements in medieval urban areas. Cities around the Mediterranean were much more densely populated than those in northern Europe, with populations many times larger. Mediterranean cities had been around a great deal longer than those in northern Europe, as well, and living patterns had been more or less fixed from the Roman period. As a result, domestic structures were (and continue to be) remarkably similar to those that had existed for millennia.

The typical house for the wealthiest members of the urban elite was undoubtedly more spacious than that of the working classes, but the greatest difference between them was probably the fact that the wealthy were able to have large enclosed courtyards in their compounds that provided fresh air, privacy, and a cool place to live and sleep in the heat of a Mediterranean summer. Wood was rarely used in house construction in areas where forests simply did not exist, so rubble, stone, and stucco walls, and roofs made of terra cotta tiles, gave Mediterranean cities a distinctive look. Furnishings even among the wealthy urban classes were likely to have been quite simple and minimalist, since a cluttered house meant a stuffy house.

The poor in Mediterranean cities were just as badly off as those in the north, but they had a distinct advantage over their northern European peers: the climate. There were slums galore in Mediterranean cities, with beggars, thieves, and prostitutes massing in the streets, but people did not generally freeze to death in the winter, and the need to heat ramshackle wooden houses, which often resulted in fires that decimated entire quarters of northern cities, was less an issue in the south. In addition, both Muslim and Byzantine cultures retained Roman practices of distributing grain and oil to the poorest inhabitants as acts of charity. This was institutionalized in the government, rather than overseen by the church, as it was in western Europe.

One thing probably missing from many urban houses in the Mediterranean was a kitchen. From the Roman period, the preparation of food was often a commercial venture, with restaurants and food counters on every street corner offering cooked food for a reasonable price. Since charcoal and wood for cooking fires was likely to have been somewhat scarce and expensive, it is likely that this kind of system prevailed in much of the Mediterranean world, at least for the working poor, into the medieval era. Certainly, Muslim and Byzantine sources describe urban environments in which men remain outside their homes for virtually the entire day and evening, returning only to sleep, and they seem to have frequented shops selling prepared food and drink—just as the typical Mediterranean male does to this very day.

Recent excavations in the former Byzantine Empire has revealed more of the urban landscape in the Middle Ages. Uncovering the medieval past in the western Mediterranean region has been somewhat more difficult, in part because of a lack of interest in the medieval remains that lie atop Roman ruins, but also because Renaissance and Baroque structures that are highly valued utilize the same space as the medieval cities. Nevertheless, it is likely that the houses of the middle classes revealed in eastern Mediterranean excavations were not all that different from those in the western Mediterranean or the Muslim Middle East. In the east, the most common houses were small, with a few rooms grouped around a central corridor. Kitchens seem to have been absent, so any cooking by the family might have been done on open fires in the interior courtyard. Furnishings were very sparse. In medieval Damascus, houses sometimes had second floors that were built out over the street, much the same as urban dwellings in the west. This provided more spacious interiors for the people (usually women) dwelling in the upper floors, but meant that the streets resembled dark tunnels.

An element of medieval Muslim cities that did not appear in either Byzantine or western European ones was the caravansary. This was a section of the city devoted to serving the caravans of Bedouins who engaged in long-distance trade from North Africa to India and even China along the so-called Silk Road through central Asia. Caravansaries were like inns in that they provided places to eat and sleep for the itinerant Bedouin. They also formed temporary market centers for the selling of the goods the Bedouin transported. Finally, they could be come semi-permanent or even permanent settlements in Muslim cities, where Bedouin could live in an environment that approximated that of living in their traditional desert communities.

The poor throughout the Mediterranean world could not avoid the squalor evident in all medieval cities. It is almost impossible to reconstruct the domestic lives of the poor: their meager dwellings have long since been confined to oblivion.

Roman traditions of personal hygiene persisted in the medieval Mediterranean, and so the availability of public baths, latrines, and even saunas, at least for men, continued to be high. Indeed, the crusaders from western Europe who settled in the eastern Mediterranean apparently became so accustomed to bathing frequently and to wearing clean, easily washable cotton and linen clothing (unlike the heavy woolen clothing typical in the west) that western religious leaders accused them of decadence and of going native. Certainly, the sewage systems in many Mediterranean cities were considered superior to those in northern Europe, although cities such as Acre, to which Christians fled in the years following the Muslim recovery of Jerusalem, were described as teeming slums of filth, disease, and crime.

For some female family members, living in these urban environments was probably less delightful than for men. Muslim and (according to many historians) Byzantine culture required a strict separation of women and men and discouraged so-called respectable women from appearing in public. As a result, women were far more likely to be confined to their houses, even to the stifling upper floors, than were men. Although the image of the royal harem relates only to the highest levels of the elite, the confinement of women in Muslim culture was very important to the maintenance of family continuity. Women from wealthy families certainly benefited from the availability of their open courtyards, which provided both the privacy required from the culture and the fresh air people craved. Women from less wealthy families were not so lucky. Women from poor families could not afford to worry about perceptions of respectability: they had to work to sustain their families, so they presided over shops, prepared and sold food, and worked as domestic servants. These women occupied the public spaces just as consistently as did men, but unlike men they did not have the advantages of bathhouses and cafes to provide a much needed respite from the hot sun. Byzantine women below the level of the elite also could not afford to maintain the respectable separation from both males and public spaces that the religious literature tended to demand. Their labor, in the preparation and selling of food and in the making of textiles, was essential for family survival just as it was in other medieval cultures.

Jewish Quarters in Medieval Cities

The image of the Jewish ghetto, so visible in early modern Rome and Venice, was not really the case in medieval Europe. Jews did tend to cluster in certain areas of urban spaces for the simple reason that they were limited in the kinds of work they could engage in, so moneylenders', jewelers', and goldsmiths' districts were occupied by Jewish families. In addition, Judaic practice required Jews to live within walking distance of a synagogue, so they tended to live in small enclaves within larger Christian districts. In some areas, such as Christian Spain and parts of Germany and the eastern Holy Roman Empire, royal and city law sometimes restricted Jews to certain sections of the city, but the image of the squalid ghetto, where Jewish families were crammed into filthy quarters surrounded by high walls and a locked gate, belongs more properly to the era of the sixteenth and seventeenth centuries, when Christian anti-Semitism expanded.[14] Without any physical separation between them, Jewish homes were thus often interspersed among Christian homes in many cities in Europe. This sometimes was a source of anxiety, even paranoia, on the part of the Christian leaders in a city, who sometimes suspected Jews of poisoning wells used by Christians (there were wells and fountains prominently displayed in the better parts of the city in order to ensure reasonably clean drinking and cooking water for the inhabitants). The mass murder of the Jews of Mainz and Cologne by crusaders on their way to Constantinople might have been prevented if Jews had been living in an enclosed quarter of the city, with a gate that locked.

Jewish homes were not very different from Christian homes. In western European cities, their home were multistory and with the same kind of overhanging second and third floor, with the only differences in the houses being dictated by Judaic traditions. There is some evidence that wealthy Jews tried to build houses of stone, perhaps as a protective measure in an era when attacks on Jewish homes by Christian mobs included setting them on fire with all the inhabitants being barricaded inside. The kitchen might have been somewhat more elaborate, especially in wealthier homes, since kosher laws required two sets of dishes and different cooking pots for preparing meat and dairy-based foods. In less wealthy homes the kitchen facilities might have been much simpler, because communal ovens and cauldrons for cooking were sometimes provided in a central location, much as they were in Christian quarters. Jews also were not permitted to use Christian public latrines (which might not have been such a hardship, considering how awful they must have been), so sanitary facilities in homes might have been more elaborate. Jews also bathed more frequently—the ritual bath, or *mikvah,* was required after all kinds of activities, from sexual relations to menstruation—and so bathhouses with separate facilities for men and women were nearby Jewish districts or areas where Jewish families clustered. Unlike bathhouses for the Christian community, these were not fronts for prostitution, but in fact places connected to religious observance.

The furnishings in Jewish households were likely to have been more or less identical to Christian households of the same social classes. Although occasionally restricted in the kinds of luxury goods they could own— most medieval cities had sumptuary laws that were designed to identify different social groups on the basis of the clothing they could wear and even the number of windows their houses could have—it is doubtful that anyone entering a Jewish home would see a significant difference in its layout and décor from a similar Christian home. Wealthy Jews in the later

Middle Ages might have displayed such luxuries as carpets, draperies, upholstered furniture, and paneled walls somewhat earlier than Christian elites' homes. Such domestic luxuries were popular in areas where Jewish trade predominated, such as the Mediterranean cities and the flourishing urban centers of Flanders and the Netherlands. One difference would have been that every Jewish home had a *mezuzah* hanging on the door frame of the front door. This was a small scroll, sometimes encased in a metal or wooden housing, upon which was written, in Hebrew, a prayer for the prosperity of the household. These were blessed by rabbis every year before Passover, and they identified a Jewish home from a Christian one. This could have been a significant disadvantage during time when Christian hostility toward Jews erupted in violence, but the tradition of the *mezuzah* remained nonetheless.

In central Europe, where Jews were somewhat less restricted, their houses might have been larger and more spacious, but these dwellings were also probably occupied by more than one family at a time. This is in direct contrast to houses in older areas of Jewish settlement—areas such as England, France, and the Rhineland from which Jews were expelled beginning in the later thirteenth century—where nuclear families were more the norm. At the same time, the homes of poor Jews were probably just as cramped and squalid throughout Europe as were the homes of the Christian urban poor. When, at the very end of the Middle Ages, Jews still living in western European cities, such as Rome, began to be pushed into specific quarters of the city, the quality of their living spaces deteriorated. The ghetto of Rome, for example, by 1600 had a population estimated to be as high as 10,000 in an area of only a few kilometers in size. The early modern ghettos in eastern Europe, such as those that existed in Prague and Warsaw, were also very crowded.

In the Byzantine and Muslim empires, Jewish homes were also more or less identical to those of their Christian and Muslim neighbors. Jews were geographically restricted in Constantinople, possibly because of their own preference, but in the rest of the Mediterranean, from al-Andalus to the Holy Land and Byzantine Anatolia, Jewish homes intermingled with those of everyone else. In addition, whereas Jews in most of western Europe were not allowed to own land, in other parts of the medieval world, such as Muslim Spain, they were not restricted in this way. Jews are recorded as owning vineyards and olive groves, for example. Nevertheless, the dominant Jewish domestic unit would be in an urban environment and Jewish landowners usually hired stewards to maintain and run their rural properties.

Domestic Arrangements of the Rural Peasant

The rural village was the principle living environment for the vast majority of medieval people. Agriculture was the largest portion of the medieval economy, and agricultural labor the largest element of the labor force. In western Europe, most peasants lived in villages clustered around arable fields, pasture, and waste—a system known as a manor—in which they worked in exchange for land to grow their own food and a dwelling. Peasants, whether free or unfree, were generally under the authority of lords (who could be a lay person or the leader of a monastic house) who actually controlled the land on which the peasants lived and worked. Thus, the village and its buildings (including the church) were the property of the lord of the manor, and the villagers who lived there were either tied to the land as serfs or were rentiers, who paid rents for their property in the form of sharecropping.

Unlike the rise of cities in the High Middle Ages or the development of feudalism and its transformation of the aristocracy and knightly class, peasant culture was much slower to change. Indeed, the lives of peasants did not change significantly from the late Roman period to the Industrial Revolution, when life changed very dramatically. The same can be said for peasant dwellings. Peasant houses in the west were usually made of timber, rubble, mud, and straw—a collection of building materials known as wattle and daub—and were roofed with thatch. The poorest houses were small, perhaps only one room, sometimes with a sleeping loft accessed by a ladder (references to people sleeping "in the roof" appear in coroner's inquests because they sometimes fell out of the rafters while asleep and died). These cottages usually had a small plot of land attached where the family grew vegetables for the cooking pot, since the arable land was entirely taken up with grain production. The back garden was also used for keeping chickens, and probably as a latrine. Kitchen facilities were primitive: an open hearth with perhaps a venting hole in the thatched roof, and an iron support for a cooking pot. Ovens for baking were usually communal, located in the village in an area devoted to baking and beer brewing.

Wealthier peasants, such as those who left inventories of their household goods in the later Middle Ages, lived in more spacious houses, although they were still quite small by modern standards. Some had two or three rooms, with partitions for the largest room, called in such inventories the hall. Fireplaces with chimneys might replace the open hearth, making it possible to have a room dedicated to sleeping. These wealthier houses could be made of stone, rubble and mortar, and other more durable materials. Indeed, some have survived for centuries, being converted into quaint cottages for summer tourists.

In the Mediterranean world, peasant houses resembled those of wealthier country folk, but on a much smaller scale. The opulence of the wealthiest was obviously not a part of peasant life, but the houses of the rural poor were likely made of brick, stucco, and tile much like those of the wealthy. They were limited in size, but probably retained the interior courtyard of more spacious homes since that space was used for both cooking and sleeping.

The Mediterranean climate was less suitable for growing grain than areas farther north, but the centuries-old production of olives and grapes made peasant communities successful as long as they worked together. Grain probably had to be imported into many communities, especially in the eastern Mediterranean, although wheat and other grains were grown even on the most marginal land. Peasant communities grew other food, such as root vegetables, rice, and green vegetables for their subsistence, maintained groves of fruit trees, and raised livestock, especially pigs and goats. Areas near the coast also were engaged in fishing. Thus the peasant communities ringing the Mediterranean, like those of the north, survived through communal labor and, to some extent, communal living.

Furniture in the peasant home was also minimal. If the family was reasonably well off, there might be a bed for the husband and wife. Children bedded down on straw-stuffed mattresses that were stored under the bed during the day. A table and benches and a storage press might be all that the family was able to afford. Indeed, flexibility would have been more important in peasant houses than having them stuffed with furniture, especially since they often brought the smaller animals, such as chickens and goats, into the house in the cold winters to protect them.

There were many economic levels within the general rubric of peasant in the Middle Ages, so this vision of the typical peasant house does not necessarily represent the lifestyles of the wealthier members of the peasantry, who undoubtedly lived in dwellings that were more like those of the gentry than of their poorer neighbors. This depiction does not represent the dwelling places of poorer peasants, either, since they probably had even less comfortable and less safe places to sleep. In the fourteenth century, the poet William Langland, in his work *The Vision of Piers the Plowman,* depicted peasant life as beset by hardship and deprivation.[15] Most historians would be hard put to contradict him. Moreover, the depiction of peasant life found in *Piers the Plowman* has as much relevance for the Muslim or Byzantine peasant as it does for the English plowman living in the late fourteenth century.

Conclusion

The domestic spaces of medieval families varied significantly according to geography, culture, and social class. Nevertheless, certain general conclusions are possible. The wealthier classes always built their homes—whether villa, tower, or castle—from the most durable materials available. Even the most elite domestic spaces were designed, however, more for work than for leisure. Women's quarters hummed with activity, while the exterior spaces were full of men engaged in their pursuits. Interior furnishings tended to be spare and simple, even among the elite, simply because the dwelling spaces had to be versatile and large, heavy furniture would have been difficult to move.

Among the urban classes of the medieval world, domestic and work spaces were literally combined. Shops occupied the ground floor, living areas the upper floors. Urban areas were always cramped for space, and the domestic arrangements of all urban classes had to place a premium on its efficient use. For the wealthy, this did not prevent a certain level of luxury from existing, in the form of upholstered furniture and comfortable beds. For the poor, life in medieval cities must have been, to use a famous phrase, "nasty, brutish, and short."

Peasant communities benefited from being in the open air, but that does not mean they lived in luxurious surroundings. Peasant dwellings were small, often made of non-permanent building material. Families were undoubtedly cramped, but this probably encouraged more communal activities. The typical peasant dwelling, with its wattle-and-daub walls and thatched roof, could be seen in western Europe from the Roman period to the eighteenth century. The same could be said for the stucco farmhouse of the Mediterranean peasant.

Notes

1. For an extended discussion of Merovingian nobles' dwellings, see Ross Samson, "The Merovingian Nobleman's Home: Castle or Villa?" *Journal of Medieval History* 13 (1987): 287–315.

2. For more information on these excavations, see "Anjar," at *Al Mashriq—The Levant,* http://almashriq.hiof.no/lebanon/900/910/919/anjar1/emergence.html and its following pages.

3. The excavations of these palace structures can be seen at "The Umayyad Palaces," http://jeru.huji.ac.il/ee23.htm.

4. See Robert Gilchrist, "Medieval Bodies in the Material World: Gender, Stigma and the Body" in *Framing Medieval Bodies,* ed. Sarah Kay and Miri Rubin (Manchester: Manchester University Press, 1994), 43–61 for an analysis of this issue.

5. See *The Castles of Wales,* http://www.castlewales.com/home.html for many interesting facts about and excellent photographs of castles in Wales and the borderlands between England and Wales (known as the Marches).

6. For more information on aristocratic tower-building in the High and later Middle Ages, see Lauro Martines, *Power and Imagination: City-states in Renaissance Italy,* Reprint Edition (Baltimore: The Johns Hopkins University Press, 1988), especially chapters 1–3.

7. For more information on Roman aristocratic towers and villas from the Middle Ages, see Richard Krautheimer, *Rome: Profile of a City, 312–1308,* New Edition (Princeton: Princeton University Press, 2000).

8. See Simon Ellis, "Early Byzantine Housing" in *Secular Buildings and the Archaeology of Everyday Life in the Byzantine Empire,* ed. Ken Dark (Oxford: Oxbow Books, 2004), especially 37–42 for a discussion of the peristyle house.

9. This is discussed by Lefteris Sigalos in "Middle and Late Byzantine Houses in Greece (Tenth to Fifteenth Centuries)" in *Secular Buildings and the Archaeology of*

Everyday Life in the Byzantine Empire, ed. Ken Dark (Oxford: Oxbow Books, 2004), 53–63.

10. Sigalos, "Middle and Late Byzantine Houses," 65–70.

11. Virtually the only discussion of the interiors of Byzantine houses in English is found in Nicolas Oikonomides, "The Contents of the Byzantine House from the Eleventh to the Fifteenth Century," *Dumbarton Oaks Papers* 44 (1990): 205–214.

12. This debate is outlined efficiently by Alexander P. Kazhdan in "Women at Home" *Dumbarton Oaks Papers* 52 (1998): 1–17.

13. Several Web sites show examples of the décor of medieval Muslim houses: "Old Damascus," http://www.oldamascus.com/home.htm and "Horace Mann's Architecture in Medieval Islamic Empires," http://www.sfusd.k12.ca.us/schwww/sch618/Architecture/Architecture.html.

14. The classic discussion of the development of the ghetto is that of Israel Abrahams in *Jewish Life in the Middle Ages,* Reprint Edition (New York: Meridian Books, 1958 [1898]), 62–72.

15. A good edition, one which includes both a translation from the original Middle English and selections from the original text, is William Langland, *Piers Plowman* (Norton Critical Edition), trans. E. Talbot Donaldson, ed. Elizabeth Ann Robertson and Stephen H.A. Shepherd, New Edition (New York: W.W. Norton and Company, 1996).

7

Grooms and Brides, Husbands and Wives, Fathers and Mothers

Throughout the medieval world, the most common family arrangement included both husbands and wives, although one of the spouses might not be the parent of the children in the family. The modern Western notion of a love match arranged by a couple who has met, dated, and decided to marry has no parallel in medieval realities: marriages were almost always arranged by the parents of the prospective couple or by the future husband and the parents or guardian of his desired bride. In some cases, the couple did not even meet until shortly before the ceremony and, in the case of royal marriages, sometimes proxies were used to perform the ceremony. As mentioned in section 1, marriages in some medieval societies—especially Muslim culture and Jews living in Muslim-dominated regions—were fairly easily dissolved, but in other societies—especially Christian Europe—they were far less easy to break up. In all cases, the goal of marriage was supposed to be the production of children, although economic, social, and emotional reasons were often more important than the ideal as stated by the main religions of the day.

This chapter focuses on the formation of marriage and the kinds of relationships that developed between husbands and wives, how these relationships influenced the experience of being fathers and mothers, and how changes in family structure through death and divorce also altered these relationships.

Brides and Grooms

Once a marriage had been arranged by the interested parties, the wedding did not necessarily take place immediately afterwards. Betrothals could be arranged long before the couple were old enough to marry. Even though the legal age of marriage was around 13 for females and 16 for males in the two Christian cultures and even younger in Jewish and Muslim cultures, betrothals in infancy were not uncommon among the wealthiest members of medieval society. In all the medieval cultures the process of marriage from betrothal to wedding could be nullified if the couple was completely unsuited to each other. Also, the consent of both parties had to be announced formally. Indeed, many of the traditions involved in modern western marriage ceremonies contain rituals invented in the Middle Ages to guarantee that the couple's consent was not coerced, that witnesses were present, and that there were no other impediments to the marriage—such as another spouse lurking in the wings. Such ceremonies also existed in Muslim, Byzantine, and Jewish cultures with differences appropriate to each.

One essential element that existed in all four medieval cultures in the process from betrothal to wedding was the marriage contract, either in writing or in oral form. This contract could become quite elaborate. In the Byzantine Empire, marriage contracts were required and had to include specific stipulations about the material settlement—both land and moveable wealth especially among the elites—that both parties were willing to make on the potential bride and groom. In the Christian west, such settlements were often embedded in deeds that established the transfer of property to a daughter as part of her *maritagium* or dowry. In Italy, the dowry contracts were closer to the Byzantine system than they were to those in northern Europe, but the intention was the same: to establish a public record of the transaction that made a marriage legal in the eyes of civil society, even if consent was the only stipulation required by the church. Jewish marriage contracts stipulated not only the material exchanges that would occur, but also the rights of the wife to expect her husband not to abandon her. Muslim contracts could include stipulations made by the bride or her family that prohibited the groom from taking a second wife. Another element that was universal to all four medieval cultures was the exchange of rings, either at the time of betrothal or during the wedding ceremony, or both. These were most often made of gold or silver, but in the Byzantine betrothal and marriage ceremonies, although betrothal rings were apparently considered essential, they could be made out of almost any material—gold, silver, iron, bronze, even glass—so the cost of these rings was not necessarily too high for poorer couples to afford.[1]

In some parts of the medieval world, a betrothed couple, especially if they were children, were then housed together. In other parts, this was not considered as important. The familiarity of potential spouses could backfire if they took a dislike to each other as children, but in most cases, the betrothed couple had some acquaintance with each other before they had to endure the wedding night. Marriages of aristocrats contained many more rituals and arrangements than those of peasants for the simple reason that the wealthiest members of medieval society had more property to arrange. Peasant marriages were far more casual: church records from medieval England describe weddings that occur in haystacks, by the side of the road, and in the middle of a village market without witnesses, rings, or a priest in attendance. Obviously, the preferred method would include all these elements, but the medieval church required only the consent of both parties for the marriage to be valid.

Although the potential groom was usually older—sometimes significantly so—than his intended bride, there was no real stigma attached to marrying a woman who was (slightly) older. When Maud Braose married her step-grandmother's son, Roger de Mortimer, the fact that she was some years older than he was irrelevant to the far larger importance of the conjoining of her significant inheritance to his own. Maud's more advanced age was also not a bar to her longevity: she outlived Roger by a decade.[2] Men could be subject to ridicule, however, if they married women significantly older than they. They could be accused of marrying for money, especially if the production of children was unlikely. Such marriages could prompt some nasty practical jokes in a custom known in France as the *charivari*.[3]

Byzantine culture differed in its wedding rituals from those of the Christian west but both ceremonies have persisted to the present day in Catholic and Orthodox ceremonies. In the west, the marriage was performed usually in a public place—often outdoors—in order to guarantee the largest number of witnesses, both invited guests and passersby. The ceremony was ideally performed by a priest and included all the elements of the modern western wedding ceremony: the pledges made by both the bride and the groom, the groom's promise to endow the bride, the use of a belt to tie the right hands of the couple together during part of the ceremony, and the exchange of rings. Orthodox wedding ceremonies include these elements, but also includes the suspension of crowns over the heads of the bride and groom. These elements appear in Byzantine iconography, both in paintings and illuminations depicting marriage ceremonies and in the depiction of couples wearing crowns on the actual betrothal and wedding rings.[4]

Jewish wedding ceremonies were different from those of their Christian neighbors in that marriage was not considered a sacrament but was, rather, a civil obligation. Jewish brides and grooms tended to be very young: girls being betrothed at 9 years of age and married at 12 was not an uncommon occurrence and boys could be married as early as 14. Their marriages were usually arranged and they might not have known each other well before the ceremony took place, in particular if the marriage was arranged between unrelated people. The Jewish marriage ceremony of the Middle Ages was not all that different from that of today, but the evolution of the ceremony, including the use of a huppa, or

wedding tent, and the breaking of a glass under the groom's foot, seems
to have occurred gradually. The huppa was originally the prayer shawl of
the groom, held up by four attendants so that the wedding couple could
stand underneath it. The ritual of the breaking of the glass (after which
the witnesses to the wedding congratulate the couple with cries of "Mazel
tov!") has a murkier history, but might symbolize the tribulations of marriage and the ephemeral nature of material goods in comparison to the
devotion the married couple must experience for each other. The tradition
of rings and crowns that existed in Christian wedding ceremonies existed
as well in Jewish ceremonies, although the significance of the symbols
was less overtly religious. For Jews, the crowns mimicked the wedding
of Esther and Ahasueras, king of Persia, depicted in the biblical book of
Esther, and celebrated during the festival of Purim.

The betrothal and wedding ceremonies of Muslim regions in the
Middle Ages combined both local pre-Islamic traditions and Arab ceremonies promoted by the Prophet. All Muslim regions engaged in shared
ceremonies and rituals, but there could be variations depending upon
both local culture and socio-economic level. Although, like Christian and
Jewish laws of marriage, Islamic legal marriage was in theory a simple act
of claiming mutual consent in public, actual ceremonies were, like those
in Christianity and Judaism, quite elaborate.

Betrothals among Muslim families occurred when girls were very
young, usually well before the potential bride reached puberty. Since
polygamy was permitted, the age range between brides and grooms—
and between multiple wives—could be quite extreme. Marriages were
arranged by parents, if both bride and groom were under age, or by the
girl's parents and her intended husband. The betrothal contract could
be a complicated document, especially if the families being joined were
wealthy.

Unlike medieval Christian societies, which barred marriage between
people closely related by blood, both Islam and Judaism permitted marriage between first cousins, especially those on the father's side. This was
often a strategy to keep property within the family confines and might
have been common among Muslim families, since the dowry the bride
brought to the marriage could be quite expensive or valuable. In addition,
the groom or his parents gave the bride and her parents a payment called
a bride price.

Once the betrothal contract had been arranged and approved, the wedding could take place. Girls could be married as early as the age of 10,
but grooms were generally adult men. Girls were expected to be virgins
unless they were widows. Wealthy widows were popular marriage partners: Muhammad, although he had 11 wives, married only one virgin,
Aisha, who was probably around 12 years old at the time. According to
the standard sources, his first wife, the wealthy widow Khadijah, actually
proposed to him.

The marriage ceremonies in the Islamic world of the Middle Ages varied considerably, but several rituals seem to have been consistent. Before the wedding, the bride's female relatives decorated her hands and feet with henna, using elaborate designs that depended upon local custom. In some parts of the Muslim world, the groom's hands were also decorated. In Egypt, ancient traditions were blended with Muslim social requirements in the creation of elaborate and expensive rituals that continue to the present day. After the terms of the betrothal were finalized, the groom gave a ring to the bride, in addition to the regular marriage gift and bride price. The betrothal was then celebrated publicly. When the wedding day arrived, the bride's hands and feet were decorated with henna, she was clothed in an elaborate dress and jewelry, and she was transported to her new husband's house on the back of a horse or camel, enclosed in a tent so that no one on the route could see her. The wedding was a celebration with food, music, and dancing that could go on for days, but in the Middle Ages it is likely that the celebrations were segregated by sex, with the women feasting and dancing with the bride, and the men with the groom.[5]

Once the wedding ceremony—such as it was—had been performed, the newlyweds did not necessarily launch into married life immediately. The western church actually opposed the celebration of the wedding night—and the obligatory display of bloody sheets that indicated the bride's virginity—because they feared that the newlyweds would become obsessed with sex. Instead, they pronounced that any sexual activity between newlyweds for the first three days was sinful and required absolution and penance. Needless to say, most couples ignored these strictures and the common culture, complete with raucous celebrations and the display of the bloody sheets, even the observation of the parents of the newlyweds to the sexual act itself, were far more typical. These celebrations could go on for days. Among the wealthier members of society, it was traditional for the families of the newlyweds to give alms to the poor, including food from the wedding feast, money, and clothing. Wedding feasts in peasant culture involved entire villages and it is likely that multiple marriages took place at one time, since many villages did not have resident priests and anyone who wanted a formal marriage needed a priest to perform it. In Muslim culture, the wedding feast was an important milestone for the married couple as well with celebrations going on for days and rituals involving female members of the bride's family visiting her daily for a week to ensure her wellbeing after the wedding night. Among European Jewry, the youth of the newlyweds might mean that they neither consummated the marriage after the wedding nor lived together for some years afterwards. Sometimes the bride and groom returned to their respective homes or the groom went off to school for an advanced education. They might not begin conventional married life for years.

   Once married and settled, newlyweds did not necessarily occupy their
own homes. Young couples often lived with the groom's parents; in western peasant culture young people often were barred from marrying until
the groom's father (usually) was dead because there was no other way to
establish a household. The medieval aristocracy usually set aside either a
portion of the family residence or, if there was more than one, a separate
residence for the new couple, but they did not achieve true independence
until either the new husband or the new wife had attained his or her inheritance. Indeed, widows and heiresses were very popular marriage partners
for young men because they had their own property where the couple
could establish their independence. The situation was quite similar in
Byzantine and Muslim culture, although the practice of polygamy among
the wealthiest Muslim families changed the relationship between husbands and wives significantly, and both cultures frowned upon the remarriage of widows unless they were still fertile and childless. Jews in western

Harem scene from the Persian *Book of Kings.* From
Firdousi, Shah Nameh. Mamluk dynasty, 15th c.
National Library (Dar-al-Kutub), Cairo, Egypt.
Photo Credit: Bridgeman-Giraudon/Art Resource,
NY.

Europe tended to avoid living in multi-generational households. Evidence from the martyr lists of the Rhineland Jews suggest that most households were comprised of parents (or a single parent) and children, with grandparents only rarely included. There was no significant stigma attached to widow or widower status, and Jews whose spouses had died were neither encouraged to remarry—unless they did not have any children to succeed them—nor discouraged from doing so. Remaining single—that is, never marrying at all—on the other hand, was frowned upon as being antisocial. Jews were mystified by the Christian promotion of celibacy as a moral and religious benefit. To them, the sexual relationship between husband and wife cemented both the family and the society.

Husbands and Wives

All four medieval cultures embodied very specific views on the roles played by husbands and wives. The male venue was conceived of as public: outdoor pursuits, public buildings, duties in administration, jobs in commerce and agriculture. The female venue was conceived of as private: domestic responsibilities such as cleaning and cooking or overseeing servants in such pursuits, child care, maintaining the kitchen garden where herbs, small fruits, and vegetables were raised, taking care of poultry, producing cloth for the household's use, and so on. Indeed, in Muslim culture and possibly among elite Byzantine families, the separation of spheres was, at least in the ideal form, quite severe, with men being barred from the women's quarters unless they were directly related to the women in question (either husband, brother, or son) or were eunuchs. Although this separation of spheres can be seen as something of an ideal in the Middle Ages, the reality was far more fluid. Peasant women were indeed responsible for all of the myriad jobs around the house, but they also had to supplement male labor in the fields during planting and harvest and they also sold goods in the weekly markets. Aristocratic women had to oversee the running of the household, but they also often had to oversee the running of the rest of the family estates, including instructing the stewards who were in charge of agriculture, investing family income, and acting as patron for the wellbeing of the workers and their families on their estates. Jewish wives were often involved in money lending and trade, and, unlike Christian wives, they did not have to have a male representative to conduct business for them or secure the permission of their husbands. Poor Muslim women were seen in the public markets all the time, both as sellers in the market stalls and as servants buying for their employers' needs. We know far less about the daily lives of Byzantine women, but it is reasonable to assume that peasant women in the Byzantine Empire lived similarly to those living in other parts of the medieval world. Poor people did not have the luxury of separating their public and private spaces and roles; wealthy people often saw those spheres overlap by sheer necessity. Among Jewish families, the separation of the sexes was far less significant. Both men and women engaged in business, with women becoming moneylenders, investors, and businesspeople in trades in which their husbands might or might not be engaged. One significant difference was that only men could attain any higher education and this restriction meant that the male-only environment of the yeshiva and the synagogue's rabbinate remained the case until the modern period. There were certain jobs, however, that were considered exclusively female, as will be discussed in chapter 9, on work and the medieval family. In the Jewish home, there was a similar blending of the sexes. There was no traditional or physical barrier between male-only and female-only spaces.

Relations between husbands and wives were as complex in the Middle Ages as they are today. Couples enjoyed each other's company and squabbled over everything. Wives were careful household managers and solicitous spouses and were also nags and scolds. Husbands were loving

An urban family runs a tailor shop. Manuscript illustration from the 15th c. Ms.N.A.L. 1673, Fol.95. Bibliotheque Nationale, Paris, France. Photo Credit: Snark/Art Resource, NY.

and kind and they also abused their wives and children. In other words, the full range of behavior that exists today existed six hundred years ago. In wealthier households, spouses were often separated for long periods of time. Noblemen had to attend royal courts, knights had to attend their lord's court. Men had to perform military service. Merchants had to travel over long distances. If the lengthy correspondence of the Paston family, a fifteenth-century English gentry family who also had significant business interests in the wool trade, is an example, the men in the family often were away for years on end because of litigation in which the family was engaged. This not only limited the time spouses spent with each other, it also limited the number of children who were born into the family. Peasant couples had to operate as partners to insure the survival of their families. This did not prevent the kinds of domestic violence that still occurs today, but the need to operate as a unit probably did encourage the couple to try to work out differences and conflicts constructively.

Although medieval people rarely left behind obvious indications of the regard they felt for spouses, it is possible to talk about their emotional lives, even if some of what follows is speculative. Conventional expressions of regard exist, such as including the names of wives or husbands in prayers and in donations to monasteries and churches. Letters written by merchants and urban leaders in medieval Italy indicate that many missed their wives and families when they traveled and that they held their wives in high regard. A famous work on household management, written by an elderly merchant in Paris for his teenage bride, contains personal touches: the young wife is instructed to learn her lessons well because when her current husband dies, she will be better able to attract and care for a new husband, someone of higher social status as well.[6] The Paston letters provide a great deal of information on the doings of well-off but not noble families in late medieval England. The family was very close-knit, with many family members engaged in both trade and estate management together. Margaret Paston's letters to her husband, John, and his replies contain much more news about business than expressions of affection, but the couple do express worries about each other's health, concerns about their children and other members of the family, happiness at the idea of seeing each other, and appreciation for the hard work each was doing.[7]

One of the most famous expressions of marital devotion was that created by Rabbi Eleazar ben Judah of Worms, Germany, known as the *Rokeah,* in the dirge (a funeral poem of mourning) he wrote for his wife, Dulcia, and two daughters after they were brutally murdered before his eyes by Christian crusaders in 1197.[8] In this poem, which focuses especially on his wife, the Rokeah describes the ways in which Dulcia earned his everlasting devotion and praise. She purchased parchment to make books, sewed Torah scrolls, took care of the students attending his yeshiva school, taught the women of the community, sewed dresses for brides, and prepared the dead for burial. Her death was devastating to her

ṁbulacionem ꝉ dolorem inuem:ꝉ
omen ḋomini inuocaui.

Sir Geoffrey Luttrell dining with his family. From the Luttrell Psalter, England, c.1340. Add. 42130, f.208. British Library, London, Great Britain. Photo Credit: Art Resource, NY.

husband: "Her husband's heart trusted in her; she returned [his kindness] with goodness . . . She was glad to do the will of her husband and never once was she angry [with him]; she was pleasant in her ways."[9]

Other medieval documents show less happy and productive marital relationships. Dhuoda, a ninth-century Carolingian-era noblewoman who wrote an educational manual for her elder son, had had a very unhappy life. Her husband, Bernard of Septimania who was a cousin of the emperor Charlemagne, was keeping her a virtual prisoner in one of his residences and had taken her son, William, away from her while he was still a small child. She was more or less forbidden to have contact with her child, but this did not prevent her husband from visiting her at his convenience. One result of these visits was pregnancy—but Dhuoda did not attain any happiness as a result. As soon as her husband received the news that she had given birth to another boy, he arrived and took the baby away. Dhuoda did not even know the name of her infant son. A prisoner of her husband and subject to his every whim, Dhuoda never saw her children again and had to content herself with writing the lengthy letter of instruction to her older son as a way of influencing his behavior. In her letter she emphasized that William should take care of his younger brother, that the boys should not hate their father for his inability to love his family, and that the boys' obligations ultimately were to God.[10]

A Jewish family's Passover meal. Haggadah for Passover. Collection of Texts on the Script and Prayer. German manuscript, c. 1400. Israel Museum, Jerusalem, Israel. Photo Credit: Bridgeman-Giraudon/Art Resource, NY.

A more complex picture of marital life appears in *The Book of Margery Kempe*.[11] Margery was an early fifteenth-century member of the urbanized gentry in England: her father had been the mayor of Bishop's Lynn (now called King's Lynn), Norfolk. She was married to a prominent merchant, John Kempe, and they lived sometimes in Bishop's Lynn and sometimes in Norwich, the county seat of Norfolk. Margery's famous autobiography contains fascinating information about married life among the late medieval gentry. She was something of a crackpot, but her experiences were not necessarily all that different from those of other women of her class even if her presentation of them is a bit weird. Margery and her husband were married when she was about twenty years old and she was soon pregnant. After enduring an extreme post-partum depression following the birth of her first child, Margery began to hear voices, which she claimed were those of the Archangel Michael, Saint Ann, and Jesus himself. Eventually, she began to see these heavenly beings as well. Throughout her catatonic state after the birth and afterwards, Margery's husband held the family together. He paid Margery's debts when she started—and failed at—a brewing business. And when Margery tried to convince him that they should stop having sexual intercourse, he resisted and negotiated until they both got more or less what each wanted: Margery was given leave to travel on pilgrimage (her husband occasionally accompanied her) and he got her in his bed. He did not give into her entreaties to stop engaging in sex until after their fourteenth child was born. Margery's husband even endured a period of time in which she fell in love with another man, and treated her with kindness and consideration when her heart was broken. In return, Margery was for the most part a good household manager, a considerate wife, and an active developer of business and political relationships that would help her husband. There was clearly a sexual spark between them as well: she describes her sexual life as energetic and satisfying, which alarmed her because good Christians were not supposed to enjoy sex. In one memorable scene, she describes the two of them sitting at the base of a cross in the king's highway to Bridlington arguing about whether Margery's desire for chastity outweighed the social companionship John viewed as essential to the marriage.[12] Certainly, Margery's view of the afterlife seems to have been more earthy than ethereal. After a particularly pleasant night, Margery awoke beside her husband saying "Alas, that ever I did sin; it is full merry in heaven" (that is, people in heaven must be very happy and be having a good time).[13] The conflict between sexual pleasure and those of a heavenly afterlife weighed very heavily on Margery, and forms one of the main discourses in her book.

Given the fact that most married people did not choose their spouses on the basis of personal attraction, it is not surprising that medieval records do not demonstrate many significant emotional connections between husbands and wives. Certainly, the passionate love poetry enjoyed by the aristocracy was not about married couples very often; instead it focused on an idealized relationship of service and duty between a knight and a lady—usually the wife of his overlord. The documents that demonstrate how husbands and wives behaved toward each other are largely legal or literary, with few personal letter collections or diaries available to provide an inside view. As a result, conclusions about the emotional lives of husbands and wives must be tentative.

In the letter collections, diaries, and autobiographies that do exist, it is often hard to tease out expressions of real emotions. For one thing, virtually all such sources were dictated to secretaries or clerks, which means that expressions of emotional connection would have been considered inappropriate. For another thing, the cost of writing paper or parchment was very high, so it would have seemed wasteful to go on elaborately about feelings when important business needed to be discussed. Finally, the nature of marriage worked against such emotional displays, since the couple's marriage was likely at best an affectionate partnership rather than an engrossing and intimate relationship. Indeed, it is far more likely to find evidence of emotional displays in unhappy marriages than in happy ones.

These kinds of evidence suggest that people's emotional lives were not necessarily bound up in their marriages, although devotion to children was commonly mentioned in them. Spouses were devoted to each other, but their devotion was determined by factors relating more to day-to-day life needs than by emotional needs. As Margery Kempe described, the ideal husband was generous, kind, willing to negotiate, a good provider, and a good father. As described by the Menagier of Paris, the ideal wife was thrifty, industrious, kind to her husband, indulgent of his whims, uncomplaining, and a good mother. The Paston letters suggest that the best marriages were those where business interests and the continued success of the family were goals shared by everyone, especially by the husband and wife heading the household. Indeed, when a young couple did fall in love, the careful plans of their families could be severely disrupted, leading to enormous tension. When Margaret and John Paston's daughter Margery fell in love with the family's steward, Richard Calle, who was considered a social inferior, and they married in secret, the furor caused by her insistence on marrying a man of her own choice was extreme. Margaret tried to force her daughter to give up her marriage, tried to have it annulled, and even tried beating Margery into submission, but to no avail. The result was extremely distressing and disruptive to the entire family dynamic at a time of political turmoil as well, when the family's business interests were at risk, and Margaret's and John's relationship with their daughter never lost an overtone of bitterness, even when they reconciled.[14]

It is harder to assess marital life on both higher and lower social class levels. Marriage among the wealthiest and most influential people of the Middle Ages was so much a politically motivated act that very few people had the luxury of the kinds of debate and compromise that seems to have been present in Margery Kempe's marriage. Peasants left so few records behind that it is difficult, if not impossible, to assess their preferences and the ways in which choices were made. Aristocrats throughout the medieval world probably had few expectations that they would be happy in their marriages (at least in our sense of the term) but they could expect reasonable partnerships with their spouses. In addition, remarrying after the death of a spouse could make it possible for two people who actually knew and liked each other to form a union. The records relating to several famous (and a few infamous) marriages as well as less well-known connections can serve to illustrate the probable range of relationships.

Among royal marriages, this range can be seen in the full glare of the public eye. King Henry II of England and his wife, Eleanor of Aquitaine had a famously passionate marriage. They had eloped almost immediately after the annulment of Eleanor's marriage to Charles VII of France, a public scandal especially since Eleanor was nine years older than Henry, he was not yet king of England (although soon destined to be), and he technically ought to have asked King Charles's permission to marry. All accounts of their marriage describe this event as driven by a grand passion, one that, after the production of eight children and the consolidation of their holdings into the most massive and formidable empire of the era, was transformed into an equally passionate dislike. Henry even resorted to imprisoning Eleanor in one of his castles after she plotted with her sons to overthrow him. She would eventually outlive him to see her favorite, her second son, Richard, attain the English throne.

Charles VII's son (by his third wife, Adela of Champagne) and successor, Philip II (known as Philip Augustus) was married (officially twice, but unofficially three) times, but his second wife, Ingeborg of Denmark, brought him the most notoriety. Although the marriage had been carefully arranged—and was a good political match—something dreadful apparently occurred on the wedding night, because Philip refused even to see Ingeborg afterwards and demanded an annulment. When she resisted and insisted the marriage had been consummated, Philip imprisoned her and declared himself un-married. He then married his mistress. The pope, Innocent III, was not pleased by all this mayhem and demanded he take Ingeborg back, even to the point of placing an interdict on France and excommunicating Philip. In the end, the king was forced to abandon his third wife (whose marriage was declared invalid on the grounds of bigamy) and to take back Ingeborg. She actually outlived him, although she probably never saw her husband after that first harrowing night.

In contrast to his cousin Philip, Henry III of England was married once, was never unfaithful to his wife Eleanor of Provence and even was accused by some contemporary chronicles of being dominated by her. Their relationship, although begun when Eleanor was barely 12 and Henry was 28 (he was a very late bloomer, and a mere year younger than Eleanor's own mother, Beatrice of Savoy), was both companionable and productive. Indeed, Eleanor's influence on her husband the king was considered dangerously significant by some members of the royal court. Henry and Eleanor's son, Edward I was also famously faithful and devoted to his first wife, Eleanor of Castile. When she died in 1290, not only did he erect crosses at every stop her funeral procession made from York, where she died, to Westminster, where she was interred, but he also deported the entire population of Jews from the country, as a partial commemoration of this famously anti-Semitic queen. Although Edward did remarry, this was largely a political move, since his new bride was the king of France's sister, Margaret. Edward was noted as a very considerate and attentive husband, unlike his son, Edward II, whose reputation during his life was nearly as unsavory as his characterization in Mel Gibson's completely unhistorical movie, *Braveheart*. Edward II's wife, Isabella of France, seems to have had good reasons to abandon her husband in favor of promoting her son as king, although her affair with the earl of March, Roger de Mortimer, was looked upon less kindly by the political community.

The marriages of Byzantine emperors and empresses were, if anything, even more convoluted than those of the western European crowned heads. Byzantine chronicles abound with descriptions of emperors divorcing infertile wives, desperate for a male heir; of wives becoming empresses upon the deaths of their husbands and ruling over sons; even of devoted imperial couples operating as co-rulers over their territories. In the Muslim world, the prevalence of polygamy completely altered the relationship between husbands and wives, but certain wives could become quite prominent during a particular reign. The famous Kurdish general Saladin was notable as a devoted husband and father, as was his commander, the Turk Nur ad-Din. Indeed, even western chronicles remark on the contrast between Saladin and his contemporary, King Richard I of England (Richard Lionheart), whose behavior as a husband was nothing short of scandalous.

Aristocratic marriages were not all that different from royal ones, although on a less grandiose scale. Stephen, the count of Blois, is often depicted as being ruled by his wife, the formidable Adela, whose father was William the Conqueror. Roger de Mortimer of Wigmore and his wife, Maud de Braose, and their contemporaries (and cousins) William de Valence and Joan de Munchesney each exemplified the kinds of cooperative relationships between spouses that probably illustrate the best an aristocratic marriage could hope for. Even when, during the baronial rebellion against King Henry III led by the earl of Leicester Simon de Montfort, both Roger and William were exiled and threatened with imprisonment, their wives not only managed to keep the family properties safe, they engineered their husbands' return from exile and were acclaimed as devoted partners. Aristocratic marriages could also go badly awry. When, in the fourteenth century, John of Gaunt, the duke of Lancaster, married his daughter Elizabeth to the much younger John de Hastings, earl of Pembroke, he did not count on his daughter spurning her teenage husband (she was some years older) and eloping with her lover, John Holand, to Spain, where Duke John was trying to settle in as co-ruler of Castile with his own young bride.

Examples of aristocratic marriages outside the Christian west are harder to tease out of the sources for Byzantine and Islamic history. For Byzantine aristocrats, marriage was not merely the union of two individuals or even of two families, it was "the business . . . of an entire social class."[15] Sources emphasize conformity with legal and social concerns, such as consanguinity (the degree of kinship between a potential couple), the size of dowries, and the ages of the betrothed couple. Church sources, especially saints' lives, emphasize the difference between so-called normal and abnormal sexual activity. While it was believed that sexual desire was a normal part of being human, being highly sexed was considered a dangerous abnormality that could lead to adultery or an inability to live chastely after the death of a spouse. Emperors Constantine VI and Leo VI were both accused of failing to control their sexual urges, to the detriment of their married lives.[16] Women's sexual urges could also wreak havoc in a marriage. The empress Theophanu was accused of both adultery and of plotting the murder of her husband, Nicephoras I.[17]

The depiction of sexual aberration in Byzantine imperial families has a long history, however. The empress Theodora, wife of Emperor Justinian I, was slandered by the court historian Procopius, who claimed that she had been a circus performer and notorious prostitute before she married Justinian. Nicetas Choniates, the twelfth-century historian, described in lurid detail the sexual escapades of the magnate class, but this can be seen more as social and political commentary on the decadence of the imperial government than as an accurate portrayal of the married lives of Byzantine aristocrats.

Other sources, such as eulogies and funeral orations, while idealized— no one wants to speak ill of the dead, after all—might be better windows into married life among the medieval Byzantine aristocracy. In such sources, at least the outline of what constituted an ideal marriage can be discerned. Married couples ideally were close in age, of good and honorable parentage, and physically attractive. Ideal wives spoke in low tones and rarely laughed. They were exemplary mothers, loved their husbands unconditionally, behaved modestly, and exhibited wisdom, never arguing with their husbands. Clearly, this ideal would have been difficult for most individuals to achieve.[18] The most important elements, according to these ideals, for a successful marriage were fertility—success in producing many children—and conjugal affection: that the couple both love and appreciate each other. This ideal, which appears throughout all the cultures of the medieval world, could have been somewhat difficult to achieve since arranged marriages between near-strangers was the norm.

So how close to these ideals were real marriages in Byzantine culture? Like the relationships between husbands and wives in western Europe, the reality was likely to have varied widely. While many marriages undoubtedly achieved the ideal of conjugal affection, others did not. Since divorce under certain circumstances (such as infertility) was possible in Byzantine law, bad marriages could be—and probably sometimes were—dissolved, but still others must have persisted.

Spousal Abuse in the Middle Ages

How prevalent was spousal abuse in the Middle Ages? This question has occupied the energies of many historians, especially in the last twenty years. Historians have always assumed that the level of casual violence—slapping, yelling insults, arguments that escalate into violence that causes some injury but is impermanent—that we would consider abuse today was more or less ubiquitous. Husbands were given many more rights over their wives and children in the Middle Ages than today and the social authorities actually encouraged (at least in writing) the so-called chastisement of wives for supposed infractions to the social order. Historians assume, however, that levels of extreme violence, in which (mostly) wives were subjected to life-threatening beatings, extreme mental abuse, and the like were rarer. Recent studies of abuse in families suggest that this was likely the case. In addition, there is some evidence that other people—members of the family, even fellow-villagers— considered it appropriate to intervene when violence escalated. In late medieval Provence, Christian neighbors even intervened when a Jewish serial abuser was beating his wife in the confines of their home: several neighbors rushed into the house and physically separated the couple. In another case, a mother physically barred her son-in-law from her home, to which her daughter had fled following a particularly brutal beating.[19] Jewish families seem to have experienced similar levels of abuse and mistreatment, although Jewish law considered it a requirement that husbands treat wives with respect and the communities might have policed (or tried to police) their membership for signs of abuse.

In the High and late Middle Ages, especially in the Mediterranean and England, legal records attest to the prevalence of wife-murder and spousal abuse. Although wives did occasionally also kill their husbands, the opposite was far more common. In addition, although the punishment for killing one's husband was burning at the stake—it was considered petty treason in English law—the killing of a wife had far fewer and far less stringent consequences. Husbands often got away with a fine or penance. There is some evidence that wife sales also occurred occasionally, in which husbands took their wives to a market center and sold them to another man. Although some historians see this as a form of informal divorce, this demonstrates how few options wives actually had if they were unable to develop a reasonable working relationship with their husbands.

Lest we feel smug that such episodes of horrific abuse no longer occur in so-called civilized portions of the developed world, it is quite likely that the level of extreme violence within families in the Middle Ages parallels the kinds of statistics that measure such violence occurring today. Indeed, some historians have suggested that the statistics concerning spousal violence in the Middle Ages demonstrate that, while the daily behavior patterns of married couples might have been more harsh, the prevalence of extreme levels of violence, torture, and abuse were lower at that time than they are now in our supposedly advanced society.[20] Husbands (and to a certain extent, wives) are still given a kind of societal permission to control unruliness in families and some men (and, indeed, some women) interpret this unspoken permission as an open door to beating their wives (or husbands) and children. Indeed, in some sub-cultures in the developed world, the traditional notion of the husband ruling the household still stands, and this idea makes it possible for husbands to chastise wives with impunity. In the Middle Ages, as now, violence perpetrated by one family member against the others worked against family cohesion. Family members would be unwilling to go the extra mile for someone they hated because of his violent behavior. As a result, it would have been important to members of the extended family, such as in-laws, cousins, brothers, and sisters, to control this kind of deviant behavior and it is likely that such controls would have occurred under the radar of the legal system.

When a Partner Died: Widowhood and Remarriage

The medieval family was unusually susceptible to the kinds of life-changing events that can cause enormous disruption and anxiety. Although such events were—and can continue to be—disruptive in all cultures and at all times, the cultures of the medieval world might have been somewhat less well equipped to address them both publicly and privately. All the life stages of the medieval family could bring both happiness and sadness and the ways in which people coped reflected this tension. The birth of children always brought with it the possibility of their early deaths or the death of the mother in labor. The death of a parent could mean the possibility of marriage for members of the next generation, who had to wait for financial reasons until such an end in order to afford to marry and start a new family. The death of a spouse could confer independent status and wealth on the survivor, who might experience that security for the very first time by becoming a widow or widower.

The death of a spouse was not only traumatic for the entire family, it changed the family's economic and social dynamic dramatically. The incidence of early death was very high in the Middle Ages among all social classes: women died as a result of childbirth in large numbers and men died as the result of accidents, war, and illness in similar numbers. Indeed, long term marriages of two decades and more were more the exception than the rule simply because it was so often the case that one of the partners died young. All four medieval cultures had extensive rules regarding the process of recovery and remarriage following the death of a spouse. Perhaps surprisingly, these systems were more alike than different, especially in the radically different ways in which men and women were treated during a period of widowhood. In addition, emotional considerations following the death of a spouse—grief and distress—were often not mentioned in official documents about the obligations of the survivor, although these emotions are mentioned occasionally in chronicles and letters.

In all four cultures, men were given far more freedom to remarry following the death of a wife than were women after their husbands' death. From western Europe to the Near East, men were generally permitted to remarry quite soon after a wife's death, sometimes as soon as three months after the funeral. In contrast, the typical period of mourning for widowed wives was one year, although in Muslim culture the wait was much shorter: four and one-half months. Marriage before the period of mourning ended could result in everything from monetary fines to, in Christian lands, excommunication. In addition, men could choose to remarry or not, while women often had to negotiate strenuously to remain single if members of their families—or their overlords or the king—were determined to marry them to other men. Indeed, one of the most important clauses in the original Magna Carta of 1215 between King John of England and his barons (and one that features prominently in all versions of the charter thereafter) emphasizes that the king could not marry a widow against her will to another man. This eventually developed into a system whereby a widow "in the king's gift" could pay a nominal fee to gain control of her own remarriage and therefore choose—perhaps for the first time in her life—whether or not she wanted another husband and who that man might be. In addition, since England's system worked from the top, down, it became standard practice for free widows of all social classes to gain at least nominal control over their remarriage. This was different from almost any other region in the medieval world, where widows were limited in their choices, some denied remarriage, and others compelled to marry again.

In medieval Italy, widows were actively discouraged from remarrying, especially if they had grown children. For example, in late medieval Florence, "two-thirds of women widowed in their twenties, and nine-tenths widowed at thirty or older" remained unmarried, even though quite a few of them lived for a very long time.[21] Under most Italian law, widows who remarried lost guardianship of their children and husbands often added monetary incentives to their wills in order to discourage their wives from remarrying.

Widows were popular as marriage partners in both the Islamic and Jewish communities. In both cultures widows acquired independent control over their marriage portions and property acquired from their late husbands. In addition, a widow with children thereby proved her fertility, an important consideration for both Muslim and Jewish men.

Significantly, the rates of remarriage among men of all social classes tended to be quite a bit higher than that of women throughout the medieval world. This might seem counterintuitive, since it could be thought that men could hire women to do the same jobs their wives performed, and women needed husbands to protect them, but in fact the opposite seems to have been true. Men were far more likely to remarry in part because they might want to have more legitimate children to guarantee the passing of their property to another of their line, in part because there was a certain social stigma attached to men who were unmarried but continued to be sexually active—and the children of such unions would be condemned as illegitimate—and in part because social concerns about the reliability of hired help in caring for children and the household were very real. Women, on the other hand, might be grateful to be able to take vows of chastity, which were necessary in the Christian west in order to remain both unmarried and respectable, and thereby prevent the real possibility of dying in childbirth, and they were able easily to hire efficient managers of their estates or workshops. Indeed, statistically, widows outlived married women by large margins. Almost every woman who reached the age of 60 and beyond in the medieval world had probably been widowed for a number of years. Some of the most long-lived women who lived outside the cloister had been widowed for many years. In contrast, men who did not remarry often did not long outlive their dead spouse. Ironically, a similar contrast occurs even today, with widowers dying younger than their female counterparts.

Second (or even third) marriages could have significant repercussions for the family, as mentioned in section 1. The stress of blending families could be high and the birth of new half-siblings could be threatening to the older children. On the other hand, some second marriages were considerably happier than first marriages, especially when widows could make their own choices of marriage partner. One notable example occurred in the fourteenth century. Alice Lacy, the daughter of Henry Lacy and Margery Longespee and heir of two earldoms—Lincoln and Salisbury—had been married while very young to her cousin, Thomas earl of Lancaster. This was a very unhappy marriage. The couple disliked each other intensely, and Alice soon removed herself from Thomas's presence and settled on one of her own estates. Thomas's political activities led his enemies to take their revenge by abducting Alice and holding her to ransom—a situation that might have included a physical assault as well (the term "rape" in medieval Latin had a number of meanings, in part because abduction and sexual assault were seen to go hand in hand). When Thomas was executed for treason as the leader of the baronial party against King Edward II, Alice's safety was in serious jeopardy. She secured her own independence, in part because of the all too public animosity the couple had displayed during Thomas's life, and eventually married a member of her household, Ebulo Lestrange, who was of noble birth but not at all the social stature of Alice. In contrast to her first marriage, this union was apparently both loving and satisfying, so when Ebulo died tragically, Alice was devastated. To make matters worse, she was again in danger of abduction: the kingdom was in an uproar following the overthrow of Edward II and the minority of Edward III. An ambitious knight, Hugh le Fresne, abducted Alice, raped her, and then demanded that he be permitted to marry her (this was unfortunately the church court's most usual punishment for rapists). Edward III agreed to the demand, probably to save Alice's reputation, and then shipped Sir Hugh off to Scotland, where he was soon killed during the military campaign against the Bruces. Alice was then able to live the rest of her life in comparative safety, but upon her death she insisted on being buried next to the body of Ebulo, her second husband, the only one with whom she had been happy.[22]

Other second marriages among the aristocracy could be seen as combining political expediency with social ambition. When Eleanor de Ferrers inherited a small portion of the vast earldom of Pembroke from her mother in 1245, she promptly eloped with one of her father's household knights, one William de Vaux. Upon his death, Eleanor used the opportunity to again elope, but this time in spectacular fashion: she married the elderly earl of Winchester, Roger de Quency. His death resulted in a significant rise in her personal fortunes, so Eleanor was able to be more conventional in her third marriage in that she did not elope, and she settled for a man, Sir Roger de Leyburn, of whom the king approved. Thus, Eleanor was able to gain a significant benefit from flying in the face of royal restrictions, a relatively modest fine being all the punishment she endured.[23] Other women and men were not so lucky.

In the Byzantine, Muslim, and Jewish worlds of the Middle Ages similar situations occurred. Very little is actually known or understood about the marriage culture of the Byzantine world beyond that of the imperial and noble households, but the process of remarriage following death was similar to that of western Europe, with one important exception. According to Byzantine law, it was considered very irregular and highly suspect to marry more than twice: third and fourth marriages were forbidden by the Byzantine Church and could result in excommunication. This presented significant problems for Byzantine emperors whose second wives had died or failed to produce the necessary male heir. Indeed, a number of Byzantine emperors who remarried three or four times found themselves at loggerheads with the leaders of the Byzantine Church and several were condemned for their marital activities.[24] Widows, in contrast to the west, were far more restricted in their choices. They were actively discouraged from remarrying unless they were still young and childless. If they were, indeed, still fertile, then their parents invariably arranged subsequent marriages for them, but their social status was adversely affected by a second marriage. In Byzantine Christianity, the ability of women to control their sexual urges was a hotly debated topic and widows who remarried were assumed to be unable to control their sexuality. This assumption placed them in marginal positions: constrained by the requirements of the society to produce children, they were nonetheless vilified for failing to maintain their chastity following the death of their first husbands.

Unlike Christian Europe, both Muslim and Jewish cultures permitted divorce, although this was far easier to obtain in the former than in the latter. The dissolving of a marriage under Islamic law had to be initiated by the husband, and the result was not only a separation of the spouses but also of the material assets of the married couple. The husband returned the wife's dowry to her and she retained the marriage gift unless she was divorced on account of adultery. Both parties were free to remarry after such a divorce. Nevertheless, it is likely that divorce benefited men more than women. It is not clear whether there were large numbers of single-female households in the Muslim regions of the medieval Mediterranean, but such households were likely to have been significantly disadvantaged from an economic standpoint. In addition, the children from the marriage probably stayed with their father, so divorced wives could be compelled to abandon their own children.

Medieval Jewish couples were sometimes known to practice something known as conditional divorce. If a man was going to be away for an extended period of time, for example on a long business trip to far away lands, he might divorce his wife on condition that the marriage would resume upon his return within a specific period of time. The reasons for this conditional divorce lay in the dangers of long-distance travel and trade. If a man died while away from home, his wife might never know what became of him and she would be unable to secure her dowry and marriage portion, gain guardianship of her children, or remarry. The conditional divorce made it possible for her to gain control of her finances and her family for the time her husband was away and in the event that he failed to return.

Since divorce was almost non-existent outside the Muslim world, the problem of single divorced women in Christian culture did not often appear. Nevertheless, more informal—and illegal—arrangements for dissolving marriages that occurred especially among the lower classes did result in a phenomenon that has become very useful to the medieval historian: litigation concerning marriage (especially charges of bigamy) that was heard in the diocesan courts of Europe. Bishops were responsible for adjudicating marriage disputes in their regular court sessions, and these form a significant bulk of documents from those courts, especially in England, where record-keeping was far more advanced than on the continent until the fourteenth century. This litigation reveals that people made far more informal alterations to their living arrangements than the legal ideal would suggest and that it could sometimes be difficult to determine even if a legal marriage had occurred! Cases of bigamy were fairly common occurrences in the bishops' courts all over England, although they represent only a small portion of the daily business of the courts. Such charges also appear in other contexts. For example, when a widow sued the heir (usually in this case not her own child) for dower in the central courts of Common Pleas, the defendant-heir occasionally argued that the widow had no claim to the property on the basis that she was not actually married to the man she identified as her late husband. When this occurred, the case had to be adjourned to the bishop's court, where the determination of valid marriage had to be made. Only after the marriage had been declared valid could the dower plea continue. In most of these cases, the marriages were in fact determined to be valid, so this could be seen as a useful delaying tactic on the part of the heir who resisted turning over a third of his property to the widow.

Conclusions: Husbands and Wives in Law and Literature

In the legal literature, the discussion of marriage in the Middle Ages can look bleak indeed. In all the legal systems of the medieval world—Roman, civil, Christian, Common, customary, Byzantine, Muslim, and Judaic—the fundamental basis of the relationship between husbands and wives was their legal inequality. In all these systems, wives had no legal personality: they were not considered to be individuals separate from their husbands. English common law makes this inequality quite explicit: "Common lawyers. . . agreed that in the eyes of the law, the husband and wife were one person, and that person was the husband."[25] This meant that wives could not make contracts or wills, could not sue in court, could not charge their husbands with abuse, could not sue for divorce (although in Muslim and Jewish culture this was somewhat moderated), and often could not gain custody of their children if their husbands died. Indeed, the institution of marriage as described in the legal systems of the Middle Ages place all the advantages in the hands of males and virtually all liabilities in the hands of females. This is one reason why widowhood could be seen by many women as a moment of true liberation from an oppressive system.

In terms of specifics, the emphasis in all legal systems was placed on problems that could occur between husbands and wives (as, indeed, legal systems do today). These included not just the obvious issues of abuse and infertility, but also such things as whether a wife was liable if her husband was a thief and brought stolen goods home with him from a heist. In this circumstance, the wife was liable only if the stolen goods were found in a locked cupboard because the wife was the keeper of the keys (in fact, the key-ring worn by noblewomen in France was known as a *chatelaine* for this very reason) and so was responsible for the secreting of the stolen property. In cases of abuse, the law in England—which was not that different in this context from laws of other western kingdoms—was that a husband was permitted to chastise his wife (that is, beat her) but he was not permitted to do permanent damage to her physically or mentally. Nevertheless, it must have been very difficult to enforce even this law, even as modern laws against spousal abuse were until very recently extremely difficult to enforce.

Since the wife's legal personality more or less did not exist, wives were protected—at least theoretically—from punishment for certain kinds of offenses perpetrated by their husbands. Wives were usually not liable for their husbands' debts (at least while he was still alive) and could not usually be accused as an accessory to crimes committed by their husbands. On the other hand, husbands controlled all the property their wives brought to the marriage, and wives had no say in what happened to it: it often could be sold, given away, or destroyed without their permission, even when the law demanded that it be preserved. Occasionally, widows sued for a return of property that had been taken against their will, but often those suits were unsuccessful, because wives could not gainsay (i.e., disagree in public with) their husbands while the latter were alive and could be forced to sign contracts which bound them as independent actors in such agreements. One exception to this standard situation occurred in medieval France, which had retained a notion of community property that gave wives a bit more say in what happened to the property they brought into a marriage. Nevertheless, it was as true of France as elsewhere that wives experienced far less independence than did widows.

It is important, however, to reiterate that the legal systems of the medieval world focused on areas of conflict, not on defining what constituted a typical relationship between husband and wife. If we look too much at the highly negative picture of marriage that the legal literature presents, we can lose an essential perspective about medieval marriage: that it was probably most frequently a partnership in the best sense of the term. Married partners had no choice but to try to get along as best they could. They had to divide the labor of the marriage rationally. They had to raise their children together. And when one spouse died, they mourned. Perhaps the most positive description of a married couple for the Middle Ages can be found in the romance, *Erec and Enid,* written by Chretien de Troyes around 1170:

A perfect match they were in courtesy, beauty, and gentleness. And they were so alike in quality, manner, and customs, that no one wishing to tell the truth could choose the better of them, nor the fairer, nor the more discreet. Their sentiments, too, were much alike; so that they were well suited to each other. Thus each steals the other's heart away. Law or marriage never brought together two such sweet creatures.[26]

Notes

1. This is discussed by Gary Vikan, "Art and Marriage in Early Byzantium" *Dumbarton Oaks Papers* 44 (1990): 145–163.

2. For an extended discussion of Maud and Roger Mortimer, see Linda E. Mitchell, "Noble Widowhood in the Thirteenth Century: Three Generations of Mortimer Widows, 1246–1334," in *Upon My Husband's Death: Widows in the Literature and Histories of Medieval Europe,* ed. Louise Mirrer (Ann Arbor: University of Michigan Press, 1992), 169–192 and Mitchell, "Heroism and Duty: Maud Mortimer of Wigmore's Contributions to the Royalist Cause," in *Portraits of Medieval Women: Family, Marriage, and Politics in England 1225–1350* (New York: Palgrave Macmillan, 2003), 43–56.

3. Natalie Zemon Davis discusses this in "The Reasons of Misrule," in Davis, *Society and Culture in Early Modern France* (Palo Alto: Stanford University Press, 1977), 97–123.

4. For an extended discussion of these depictions, see Gary Vikan, "Art and Marriage in Early Byzantium."

5. Several Web sites describe Muslim wedding ceremonies. See Ahmed Negm, "Egyptian Marriage Customs of the Past and Present," in *Wedding Customs Around the Muslim World,* http://www.zawaj.com/weddingways/Egypt_customs.html and *Wedding Ceremonies and Customs in Various Islamic Lands—Past and Present,* http://www.sfusd.k12.ca.us/schwww/sch618/Women/Weddings.html.

6. A good, albeit abridged, translation is *A Medieval Home Companion: Housekeeping in the Fourteenth Century,* trans. and ed. Tania Bayard (New York: HarperCollins Publishers, 1991).

7. A good edition of selections from the voluminous correspondence of the Pastons is *Illustrated Letters of the Paston Family: Private Life in the Fifteenth Century,* ed. Roger Virgoe (New York: Weidenfeld and Nicolson, 1989). Hereafter referred to as *Paston Letters.*

8. Mentioned at length by Kenneth Stow in both "The Jewish Family in the Rhineland in the High Middle Ages: Form and Function" *The American Historical Review* 92, no. 5 (1987): 1085–1110 and in *Alienated Minority: The Jews of Medieval Latin Europe* (Cambridge, MA: Harvard University Press, 1992), 196–198.

9. Stow, "The Jewish Family in the Rhineland," 1085–1086.

10. For a lucid analysis of Dhuoda's work, as well as lengthy quotations of it, see "Dhuoda" in Peter Dronke, *Women Writers of the Middle Ages: A Critical Study of Texts from Perpetua to Marguerite Porete* (Cambridge: Cambridge University Press, 1984), 36–54.

11. The best recent edition is *The Book of Margery Kempe,* Norton Critical Edition, trans. and ed. Lynn Staley (New York: W.W. Norton and Company, 2001).

12. *Book of Margery Kempe,* 19–20.

13. *Book of Margery Kempe,* 10.

14. *Paston Letters,* 179, 180, 183, 184, 186–187.

15. Angeliki E. Laiou, *Mariage, amour et parenté à Byzance aux XIe-XIIIe siècles* (Paris: De Boccard, 1992), 9, translation mine.

16. Laiou, *Mariage, amour et parenté à Byzance,* 70.

17. Laiou, *Mariage, amour et parenté à Byzance,* 74.

18. Laiou, *Mariage, amour et parenté à Byzance,* 91–93.

19. See Steven Bednarski, "Keeping it in the Family? Domestic Violence in the Later Middle Ages: Examples from a Provençal Town (1340–1403)" in *Love, Marriage, and Family Ties in the Later Middle Ages,* ed. Isabel Davis, Miriam Müller, and Sarah Rees Jones (Turnhout: Brepols, 2003), 277–299.

20. For a discussion of the differences between medieval and modern spousal abuse, see Bednarski, above, Martha A. Brozyna, "Not Just a Family Affair: Domestic Violence and the Ecclesiastical Courts in Late Medieval Poland," 299–310, and Miriam Müller, "Conflict, Strife, and Cooperation: Aspects of the Late Medieval Family and Household," 311–330 in *Love, Marriage, and Family Ties in the Later Middle Ages.*

21. Ann Morton Crabb, "How Typical was Alessandra Macinghi Strozzi of Fifteenth-Century Florentine Widows?" in *Upon My Husband's Death: Widows in the Literature and Histories of Medieval Europe,* ed. Louise Mirrer (Ann Arbor: University of Michigan Press, 1992), 49.

22. See Linda E. Mitchell, "Martyr to the Cause: The Tragic Career of Alice de Lacy," in Mitchell, *Portraits of Medieval Women: Family, Marriage, and Politics in England, 1225–1350* (New York: Palgrave Macmillan, 2003), 105–124.

23. I have discussed Eleanor's career in several contexts. See, for example, "The Lady is a Lord: Widows and Land in Thirteenth-Century Britain" *Historical Reflections/Réflexions Historiques* 18, no. 1 (1992): 71–98 and "Agnes and Her Sisters: Squabbling and Cooperation in the Extended Medieval Family" in *Portraits of Medieval Women,* 11–28.

24. This situation is highlighted by Judith Herrin in *Women in Purple: Rulers of Medieval Byzantium* (Princeton: Princeton University Press, 2001).

25. Sue Sheridan Walker, "Introduction," in *Wife and Widow in Medieval England,* ed. Sue Sheridan Walker (Ann Arbor: University of Michigan Press, 1993), 4.

26. *Erec and Enid*, vv 1479–1690, trans. W. W. Comfort, 1914, http://omacl.org/Erec/erec1.html. See, also, Amy Livingstone, "Powerful Allies and Dangerous Adversaries: Noblewomen in Medieval Society," in *Women in Medieval Western European Culture,* ed. Linda E. Mitchell (New York: Garland Publishing, 1999), 7–30.

8

Children and the Family

The medieval definition of child is somewhat different from that of today. Indeed, there were many different categories used to establish both child status and adulthood. The legal systems established the categories of childhood and adulthood according to gender as well as linear age, especially when considering specific life stages, such as age of consent to marriage, earliest age of employment, age of majority, and so on. The basic formula of reaching one's majority at 18 or 21, although it did exist in the Middle Ages, had little actual relevance for most people, except for wealthy young men who were unable to take control of their inheritances before that time. In addition, the roles of children in medieval culture often carried far more responsibility than those of children in developed nations today; child labor was very common, indeed typical, throughout the medieval world. Therefore, when considering the position of children in the family, how they were raised, educated, and treated, and how they passed through the typical life stages of infancy, youth, adolescence, and into adulthood it is necessary always to keep in mind that the values of medieval society differed to a great degree from ours, and that different social classes interacted with their children differently.

Family Size in the Middle Ages

Medieval families, even the wealthiest, were usually fairly small, with two or three children surviving to adulthood. This does not mean that women gave birth to only two or three children in a lifetime. Indeed, it is likely that women experienced frequent pregnancies, but that they also experienced frequent miscarriages and infant deaths in childbirth. In addition, the physical separation of spouses that occurred among married couples of the upper classes could limit pregnancy. Elite men were required to spend several months a year attending the king, emperor, or caliph/amir, performing military service, or performing administrative services. Men engaged in long distance trade or involved in elite mercantile activities, such as the Paston men or Jewish international travelers, could be separated from their wives for years on end. This could, of course, have a significant impact on family size.

Birth control was forbidden among all medieval people except for Jews, who were permitted to use a sponge device—similar in shape to today's cervical sponge—to prevent pregnancy under certain circumstances. Even though it was illegal, however, medieval Christians did in fact make use of birth control to limit families, especially in times of hardship.[1] The most typical form was the practice of coitus interruptus, but extending the time of breast feeding, which has an impact on female fertility when the mother's caloric intake is barely adequate, could also be used to prevent pregnancy. Jewish midwives might also have supplied Christian women with the sponges approved as birth control devices by the Jewish community.

Although most monogamous households probably contained no more than two or three children, aristocratic Christian, polygamous Muslim, and some Jewish families could be quite large. Among the Christian aristocracy, healthy women might experience double-digit pregnancies with many of the infants surviving at least into their teenage years. Eleanor of Aquitaine had a total of 10 surviving children: 2 with her first husband, King Charles VII of France, and 8 with her second, King Henry II of England. William and Isabella Marshal, the earl and countess of Pembroke, had 10 children—5 boys and 5 girls—in their 28 year marriage, all of whom survived to adulthood. One of their daughters, Sibyl, who married William de Ferrers earl of Derby, had seven children, all girls. When Sibyl died, William married again and went on to have at least one more child, Robert, who inherited the earldom.

The Islamic rulers who practiced polygamy on a grand scale probably had many children, even if their wives individually did not necessarily produce a large number of progeny. In fact, most of the medieval caliphs and amirs had few wives—the famous Haroun al-Rashid had only one, the poet and intellectual Zubayda—but probably hundreds of female sex-slaves and concubines, whose children were included in the royal household. Most of these children are invisible to the historian. Haroun, himself the son of a former sex-slave al-Khayzuran and the 'Abbasid caliph al-Mahdi, might have had thousands of female sexual partners (as is rumored in the legends about him), but only two of his sons are mentioned in most sources: his eldest, al-Ma'mun, who was born of a slave, and his only legitimate son, al-Amin, born of the marriage of Haroun and Zubayda.

Historians differ in their analysis of family size in Jewish communities in the Middle Ages. In western Europe, bans against polygamy, the use of birth control, and restrictions on the size of Jewish households because of the limited space in which the communities dwelled, might have combined to limit family size. In the Rhineland and France, Jewish families seem to have averaged around two or three children: numbers more or less identical to Christian families. In the Mediterranean, family sizes might have been larger, since some historians mention families with as many as 10 children as being not uncommon.[2] The documents of the Cairo *geniza* suggest that the average Jewish family in Muslim-controlled Egypt included four or five children; that is, twice the number found among German-Jewish or French-Jewish families. There is no way to verify such numbers and the families of Middle Eastern Jews might indeed have been even larger, since girls seem to have been undercounted in the *geniza* records.[3]

Infants and Toddlers

Infancy was a risky period: disease, infant diarrhea, and accidents seem to have been so common as to make the odds of surviving the first year roughly 50/50. This is true of the children of the elites as much as of the common classes, since all experienced the lack of medical knowledge that could have made infancy a more secure period. Statistics about survival are nonexistent for any medieval culture, but coroner's inquests and other kinds of records for western Europe suggest that the first five years of a child's life were the most dangerous.

Once born, infants were swaddled—they were wrapped tightly in cloth bands so that their limbs did not move around—because it was thought that they needed that level of support to survive, at least for the first few months. Mothers or wet nurses were responsible for their feeding and infants were often nursed for two years or more. If the mother died in childbirth and a wet nurse could not be found, the infant was almost guaranteed to die. Although midwives and caretakers might attempt to save the baby by dripping cow's or sheep's milk, usually diluted with water, from a twisted rag or a nursing horn into the baby's mouth, human infants simply cannot digest animal milk efficiently. Among the elites, wet nurses were quite common. Indeed, church officials often sermonized that noblewomen were failing in their responsibilities to their children by hiring wet nurses, because it was thought that personality traits were literally absorbed through the mother's milk, and that a peasant woman who nursed a noble infant was thereby imparting the values of a peasant in the act of nursing. The mother of three famous leaders of the First Crusade, Ida of Boulogne, was, according to legend, so determined that her children would be nursed only by her that, when she discovered that a wet nurse had fed her infant son to stop him from crying, Countess Ida forced the baby to vomit the "alien" milk so that she could nurse him herself.[4] Nursing often prevented ovulation in the mother, especially when the mother's diet was low in protein and nutrients, so this was a good reason for mothers to nurse their children as long as possible. This could be one reason why noblewomen are often noted as having many pregnancies: they did not nurse, so their fertility was not affected.

Children were often put in charge of overseeing their younger siblings. It was not uncommon for a six-year-old to be given the task of caring for an infant. Mothers were usually engaged in work that made it difficult to keep an eye on their toddlers, whether it was work in the kitchen garden, in the artisan's workshop, or maintenance of the manor. As can be imagined, having such young children in charge could result in terrible accidents befalling their infant charges, especially if they were mobile: falling into the kitchen fire, overturning the soup cauldron, and other kinds of incidents are mentioned frequently in coroner's reports. For example, a five-year old boy was babysitting his one-year old brother, who died when his cradle caught fire.[5]

Once an infant was considered able to sit up, crawl, and stand the swaddling was removed and she or he was able to move around more freely. Toddlers continued to nurse, but solid food was introduced slowly into the diet: grains boiled into a kind of porridge was a common food for adults as well as children, and this was seen as appropriate for babies slowly being weaned from their mothers' or nurses' milk. Animal milk mixed with water and bread was also a common supplement to breast milk. The period between ages two and five were probably not only the most dangerous, but also the most carefree. Toddlers were treated like children: they engaged in play; they had few responsibilities; and they were probably indulged more than older children. This is also probably the period of time in which children bonded with their parents, especially their mothers.

The kinds of play in which young children engaged mimicked the activities of their parents. Little girls played at cooking or might try to help their mothers by trying to do tasks such as drawing water from the communal well. Boys played at fighting or the tasks engaged in by their fathers, such as grinding grain, blacksmithing, or cutting wood.

Historians have debated a great deal about the degree to which parents had emotional connections to their young children. In 1960, the French sociologist, Philippe Ariès, wrote a book entitled *Centuries of Childhood* in which he theorized that parents in the historical past did not feel true affection for their young children, and that instead they exploited them heartlessly. According to Ariès and his followers, parents did not begin to feel genuine (as determined by modern attitudes) love for their children until the nineteenth century.[6] Historians ever since have been disputing his conclusions, and convincingly. Although medieval parents might not have had a great deal of time to spend with their children and they might have been burdened with many other responsibilities, sources demonstrate that true affection and parental concern existed and that infants and toddlers were mourned when they died. Indeed, chronicles mention the excesses of grief experienced by noble and royal parents whose young children died. When Henry III of England and his wife, Eleanor of Provence, lost their three-year-old daughter Katherine, Queen Eleanor was criticized for the degree to which she mourned and for her very public displays of grief. The chronicler Matthew Paris, who had little love for either Henry III or his queen, was scathing about Eleanor's so-called excessive grief, not just because her distress had made her ill, but also because he considered Katherine, who might have been disabled in some way, to be an inappropriate object for such a degree of sadness, describing her as "dumb [that is, unable to speak] and fit for nothing, though possessing great beauty [or prettiness]."[7]

Certain religious and culturally traditional ceremonies welcomed infants into the community of their families, often very near the moment of their birth. Christian babies, born alive or dead, were supposed to be baptized as soon as possible following the birth, and certainly within the first year. This ritual was so important to Christian culture that midwives were given permission to baptize newborns if they were born dead or if it was thought that they would not survive long enough for a priest to perform the ceremony. In Byzantine culture, the naming of the newborn, which also designated the infant's patron saint, was an important ritual that included a priestly blessing. Similar rituals, overseen by an imam, occurred in some Muslim regions of the Mediterranean.

In Jewish culture, the circumcision of boy babies in a ceremony known as a bris was supposed to be carried out by the rabbi within eight days of the baby's birth. Similar ceremonies in the Islamic community occurred when children were older, and so will be discussed in the next section.

Childhood: Ages 5 to 12

Once past the dangerous period of infancy and toddler-hood, children began to be given more responsibility and to be more independent. Peasant children were expected to work in some capacity from about the age of five. They took care of younger children, helped in home maintenance and in the kitchen garden, helped in the agricultural labor, in the dairy, and with other kinds of chores. Elite children might have had fewer chores to perform, but they had responsibilities nonetheless. Their education began as early as the age of five, with both boys and girls receiving instruction from tutors, boys being trained in the arts of war, and girls in skills considered appropriate for females: weaving, tapestry, cooking, embroidery. It is likely that, among the elite classes, both boys and girls were taught to read the language they spoke. In areas, such as Western Europe, where the vernacular language—English, German, Italian, and so forth—was not in common use internationally, elite children also learned French, which was used by many people as an international language. European boys who demonstrated a facility for languages and an interest in furthering their education also learned Latin, especially those elite males who were destined for careers in the church. In the Byzantine Empire, where Greek was both the vernacular and the intellectual language, the western tension between Latin, the language of the church, and the many spoken languages of Europe did not exist. Similarly, although a number of non-Arabic dialects were spoken throughout the Islamic world, such as Turkish by the Seljuks and Ottomans, Coptic among the Egyptians, and Aramaic and Syriac in Syria and the Lebanon, most people became conversant in Arabic because of religious requirements as well as commercial, intellectual, and political traditions and norms. European Jewish children, who commonly spoke Yiddish (a polyglot language whose structure was Hebrew, but which contained German and Slavic vocabulary) among themselves, learned Hebrew and also picked up the vernacular of whatever country or region in which they lived. Jews living in the Islamic portions of the medieval world spoke Arabic as their everyday tongue, so they had to undertake formal instruction in Hebrew as well.

In the Muslim world, education of boys was considered essential and all boys were schooled in the Quran. Girls were not often given opportunities to become literate, but they were expected to memorize Quranic verses nevertheless. Their education was primarily in domestic skills. A similar emphasis on the education of males existed in both Jewish and Byzantine cultures, with all of these societies considering the age of seven to be more or less the optimum age for beginning a child's education.

Descriptions of the educational experiences of young children appear in some medieval sources. The Anglo-Saxon King Alfred of Wessex and his older brothers had a tutor who resided with the royal household. According to a popular story told by his official biographer, Asser, Alfred's mother challenged the boys to learn the contents of a book of English poetry. Alfred manipulated the contest by grabbing the book and taking it to his tutor, who then taught him the poems so that he could recite them to his mother.[8] The mother of theologian and historian Guibert, abbot of Nogent-sous-Coucy, engaged a tutor for him and oversaw his education quite closely.[9] Although she does not describe the process of her education, Anna the daughter of Emperor Alexios Komnenos, clearly received an unusually thorough academic education, possibly at the urging of her grandmother Anna Dalassena, since she became Alexios's official historian and biographer.

Sometimes even very young children were sent away for their schooling. Bede, the famous eighth-century Anglo-Saxon theologian and historians, was dedicated to the monastery of Monkswearmouth when he was only six or seven years old. Although the dedication of very small children to monastic life was discouraged in the High Middle Ages, Bede's experience was not radically different from boys sent to monasteries—and from girls such as Hrotsvit of Gandersheim and Hildegard of Bingen to convents—for their education.

Children of lower social status also began their education around the age of seven. In medieval cities, apprenticeships in manufacturing and trade guilds began at about ages 7 to 10. In cities that organized municipal schools, such as Florence in the thirteenth century, middle-class and elite boys were sent to school for a few years before embarking on their apprenticeships in the notarial, banking, and mercantile trades. Other guilds did not require formal education, so apprenticeships started early.

Even though the activities of boys and girls from the age of five were probably dominated by work and schooling, there was still time to play. Again, coroners' reports, by describing the ways in which children tended to die, tell us how they lived as well. Peasant children seem to have had reasonable opportunities for play, and their interests were not all that different from those of children today. They climbed trees (and fell out of them), engaged in mock battles (injuring each other in the process), caught fish (and fell into creeks and ponds), and played games. It seems that children were not necessarily closely supervised, so the danger of injury in rough play was fairly high. It is possible that boys injured themselves and each other in greater numbers than girls when engaged in play, although the tasks that girls were expected to perform, such as cooking, could be dangerous for them as well.

Apprenticeship, the beginning of formal education, and entry into domestic service were all initiated sometime between the ages of 7 and 12. In many cases, such training necessitated leaving home. Among the aristocracy in Europe, the fostering of young men from other families, and the sending of one's own male children to be fostered, was an important part of the social culture. Girls were not fostered in the same way, but it was possible for girls to become betrothed as early as the age of six (although they could not be forced to marry and they could reject the betrothal once they reached the age of consent), and they were sometimes sent to live with their intended husband's family. The other medieval cultures were less likely to send their children away from home for fostering in another's household, but people did send their sons away to school. The schools of Damascus and Constantinople were famous and people who could afford to have their sons educated in the best schools tried to take advantage of this privilege. Jewish communities in the Middle Ages maintained their own schools for young Jewish men, usually run by the community's rabbi, where they learned Hebrew and studied both Torah (the first five books of the Hebrew Bible) and the interpretive texts known as Talmud, Mishnah, and Midrash. Jewish boys were also educated in other languages—Arabic, French, Latin, German, English, Greek—to facilitate their business in international trade. Indeed, the transmission of Classical Greek texts such as those by Aristotle to the West came about because of Jewish scholars in Muslim Spain translating Arabic translations of these classics into Latin. Most Muslim boys were educated in local schools beginning at age seven. Education in Islamic society was focused almost entirely on memorizing the Quran, a process that took about two years. Graduation was celebrated by the whole community and the most gifted boys could go on to advanced education curricula in one of the great centers of learning in Damascus, Baghdad, Cairo, or Mecca.

The period of childhood between 5 and 12 was also the period when sexual separation began to have a significant effect on the lives of medieval boys and girls. Medieval society—no matter the region or culture—was profoundly concerned with highlighting differences between males and females. This was expressed for children in the form of clothing, educational opportunities, choices of profession, and even the physical environment in which they were raised. Boys, unless they were destined for professions in religion as priests, monks, rabbis, or imams, were discouraged from remaining indoors and much of their training occurred outside the house. This could involve everything from military training for the elites to agriculture and skilled manual labor such as blacksmithing or milling for the peasantry. Girls, on the other hand, were discouraged from *leaving* the house. This was more or less the case even for peasant families, where the radical separation of environments that could occur among the wealthy classes was impossible to maintain. Girls' training in the domestic arts of cooking, cleaning, spinning, weaving, needlework, and household management prepared them not only for marriage, but also for domestic service and jobs in the textile trades.

Among all medieval societies, gender identification became increasingly critical as children aged. This is likely to have been one of the principal reasons why medieval people dressed their children in clothes that mimicked adult dress. Before puberty, it can be difficult to distinguish sexual difference when children are clothed in similar attire and their hair is of similar lengths. Medieval people exhibited a profound anxiety about gender identity, especially about the possibility of girls disguising themselves as boys. This anxiety was connected significantly to concerns about female chastity and, sometimes, paranoia among religious leaders about females supposedly infecting male spaces and competing intellectually and physically with men. One of the main reasons, for instance, why Joan of Arc, a girl of only 16, was charged with heresy is because she insisted on wearing male clothing.

Some cultural rites of passage could take this anxiety about gender identity to extremes. A significant rite of passage for Muslim boys between ages 7 and 12 was circumcision. Unlike the Jewish bris, performed by a rabbi on a newborn boy, Islamic circumcision celebrated a boy's entrance into puberty. A public celebration involving the whole family, the circumcision of boys was a time of joyous anticipation, one that initiated Muslim boys into the religious and social community. A very different series of events occurred in the context of a practice known euphemistically as female circumcision, but more accurately termed female genital mutilation. Unlike male circumcision, this was (and is) not practiced by all Muslim communities. Turks, for instance, did not engage in this practice, but most Islamic societies from Syria to North Africa, including Egypt and Sudan, did—and many continue to do so today. The procedure was performed by female practitioners when a girl was around 7 to 10 years old. Unlike male circumcision, female genital mutilation was neither celebrated publicly nor even acknowledged publicly. As a result, the motive behind the practice is unclear, although it is well known that it predated the adoption of Islam by the communities that continue to practice this procedure. The control of female sexuality does, however, seem to be the major motive behind the practice, since many medieval Islamic sources claim that women upon whom this mutilation was not practiced were dangerously sexually adventurous.[10]

This emphasis on gender identification that was so important to western Christian and Islamic culture was made much more complicated in the Byzantine Empire because of the use of eunuchs to fill prominent administrative positions in both the imperial government and in the Byzantine Church. Although originally the boys subjected to castration for this purpose were predominantly non-Roman slaves, by the time of the Komnenan dynasty (the eleventh century), Byzantine families—even sometimes aristocratic ones—were known to secure professional careers for their young sons by having them castrated. Eunuchs occupied important positions in the Byzantine government; there are even examples of eunuchs who became generals in the imperial army, although this was very rare indeed. Their political importance could even give prominent eunuchs the opportunity to manipulate their office to secure members of the imperial family as partners for their own brothers and sisters. In addition, although early Christianity forbade eunuchs from becoming priests, by the middle Byzantine period this restriction was no longer an issue and eunuchs began to make up a small but politically and intellectually significant core of church administrators. Indeed, some of the most important bishops of the Komnenan period were eunuchs, men who were singled out for being especially pious and spiritual in their professional lives. This kind of decision was a deliberate choice on the part of the parents, but not necessarily on the part of the child: it is doubtful that boys would have undergone a surgical procedure that was not only dangerous—records suggest that a huge number of young boys died in the process of being castrated—but also barred them from a normal life of marriage and family. Nevertheless, parents with intellectually talented younger sons might have seen this path as attractive for the future of not only their children, but also the influence of the family.[11] Islamic culture also used eunuchs in administration and as guards over harems, but these were always slaves subjected against their will to being castrated.

Since the period between ages 5 and 12 could be considered on a broad scale a period in which apprenticeships of all kinds—not only in manufacturing among the urban classes, but also training in clerical careers, in military skills, and in domestic management among all levels of medieval society—occurred, it is not surprising that betrothals were also often arranged for children in this period of their development. Parents were very concerned about the future welfare of their children, and marrying them well was one of the best ways medieval parents could hope to guarantee a comfortable life as adults. The age of consent and marriage differed among all the different medieval cultures, and marriage practices could be radically different even within specific cultures depending on local custom and social status, but it was not uncommon for the children of elites—especially girls—to be betrothed or even married by the age of 12. This was also the case for most Jewish and Muslim women, even those of lower social and economic status.

The marriage choices for medieval children, and the criteria parents used to come up with the best candidates, were based not on love in our conventional sense of the term, but on issues such as security, wealth, political influence, and physical proximity of land. As discussed recently by Martha Howell, the "companionate marriage" was an ideal model, but the achieving of such a marriage, one based on love and respect and a sense of partnership, could be accomplished only after other more practical issues were sorted out.[12]

Parents were not always the people involved in making these choices. Among the highest levels of the aristocracy, the king had a say in the marriages of their children, especially if their father was, or parents were, dead. A good example of this is the betrothal and marriage of two sisters, cousins of Henry III of England's queen, Eleanor of Provence, to two young heirs to important lordships in the north of England, Edmund de Lacy future lord of Pontefract and earl of Lincoln, who married the elder sister, Alice of Saluzzo, and John de Vescy future lord of Alnwick (and also a vassal of the Lacy lords of Pontefract), who married Agnes of Saluzzo, Alice's younger sister. The king and queen clearly had a hand in these marriages, even though the mothers of the children involved (the chronicler Matthew Paris describes the betrothals taking place when the children were "very young") were still very much alive. Both Edmund de Lacy and John de Vescy had been fostered in the royal household, and were raised with the royal couple's own children; their closeness to Henry and Eleanor's sons Edward and Edmund undoubtedly contributed to the decision to marry them to the Savoyard cousins of the queen, thus linking them even more with the interests of the royal family. Since they were both significant heirs and officially wards of the crown, their mothers had little say in whom the two boys married. This does not mean, however, that

Margaret de Lacy, Edmund's mother, and Agnes de Vescy, John's mother, were completely uninvolved in this decision-making or that they opposed the marriages. Margaret was an intimate of the queen, and both she and Agnes had ties to the court through their magnate status. Margaret was countess of Lincoln in her own right and dowager countess of Pembroke, while Agnes was one of the heirs of the earldom of Pembroke through her mother, Sibyl la Marshal.[13]

The very early age at marriage of elite western Christian and most Jewish, Muslim, and Byzantine girls put an abrupt end to childhood for them. By the time they were 13—and often years before—girls from these cultures were considered marriageable women and more often than not either wed or betrothed. Even though young girls just reaching puberty in these cultures knew that they were destined or at least likely to be wed by age 12, no amount of preparation could prepare them psychologically for the experience, especially since very often their husbands were bound to be closer in age to their mothers than themselves. The experiences of Eleanor of Castile in the negotiations and enactment of her marriage to the Lord Edward, son and heir of Henry III of England and Eleanor of Provence, could provide a window on the difficulties girls experienced when they married so young.

Eleanor was born late in 1241 and probably had not even reached the age of 12 when she became betrothed to Prince Edward, who was only two years older. Their wedding was performed about a year later, in October 1254, and consummated immediately, since both had reached the legal age of consent. Eleanor seems to have gotten pregnant almost immediately, but gave birth prematurely seven months later: the baby died. She would not give birth to a surviving child for another five years.[14] Her inexperience and physical immaturity, and the public anxiety over her childlessness, must have made those years very stressful for the young princess. During these years, however, she developed a good relationship with her mother-in-law, Queen Eleanor, and her relationship with Edward, whom she had met for the first time literally days before they consummated their union, blossomed. Her experiences, as well as those of her mother-in-law, who was also married at 12 years of age, might indeed have been the impetus for them both to argue strenuously against the betrothal and marriage of Eleanor's and Edward's daughter in 1282, when she was only 13. The two queens were successful: the marriage negotiations were delayed.[15]

Eleanor of Castile's experiences might have been most typical for girls of European royalty, but they resonate far beyond that exalted social level. Eleven- or 12-year old girls who were married to men they did not know well, even if they were boys close to them in age, must have felt the same kinds of anxiety Eleanor experienced. Unfortunately for Jewish, Byzantine, and Muslim girls generally, social customs outweighed their own possibly terrifying experiences. Unlike the two

Eleanors, who convinced their son and husband respectively, that 13 was too young an age to marry, the daughters of most child-brides underwent the same abrupt transition from girlhood to adulthood as their mothers.

Adolescence: Ages 13 to 21

Medieval people did not necessarily recognize the years between youth and adulthood (as we would recognize it) as a unique developmental period, although the Latin term *adolescens* was used to refer to young men of this age and this period was to some extent considered to be a separate and unique life stage in western Christian society. Nevertheless, by the age of 13, most medieval people were considered to be more or less adults. The onset of puberty effectively rendered them capable of assuming adult responsibilities. Indeed, the legal age of marriage for girls in Christian Europe was between 12 and 14 and for boys, between 18 and 20. Girls this young were not only married, but could also take control of property they inherited, something boys were not able to do until they had reached their majority at 21. Ironically, boy kings could theoretically dismiss their guardians and take control from the regency council, which was usually appointed according to the will of the late king, once they had reached the age of 14 as well. This is essentially what King Edward III did when he exiled his mother, who had been acting as regent, and executed Roger de Mortimer earl of March, once he had reached the age of 14 in 1330. Thus a king could enter into his inheritance and assume adulthood at the same time as girls but much earlier than other boys.

In the other medieval cultures, adulthood was also defined, in varying degrees, by puberty for both boys and girls. Marriages occurred very early, even if the married couple did not cohabit until later, as sometimes occurred in Jewish communities. Girls received their inheritances in anticipation of marriage, in the form of dowries. It was not unheard-of for a girl to be a widow before she reached her eighteenth birthday. This in fact happened to Eleanor Plantagenet, the sister of King Henry III of England, who was married at 12 to William II le Marshal (he was considerably older) and was widowed by the time she was 16.

For most boys and many girls in the Middle Ages, however, the period we think of as adolescence was an initiation into adult life, rather than a full-blown leap. This period of time focused on intensive education and activity for both boys and girls. In medieval cities, apprentices moved from that low status to the status of journeyman (where many of them remained for their entire lives) usually between the ages of 16 and 21. Master status was much harder to achieve and few journeymen were able to gain that title. Among the elites, boys could be knighted at the age of 16; those destined for a career in the church were sent to university for advanced education sometime around the age of 14, and could begin the ordination process by becoming acolytes at around the same time. Among peasants, boys could begin to take on not just more work in the fields, but also professional training by the time they were 14 or 15.

Pubescent boys lived a kind of every-boy-for-himself existence in medieval Europe, especially those who were apprentices, workers, or university students in the cities of the period. Freed from the restrictions of parental oversight, these young men were notoriously rowdy troublemakers: medieval records detail all kinds of mayhem perpetrated by roving bands of young men. In medieval Rousillon, gangs of teenage boys and young men kidnapped respectable women from their houses and raped them, sometimes keeping them captive for days on end. These women were then dumped at one of the city's brothels since their status as respectable was destroyed by the actions of these young thugs.[16] Riots initiated by apprentices and young journeymen were common, especially during holidays such as Carnival, known in the United States as Mardi Gras.[17]

In university towns, such as Paris and Oxford, not only did hordes of drunken students rove the streets looking for trouble, but town-gown disturbances were common enough to be a source of tremendous anxiety for both city and university officials. The medieval historian and theologian Jacques de Vitry wrote scathingly about the behavior of students in Paris.

Almost all the students at Paris, foreigners and natives, wanted to do absolutely nothing except learn or hear something new. Some studied merely to acquire knowledge, which is curiosity; others to acquire fame, which is vanity; others still for the sake of gain, which is cupidity and the vice of simony. Very few studied for their own edification, or that of others. They wrangled and disputed not merely about the various sects or about some discussions; but the differences between the countries also caused dissensions, hatreds and virulent animosities among them and they impudently uttered all kinds of affronts and insults against one another.

They affirmed that the English were drunkards and had tails; the sons of France proud, effeminate and carefully adorned like women. They said that the Germans were furious and obscene at their feasts; the Normans, vain and boastful; the Poitevins, traitors and always adventurers. The Burgundians they considered vulgar and stupid. The Bretons were reputed to be fickle and changeable, and were often reproached for the death of Arthur. The Lombards were called avaricious, vicious and cowardly; the Romans, seditious, turbulent and slanderous; the Sicilians, tyrannical and cruel; the inhabitants of Brabant, men of blood, incendiaries, brigands and ravishers; the Flemish, fickle, prodigal, gluttonous, yielding as butter, and slothful. After such insults from words they often came to blows.[18]

Students were, at the end of the day, not all that different in the Middle Ages from those attending college and university today. They tended to spend their money unwisely and were forced to beg parents to pay their bills; they drank too much beer and wine; and they had favorite professors into whose classes they crowded, while less favored teachers endured inattentive students and empty classrooms.

Medieval chronicles describe the hard drinking, dicing, and whoring in which young aristocratic men engaged, often to the dismay and anger of their parents. King Edward I had a miserable relationship with his teenage son, Edward prince of Wales, in large part because Prince Edward rebelled against his strict father's insistence that he give up some of his more unsavory friends. The description of Prince Hal and his behavior in Shakespeare's play Henry IV was not unfamiliar to the Elizabethan audience, which was made up significantly of young men out for a good time.

The expectations for girls were so different that the onset of puberty had a very different significance for them. The preservation of a girl's virginity became a very serious issue for families of the middle classes and above and so control of their activities, and the confinement of them to the house, occupied parental energies. In the story of Romeo and Juliet, for example, Juliet is being introduced to the adult community for the first time during her betrothal party—at the age of 13—and every move she makes is controlled by her zealously protective mother and her not-so-zealous nurse. The preparation of a trousseau, the goods that a girl would bring to her marriage that comprised not only her personal clothing but also things like bedding, floor and wall coverings, furniture, and so on, occupied a great deal of time for daughters in elite families. Such preparations also occurred, to a certain extent, for daughters destined to enter convents or nunneries, which they generally did before the age of 16.

Parents in many parts of the medieval world did make some effort to match their daughters to men who were not only of the same social class, but also somewhat close in age. It was not unusual for there to be only a few years separating brides and grooms among the elites in northern and western Europe, for example. In other parts of Europe, however, it was customary for there to be a more radical difference in age between bride and groom. In the city-states of high medieval Italy, for instance, 14- and 15-year-old girls often married men in their thirties. This radical disparity between the ages of men and women could be beneficial in some ways: young and immature girls might be better protected by older men, whose behavior was perhaps more paternal than that of a younger man. Nevertheless, the difference in age and experience operated as a real bar to intellectual and social development for young women whose inexperience in the world was interpreted as ignorance. A paternalistic husband could easily become controlling and dismissive.

Among the lower classes, marriages tended to occur when the parties were older, often well over the age of 18, but this did not mean that girls experienced a more gradual transition from childhood to adulthood in this circumstance. Girls aged 14 often went into domestic service or became apprenticed to female-centered workshops where textiles and lace were produced. Domestic service was a pathway to independence for peasant girls. Not only did they earn wages that they could save toward the nest egg necessary in order to get married, but they also learned and expanded on skills they needed in order to run a household of their own. Indeed, there was a more or less constant stream of young women moving in and out of the labor force who used both domestic service and jobs in textile and lace manufacture as transitional stages from childhood to marriage. It was rare for young women to remain in service for their entire lives. Instead, they would leave to marry, and perhaps return to service if widowed.

In the Muslim world, the possibility of polygamy altered dramatically the life stages of children. Young men, like those in Christian cultures, continued their education during their adolescent years. They entered into different professions, from the military to more intellectual pursuits such as physician or imam; they gained experience in the world through travel and trade; they worked the family farm and planned on inheritance of land to amass the funds necessary to marry. Girls, on the other hand, experienced a profound change in their independence and their ability to achieve goals other than marriage. There were no religious houses where girls could become nuns dedicated to chastity and education. Domestic service was an option, but not a particularly respectable one, or one that could serve as preparation for marriage. Girls who attained puberty were subjected to veiling and, if anything, their activities and opportunities were more restricted than they were as children. The contrast between the lives of young men and young women was thereby emphasized by the culture, as the status of women became bound up fundamentally on the maintenance of their virginity before marriage and their chastity after marriage.

The Byzantine world occupied a kind of middle ground between the Muslim and western Christian worlds. Certainly young women of elite status were educated by tutors, as the life of Anna Komnene attests. Certainly most young women were expected to marry. Unlike the west, which offered quite a few opportunities for elite girls to reject marriage and to become nuns, the Byzantine east had fewer female monastic institutions and seem to have been more suspicious of the idea of women operating in an institution that was not under direct male control. In addition, the physical isolation of elite women was emphasized, in much the same way as it was in Muslim culture: elite women were waited on by female servants and eunuchs and contact with unrelated males was actively discouraged. This meant that the typical lot of young pubescent women, whose public labor was vital to the survival of the family and who were not able to quibble about the respectability of girls needing to work in the public marketplace, more or less automatically conferred on them a questionable status as girls of possibly low morals. This would have been in marked contrast to the opportunities that opened for young men in the Byzantine world, where the onset of puberty would have opened doors both professional and social. Chances to attain higher education, to enter into professions that were of high status, and to gain public political influence were possible for male teenagers, whose public lives became increasingly emphasized. Moreover, like medieval Italy, the age disparity between brides and grooms tended to mean that very young brides, aged 12 to 15, often married men considerably older than they.

Abuse of and Violence against Children

Just as discussed with respect to husbands and wives, casual violence directed against children was probably so common in the Middle Ages as not to be worth mentioning in any sources. Concerns about the exploitation of children are a remarkably recent phenomenon: legislation limiting child labor began to be passed only within the last 150 years. In addition, the sexual exploitation of children was not even considered an issue until very recently. Children, even more than women, were considered the property of their parents in many otherwise civilized countries until the mid-twentieth century. This attitude certainly affected the lives of children in the Middle Ages.

Sources mention occasions of violence against children, such as Guibert of Nogent's description of his mother's distress when she discovered that his tutor was beating him. Ironically, Guibert chastises his mother for wanting to fire the tutor: he felt that the beatings were beneficial to his development as a scholar. Certainly, the culture of the medieval world considered corporal punishment a teaching tool, so childhood for virtually every child must have been full of physical violence ranging from the mild to the extreme.

Unlike episodes of extreme violence of husbands directed against wives, which could prompt outsiders to intervene, there is no evidence that outsiders considered it appropriate to do so in the beating of children. Occasionally, if a child's guardian was seen to be too restrictive or abusive, someone in authority might step in. Parents who had apprenticed their children to masters for the purpose of training also were concerned sometimes about the level of abuse to which their children were subjected and could complain. It is not clear whether those kinds of interventions actually moderated the behavior of the abuser.

The sexual exploitation of children was undoubtedly very high. Sources from medieval London describe the use of children as prostitutes. In one infamous case, a young boy was dressed as a girl to be used as a prostitute and this boy grew up to be a transvestite who was very popular among the community of men (apparently including many priests and friars) who frequented prostitutes in medieval London.[19] The sexual abuse of girls in domestic service was probably very high, as well.

In a civilization where the age of marriage and puberty coincided, at least for girls, it might seem bizarre to discuss the sexual exploitation of children. Nevertheless, this was an issue of some concern among the religious leadership of both Christian and Judaic cultures. There was a great deal of discussion about trying to prevent girls married before age 12 from being sexually abused. In the Byzantine Empire, it seems the authorities actively tried to control both this problem and the related problems of child prostitution and incest.[20] It is not clear whether these concerns and attempts to control what was likely an endemic problem improved the situation. Indeed, child prostitution and the sexual exploitation of children—probably both girls and boys—was and continues to be a persistent problem throughout the world to this day.

All the medieval political systems had public and legal systems that tried to control the abuse of children, at least those that resulted in death. If a baby was stillborn or a miscarriage occurred, an investigation usually took place to determine whether the death was accidental, the result of the birthing process, or a case of infanticide or abortion. This investigation was not so much for the protection of children, however. Unfortunately, it was usually designed as a preventive measure to discourage women from controlling their fertility. In England, any death of any kind required a coroner's inquest be conducted so if a child died, the reasons for that death were revealed in at least some cases.

Conclusion

The lifecycles of children in the medieval world thus shared elements we would find familiar today: infancy and childhood were periods where families nurtured and protected their children, gave them opportunities for both play and learning, and gradually granted them more and more independence as they grew toward adulthood. On the other hand, modern parents would no doubt be appalled by some of the dangerous behavior countenanced by medieval parents. Moreover, the misbehavior of college students today probably cannot hold a candle to the kinds of mayhem thought up by medieval university students. In many ways, the lives of boys then and now were more similar than the lives of girls. The increasing restrictions on girls as they moved through their life stages is in sharp contrast to the increasing independence modern-day girls experience as they go from childhood, to adolescence, to adulthood.

What cannot be questioned is the devotion of parents with regard to their children. Although not necessarily expressed in the ways we do today, parents sought the best opportunities for their children, even in some cases to the point of having young sons castrated in order to guarantee their future professional success. Parents made enormous sacrifices for their children. The Carolingian noblewoman Dhuoda's tragic life, discussed in chapter 7, is a good example of such a sacrifice. She was unable to be directly involved in her children's lives because of her husband's abusive treatment of her, so she resorted to writing a long treatise, in the form of a letter, to them with instructions meant to guide their proper development as honorable young men. Parents also mourned babies and young children who died, celebrated their successes, and delighted at the birth of grandchildren. Children, for their part, were as complex in the Middle Ages as they are today. They were timid and adventurous, obedient and rebellious, willing to accept strict controls on their behavior and chafing at such restrictions.

Notes

1. This is discussed by P.P.A. Biller, "Birth Control in the West in the Thirteenth and Early Fourteenth Centuries" *Past and Present* 94 (1982): 3–26.

2. Such as Norman Roth, *Daily Life of the Jews in the Middle Ages* (Westport: Greenwood Press, 2005), 45.

3. See S. D. Goitein, *A Mediterranean Society: An Abridgement in One Volume,* rev. and ed. Jacob Lassner (Berkeley: University of California Press, 1999), 409–410.

4. For a discussion of nursing, see Mary Martin McLaughlin, "Survivors and Surrogates: Children and Parents from the Ninth to the Thirteenth Centuries," in *The History of Childhood,* ed. Lloyd de Mause (New York: Psychohistory Press, 1974), 101–81 and reprinted in *Medieval Families: Perspectives on Marriage, Household, and Children* (Toronto: University of Toronto Press, 2004), 20–124. See, especially 36–38.

5. This is discussed in depth by Barbara A. Hanawalt, *The Ties that Bound: Peasant Families in Medieval England* (New York: Oxford University Press, 1986). See especially 157–159.

6. Philippe Ariès, *Centuries of Childhood: A Social History of Family Life,* trans. Robert Baldick (New York: Random House, 1962).

7. Matthew Paris, *English History,* 3 vols, trans. J. A. Giles (London: Henry G. Bohn, 1854; reprint New York: AMS Press, 1968), 3: 232 and 250. This is also mentioned by Margaret Howell, *Eleanor of Provence: Queenship in Thirteenth-Century England* (Oxford: Blackwell Publishers, 1998), 101–102.

8. This is discussed in depth—including the problems with the story—by David Horspool, *King Alfred: Burnt Cakes and Other Legends* (Cambridge, MA: Harvard University Press, 2006), 17–36.

9. This can be found in Guibert's autobiography, most recently translated by Paul J. Archambaut, *A Monk's Confession: The Memoirs of Guibert of Nogent* (University Park: Pennsylvania State University Press, 1996).

10. Unlike male circumcision, which does not have a negative impact on male abilities to experience pleasure in sexual intercourse, female genital mutilation removes all the outer genitalia, in particular those organs that provide females with a pleasurable experience. An excellent discussion of this controversial issue is Jonathan P. Berkey, "Circumcision Circumscribed: Female Excision and Cultural Accommodation in the Medieval Near East" *International Journal of Middle East Studies* 28, no. 1 (1996): 19–38. Perhaps unsurprisingly, female genital mutilation is not discussed in any web sites describing Islamic culture for the use of students.

11. See Shaun F. Tougher, "Byzantine Eunuchs: An Overview, with Special Reference to their Creation and Origin," in *Women, Men, and Eunuchs: Gender in Byzantium,* ed. Liz James (London: Routledge, 1997), 168–184. for a general overview of this issue. In addition, Kathryn M. Ringrose has discussed the different ways in which eunuchs in imperial administration, known as court eunuchs were characterized in comparison to those with careers in the church, known as church eunuchs. See Ringrose, "Reconfiguring the Prophet Daniel: Gender, Sanctity, and Castration in Byzantium," in *Gender and Difference in the Middle Ages,* ed. Sharon Farmer and Carol Braun Pasternack (Minneapolis: University of Minnesota Press, 2003), 73–106.

12. Martha Howell, "The Properties of Marriage in Late Medieval Europe: Commercial Wealth and the Creation of Modern Marriage," in *Love, Marriage, and Family Ties in the Later Middle Ages,* ed. Isabel Davis, Miriam Müller, and Sarah Rees Jones (Turnhout: Brepols, 2003), 17–62.

13. Both women are discussed in Linda E. Mitchell, *Portraits of Medieval Women: Marriage, Family, and Politics in England, 1225–1350* (New York: Palgrave Macmillan, 2003). See, especially, 11–42.

14. John Carmi Parsons, *Eleanor of Castile: Queen and Society in Thirteenth-Century England* (New York: St Martin's Press, 1995) discusses Eleanor's youth extensively in chapter 1, 1–68.

15. Parsons, *Eleanor of Castile,* 21. The name of this daughter does not appear, but Parsons might be referring to Joan of Acre, whose marriage to Gilbert de Clare began to be negotiated at around 1282, but was not performed until 1290, when Joan was eighteen.

16. This is discussed by Jacques Rossiaud, *Medieval Prostitution,* trans. Lydia G. Cochrane (New York: Blackwell Publishing, 1988).

17. One such episode from the sixteenth century forms the basis for Emmanuel Le Roy Ladurie's book, *Carnival in Romans,* trans. Mary Feeney (New York: George Braziller, 1979).

18. Jacques de Vitry, "Life of the Students at Paris" in *The Internet Medieval Sourcebook,* http://www.fordham.edu/halsall/source/vitry1.html.

19. This unique case's documents can be found at the *Internet Medieval Sourcebook:* "The Questioning of John Rykener, a Male Cross-Dressing Prostitute, 1395," http://www.fordham.edu/halsall/source/1395rykener.html.

20. John Lascaratos and Effie Poulakou-Rebelakou, "Child Sexual Abuse: Historical Cases in the Byzantine Empire (324–1453 A.D.)" *Child Abuse and Neglect* 24, no. 8 (2000): 1085–1090.

9

Religion and the Family

Medieval religious practice, whether Christian, Muslim, or Jewish, was intimately connected to family life. Mothers were responsible for basic religious education at virtually all social levels, and personal piety conducted within a domestic environment was a fundamental component of religious practice. In addition, elite families in the Christian west and Byzantine east were often connected in significant ways to the institution of the church through patronage of monasteries and nunneries, the promotion of family members as professional clergy, and political associations between church elites, such as bishops, and their own families. The dedication of children to monastic houses made these associations far more intimate and helped to keep families involved in the monastic communities. It is likely that similar relationships existed in Judaism as well as in Islam, but neither religion operated under such an elaborate professional hierarchy. The more informal structures of those religions make it very difficult to uncover evidence of political and patronage associations connected to the rabbinate or office of imam. Professional religious thinkers, such as theologians and philosophers, in all four cultures took pains to analyze and discuss issues of family life that intersected religious observance, such as mixed marriages, conversion, the status and roles of men and women in the family, and so on. Finally, religious authorities oversaw many life events that medieval people experienced, from marriage and divorce, claims of legitimacy, conflicts between spouses, charges of sexual assault and abduction, and issues central to inheritance of property. These have been discussed in depth in previous chapters, so they will be touched on in this chapter only as they relate to specific religious issues.

The sources for the history of medieval religion and its relation to the family are quite varied. The vast quantity of Christian texts describing the lives of the saints, especially the very popular collection known as *The Golden Legend* (it was even more popular than the Bible, since it was written for a lay audience and appears in all the vernacular languages of Europe), are important sources not only for ideas about piety and belief, but also about relationships. Nevertheless, these are not always the most reliable sources for accurate historical information because their purpose was to emphasize the extraordinary piety of the saint, not to present him or her as a normal person. Similar kinds of texts exist for Islam, in the sense that a vast quantity of stories about the Prophet and his family and the heroes of medieval Islam—Nur ad-Din, Salah ad-Din, Sultan Baybars, Zengi, and so on—were the fodder of professional storytellers who performed these stories for public and private audiences (as they do to this day in the tea and coffee shops of Muslim countries through-out the Middle East). These are just as unreliable as saints' lives, and for similar reasons. Perhaps unsurprisingly, there are few equivalent texts for medieval Judaism, although other kinds of sources do exist, such as the interpretive writings known as Mishnah and Midrash, that focus in part on regulating religion in family life, and some popular stories that circu-lated in the later Middle Ages, such as those concerning the legendary rabbis Hillel and Akivah.

More neutral sources, such as public records, legal records, charters and deeds, chronicles, and so forth, also contain information about the medi-eval family and its religiosity. The emphasis in these kinds of sources, however, is not to describe family relationships so much as to identify ways in which either families are in conflict or the ways in which they express in physical form—such as through donations to monasteries—their piety. Thus, using a combination of sources, but keeping in mind at all times that their emphasis is not always on providing factually accurate information, can help to create a more complete picture of the ways in which medieval families experienced their religious practice.

Christianity and the Medieval Family

From its inception, Christianity was conceived of as a family-based reli-gion. In the first century of its existence, Christian rituals were performed almost always within the confines of private homes, developing public spaces for religious practice only in the second or even third century. The stages of Christian life, from baptism (during at least the first four hundred years of Christianity, people received baptism not at birth, but at adulthood) to death are connected to long-standing family rituals: wel-coming new babies into the family unit, the transition from childhood to adulthood (corresponding with the sacrament of Confirmation), marriage, and mourning the death of a family member. The separation of Christian ritual and the family unit began to increase only after the promotion of the religion by the emperor Constantine in the fourth century, but even at the height of such separation, in the codification of canon law and the presentation of elaborate rituals within the confines of magnificent cathedrals and metropolitan churches, the practice of Christianity within the intimate confines of the family and the household was far more typical of the experience of the medieval Christian person.

Life Stages and the Christian Family

By the seventh century, baptism of infants was much more common than the older tradition of using baptism to commemorate the conversion of an adult and his or her entry into the Christian community. Baptism became, then, a far more family-oriented ritual than it was originally intended to be. Indeed, it became a self-consciously family-centered ritual: although usually performed in a church, the requirements of the ritual included the commemoration of a second set of parents: the godmother and godfather who promise to oversee the child's progress as a Christian. Ironically, although baptisms were celebrations of the family and included virtually all family members, the one person who was almost always absent was the mother. According to canon law, women who had just given birth were not permitted even to enter a church until 40 days later—the western tradition of churching comes from this prohibition—and babies were supposed to be baptized within a week of their birth.

Most Christians in the medieval world did not experience the full range of religious rituals associated with the sacramental system—baptism, confession and penance, communion, confirmation, marriage, ordination, and last rites. It is unlikely, for example, that all Christians were routinely confirmed since the rite of confirmation required extensive religious education. Members of the lower classes were not expected to confess and take communion more than once a year and their participation in weekly masses might have been inconsistent as well, especially at times when agricultural labor required working on Sunday. Nevertheless, there are clear indications that medieval Christians used the sacramental rituals to mark specific life stages related to family life, in particular baptism, marriage, and last rites. These were certainly family affairs, celebrating the original domestic focus of early Christianity in a way that was immediately accessible even to those who had little education or understanding of Christian theology.

Perhaps inevitably, the Christian focus of these rites of passage came to be intertwined with other traditional practices of European cultures, including many pre-Christian religious rituals. The use of amulets, the eating of specific kinds of food, the practice of processing around the village church in particular directions, and so on hearken back to earlier cultural traditions that have nothing to do with Christianity, yet the village priest often not only participated in such rituals, but might not even have been aware of their pre-Christian associations.

Marriage has been discussed in other contexts in previous chapters, but its religious associations and rituals marked an important life stage for medieval Christians. The marriage ceremony itself, the origin of the modern Christian marriage ceremony, is an interesting mixture of Christian and secular elements: in the English kingdom, for instance, the promise of the groom to endow his bride with his worldly goods referred specifically to common law requirements of dower for widows, something that had nothing to do with the church's laws regarding marriage. The ritual of brides wearing something old, something new, something borrowed, and something blue comes from pre-Christian marriage rituals, with each element representing hopes for a successful married life of material prosperity and many children. In Byzantine marriage ceremonies, the use of crowns came from the pre-Christian Roman practice of crowning the wedding couple with laurel wreaths, sometimes made of gold but more typically of real leaves. The wedding ring also comes from pre-Christian rituals in which the ring is symbolic of the wealth the groom brings to the marriage and his pledge to support his bride materially. Priests were expected to perform these ceremonies—in the west, they did so in front of the church door in order to guarantee as many witnesses as possible—but the ritual really was a family, even a community, affair. Since marriages were, at least according to Christian ideals, supposed to create a companionate relationship between two adults and was also supposed to produce children, marriage ceremonies could be seen as the ultimate public expression of family unity.

As the medieval Christian family grew, each child's birth would of course result in a reconnection of the family with the requirements of Christian ritual: more baptisms, more communions, more marriages, and more deaths. The rituals marking the end of life were also shared between the priest and family members and between Christian and non-Christian traditions. The priest performed the Last Rites, which were designed to cleanse the soul of sins before death. These in some ways mimicked the baptism ceremonies, a holdover from the time when Christians were baptized on their death beds, but also included a final confession. Although in many ways an intensely personal moment, the ritual of Last Rites could also include the witnessing of the rest of the family, since these ceremonies also often included oral statements of the dying person that were the legal equivalent of a Last Will and Testament. These, too, were best witnessed by a priest. Priests also presided over the funeral ceremonies, but family members oversaw the preparation of the body for burial (including placing pennies on the eyes of the corpse, a holdover from pre-Christian rituals) and the funeral feast that followed. Family members would then commemorate their recently dead members with prayers—the wealthy could pay for monks to perform masses for their dead loved ones—and remembrances on All Souls Day (November 2).

Christian Holidays

In modern times, holiday celebrations center on the family. This was more or less the case in the Middle Ages as well. However, the kinds of celebrations and the favorite holidays were somewhat different. In addition, almost all the rituals and images we associate with major Christian holidays—the Christmas tree, mistletoe, holly wreaths, Yule logs, the Easter bunny, Easter eggs, and so on—originally had nothing whatsoever to do with Christianity and were more or less appropriated by the church and integrated into the religion because there was no way to eradicate such ancient traditions.

Today, Christmas is probably the most family-oriented and popular Christian holiday, but in the Middle Ages, it was far less important than the period between Ash Wednesday and Easter. The day before Ash Wednesday was Carnival (the French term "Mardi Gras" or Fat Tuesday was invented at a later period). This was a wild celebration of life and indulgence in preparation for the sacrifices of the Lenten period. And Carnival was not just a family affair: the entire community engaged in the celebration as a kind of family writ large. Once Lent began, life became much more sober: Christians were not permitted to eat meat during Lent and marriages were not supposed to be performed during this period. Easter, celebrating the Resurrection, paralleled Carnival: a return to normal life after a long period of deprivation.

Even Easter, however, was not free of non-Christian associations. Indeed, the very name "Easter" for the holiday known as *Pasche* in the rest of Europe (to connect it very specifically with the Jewish holiday of Passover, which in Hebrew is called *Pesach*) refers not to the resurrection of Jesus Christ but to an early Germanic fertility goddess whose festival occurred around the time of the Vernal Equinox, and whose name was *Eostre* (pronounced "Ees-ter" like the Christian holiday). Celebrations of this re-awakening of the earth after a long winter often included the eating of eggs and commemoration of unusually fertile animals, such as rabbits. These rituals were combined with elements of Jewish Passover rituals, such as the eating of the paschal lamb (the youngest lambs born in the spring) and the eating of eggs with salt.

Christmas celebrations in the Middle Ages did not have the universal symbolism it has today. The Christian holiday, more accurately called the Feast of the Nativity, follows a 40-day period of fasting called Advent. Although medieval people below the level of wealthy elites did celebrate this great and important feast day, , they did so on a rather simpler basis than today.

Virtually every popular symbol of Christmas that exists today has its origin in pre-Christian celebrations surrounding the Winter Solstice, the shortest day and longest night of the year. Even the date of Christmas—December 25—existed in Roman culture as the birthday of the god Mithras long before Christianity appeared. Priests and theologians at first tried to limit all of these pre-Christian rituals and elements, but they were so pervasive that the religious authorities finally gave up and began incorporating them into Christian celebrations by reinterpreting them for Christian consumption. Indeed, Christmas celebrations contain so many non-Christian and pre-Christian elements that Oliver Cromwell, the Puritan Lord Protector of England after the English Civil War in the seventeenth century, forbade the celebration of the holiday entirely during the 20 years of his reign.

In the Middle Ages, families in many parts of northern Europe burned Yule logs for the duration of the 12 days of Christmas, from Christmas Eve to the Feast of Epiphany. They hung mistletoe, holly branches, ivy, and garlands of evergreens in their houses and in the parish churches. Although the church interpreted these symbols in ways that represented Christian theology and history, all of these elements came from pre-Christian rituals relating to the solstice, ones that dated back to the Druids, Germanic polytheism, and the Greco-Roman god Bacchus.

Families were not supposed to eat meat during periods of fasting, such as Advent and Lent, so the Christmas feast was an important celebration. Traditional foods in the west included both pre-Christian elements and elements developed at the time. The drinking to everyone's health—the word "wassail" comes from the Old English exclamation *"waes hael!"* ("Be well!") shouted before downing the tumbler's contents—was usually performed in the drinking of hot mulled (spiced) wine or the contents of the wassail bowl: a strong mixture of ale, honey, and spices that was heated. For the aristocracy, the Christmas feast included venison and other game as well as domestic duck and goose (turkey did not appear in Europe until the discovery of the Americas in the sixteenth century). For the peasantry, the European traditional feast was humbles pie, a meat pie containing the cheapest parts of the deer or other large animal—the organ meats—that were called the humbles of the animal.

Byzantine Christmas celebrations were considerably more sober than those in the Latin west. For one thing, Byzantine society tended to frown upon the kinds of riotous celebrations popular among western Europeans. For another, the Byzantine church was somewhat more reluctant than the Latin church to include patently non-Christian elements in religious celebrations. The Byzantine family also experienced the 40-day period of fasting called Advent in the West, but they called it the Phillipian Fast. The five days before the Feast of the Nativity—which was traditionally celebrated on January 6, not December 25—included a so-called strict fast, that is, not merely abstaining from meat, but also from most food, especially during daylight hours, and preparation for the feast. The Christmas feast itself included special foods, in particular a loaf of white bread decorated with a cross cut into the crust before baking that symbolized the sacrifice of Christ. Family members were supposed to recline while eating this feast, rather than sit upright as they normally did. This is probably one of the few pre-Christian traditions to persist, since both Greek and Roman and Jewish feasts were consumed while reclining (usually lying on one's side, propped on an elbow). Byzantine Christians also kept in the house a bowl of holy water and a sprig of basil suspended over it and used it to sprinkle holy water throughout the dwelling in order to keep mischievous spirits called *"killikantzaroi"* at bay.[1]

The figure of Santa Claus comes very late in Christian history, although the Greek Saint Nicholas was associated with Christmas in the Orthodox church as early as the Middle Ages, and the tradition of exchanging gifts at Christmas was not nearly as significant in the Middle Ages as now. Indeed, other holidays, both before Christmas and after, were often more important as times of gift-giving: in particular Epiphany, the celebration of the three Wise Men bringing gifts to the infant Jesus, which is still an important holiday in Mediterranean countries.

The church in the Middle Ages, even when it appropriated pre-Christian holidays to serve the interests of Christianity, was careful nonetheless to separate some Christian holidays from pre-Christian versions of them. One such holiday was the celebration of New Years Day on March 25, the Feast of the Annunciation, rather than on the traditional Roman date of January 1. This is one reason why our modern "New Year's Day" is buried in the "Twelve Days of Christmas" celebrated in the Middle Ages from December 25 to the Feast of the Epiphany, January 6.

Other holidays celebrated in the modern world have almost entirely lost their Christian associations, perhaps because the Christian overlay was very thin, indeed. A good example is Valentine's Day. This holiday, which actually is supposed to be a celebration of the Feast of St. Valentine, was designed to replace a Roman holiday called Lupercalia, which commemorated the founding of Rome by Romulus and Remus (Lupercalia refers to the she-wolf that, according to legend, suckled the twins when they were abandoned). St. Valentine's feast had nothing to do with hearts or secret messages to love-objects. Indeed, he is an unusual saint to include in these celebrations since Valentine was a Roman priest (or possibly bishop) from the third century who was martyred by being beheaded. Only much later was Valentine associated with lovers.

Families experienced all Christian holidays very differently depending upon not only their social class, but also their location. Traditions in England were radically different from those in Italy and celebrations in Byzantine Constantinople were very different from those in Papal Rome. In addition, there was a tension between family traditions, which often had little to do with Christian theology, and the church, which worked hard to transform traditional celebrations into religious events often to little avail.

Aristocratic families probably celebrated Christian holidays more consistently than poorer families because they were more closely associated with religious professionals, were more likely to attend mass daily rather than occasionally, and felt greater obligations to demonstrate their piety in a public way. Since the Christian calendar contains a feast, saint's, or fast day for virtually every day of the year, the connection between holidays and religion was much more fundamental to aristocratic lifestyles than they were for the working poor. Depictions of elaborate Christmas celebrations in late medieval France appear in illuminated manuscripts such as *The Trés Riches Heures* created for Jean, Duke of Berry in the fifteenth century. The frequent attendance at mass by the wealthy classes also connected holidaymaking with Christian practice more directly than for the poorer classes. Since aristocratic households usually contained at least one chaplain, these religious professionals routinely presided over the religious aspects of holidays. In addition, most aristocratic families contained at least one member who had taken religious vows, and their associations with their families probably emphasized the Christian aspects even of those holidays that were only loosely connected to that religion.

We have very little information about the ways in which poor families celebrated Christian holidays. It is likely that their celebrations were quite minimal—if they existed at all—simply because poor working families did not have the leisure to indulge in non-communal festivities. Poor people did, however, participate enthusiastically in community-wide holidays such as Carnival and May Day (the latter a profoundly non-Christian holiday that the church tried very hard to eradicate) and in England the urban poor formed the majority of the audience for the so-called Miracle Plays performed during Lent and Holy Week (the period between Palm Sunday and Easter Sunday) by traveling players and city guilds. These celebrations were very public, often subsidized by the city guilds and, in villages in rural Europe, by the lords of the manor. They were less about religious observance than about blowing off steam after the hard work of planting in the spring.

The Religious Culture and Medieval Christian Families

The success of Christianity was possible in large part because of the actions of female converts to the religion, and this reality continued to be important in the furtherance of Christianity throughout the medieval period. Early medieval historians such as Gregory of Tours and Bede depict the conversions of important kings such as Clovis, the first Merovingian ruler of the Franks, and Ethelbert, king of Kent, as being the result of what can only be described as nagging on the part of their wives. Although both kings then became true converts as the result of miraculous intervention, at least according to these authors, the impetus for their ultimate conversion to Christianity apparently came from their Christian wives.

Religious authors, especially writers of sermons and of manuals of instruction for chaplains and confessors, often focused on the persuasive power wives had over their husbands, not only in encouraging them to convert, but also in encouraging them—both verbally and by example—to behave more charitably: to support monasteries, to give alms to the poor, and to be nicer to their wives and children. This is thought of as a kind of religious instruction, and priests were urged to encourage their wealthy and influential patronesses to act in this way.[2]

Children were expected to receive their initial instruction in Christian principles from their mothers, who were encouraged not only to teach their children basic Christian principles but also to ensure that they learned the catechism and memorized the Lord's Prayer (the *Pater Noster*) and the Marian prayers, such as Hail Mary (*Ave Maria*), that made up the prayers connected to the use of the rosary, which was invented in the twelfth century as a tool to connect individual religious observance to the new Cult of the Virgin. Children were not necessarily taught to read Latin, but mothers might have read stories from *The Golden Legend* to their children in the vernacular, and they also hired tutors to instruct their children. Mothers were likely to be important influences on decisions by their children to become priests, monks, and nuns as well.

The important twelfth-century theologian Guibert, abbot of Nogent-sous-Coucy, considered his mother to be the most important influence on his life, especially in terms of the choices he made about his future. Guibert, in his autobiography entitled *His Own Life*, describes the circumstances of his birth, which ultimately led him to become a monk. He was the youngest child in a large family, and his mother was not in good health during her pregnancy. Her labor was so extended and painful that Guibert's father feared for both their lives. In desperation, he "with his friends and kinfolk," went to a chapel dedicated to the Virgin Mary and there "they made these vows and laid [an] oblation as a gift upon the altar that, if the child should prove to be a male, he should for God's sake and his own be [tonsured as] a cleric; but if of the inferior sex [i.e., female], that she should be dedicated to a suitable [religious] profession."[3] Even though the impetus for Guibert's future profession as a cleric came from his father, he claims that he might never have become a monk and abbot had his father survived, because he was such an attractive and precocious child that his father would have reneged on his vow and trained him for a secular career. His father, however, died when Guibert was only eight months old and his mother became both his parent and guardian. She secured a teacher for the child Guibert, and promised him that he would be free, once his education was complete, to choose between the life of a cleric and that of a knight. Guibert insisted that he was determined to become a professional religious, which pleased his mother far more than if he had chosen a secular career: "both [of us] exulted together that I should seem to aspire with all the ambition of my soul towards that life my father had vowed for me."[4]

Families also supported religious vocations of daughters as well as sons, and might have had significant influences on such life choices. The amazing career of St. Catherine of Siena began when, over the opposition of her parents, she dedicated herself to virginity at age seven. She eventually won her family over, however, and established a kind of hermit's cell in their house at the age of 16 with their approval. Catherine joined the Third Order of the Dominicans, which meant that she never lived in a nunnery and was more or less independent of supervision. Instead, she remained in voluntary seclusion in her parental home, practicing such extreme asceticism that it is likely an abbess would have tried to control her self-abusive behavior. Her family, however, apparently supported her decision, and as a result she eventually entered into a public career as an ambassador, negotiator, and one of the architects of the return of the papacy back to Rome from its voluntary exile in Avignon in the late fourteenth century. All her work earned her the title Doctor of the Church—the only medieval woman ever to gain that reward.[5]

Mothers and fathers were not the only family members to support professional aspirations of children intent on careers in the church. The daughters, grand-daughters, and even a grand-daughter-in-law of Sibyl la Marshal and William de Ferrers took an especial interest in the career of one of their nephews, James de Mohun, who had embarked on a career in the church. The sisters took charge of his education, granting him clerical livings to finance his schooling and upgrading his appointments as he moved up the professional ladder from acolyte to deacon to priest to master. What is most interesting about this particular situation is that James's mother and father had died before he had begun this educational program, and his maternal aunts and cousins, rather than his paternal relations, acted as his patrons. Clearly they all felt some obligation regarding his future, one that transcended the usual closer family ties binding parents to their children.[6]

Parents often worked hard to promote children—especially sons—who had embarked on careers in the church. Bogo de Clare was notorious in the thirteenth century for accumulating valuable church grants known as benefices in a process called pluralism that was in fact banned by the church. Many of these offices, livings, and objects of patronage were provided to him by his own mother, Maud (aka Matilda) de Clare, dowager countess of Gloucester and Hertford. She was so enthusiastic about furthering Bogo's career that she even sued her own eldest son, Gilbert de Clare, over his presentation of a cleric to a parish church she had wanted to award to her younger son.[7]

Most parents considered a career in the church to be beneficial not only for their children, but also for the family's sacral future: having a professional religious in the family guaranteed that the family would gain the boon of intercessory prayers for some time to come. Other parents, who had different plans for their children, were not so enthusiastic. The history of Christina of Markyate, an English local saint who lived in the transitional period immediately following Duke William of Normandy's conquest of England, can demonstrate the lengths to which parents might go to dissuade their children from choosing a religious vocation.

Christina, who had been christened Theodora (a Greek name meaning "gift of God" that would have been very unusual in England at that time), was born into a noble family from Huntingdon, a town in the middle of England. When she was a small child, her parents took her to the monastery of St. Alban's, where she became fascinated by the lifestyle of the monks and decided to devote herself to God in a life of inviolable virginity. She apparently never told her parents of this decision, however, because when they arranged a betrothal between her and a young nobleman named Burhtred, she refused, saying that she had made a vow of virginity. No amount of pleading, flattery, persuasion, or argument would convince Christina to renege on her vow, so her parents resorted to force: they dragged her off to church and somehow forced her (the author of the saint's life describing these details claims he did not know how they succeeded) to agree to the betrothal. Once betrothed, however, Christina still refused to go through with the wedding, even though, with the betrothal official, she was considered married in the eyes of the church. Her parents plotted to separate her from her religious vocation. They refused to allow her to talk to any priests; they locked her in her bedroom. They demanded that she participate in banquets and other festivities, even forcing her to be a cup-bearer in a skimpy costume in the hopes that the bawdy compliments she received and the tradition that the cup-bearer was to take a sip of wine from the cup every time she served someone would loosen her inhibitions. All of these tactics failed: Christine remained adamant. In desperation, her parents talked her fiancé (who, from the accounts of her life, seems to have been something of a victim himself) into trying to rape her, but instead of violating her, the two of them sat on her bed and talked about religion all night. Christina's parents finally took her to Fredebertus, the prior of Huntingdon Priory, to see if he could convince her to give up her stance against marriage. Her parents' motives, as stated by her father, had more to do with family honor than concern for Christina's welfare: "if she resists our authority and rejects it, we shall be the laughing-stock of our neighbors." Fredebertus interrogated Christina, scolding her for her disobedience, but when she told him that she had vowed to remain a virgin while still a child, and explained her own motives, the prior decided to ask the bishop of Lincoln, Robert Bloet, to adjudicate the conflict. Bishop Robert decided in Christina's favor, but then changed his mind, possibly because her parents bribed him. Christina finally elicited the aid of a local hermit, Eadwin, escaped from her family's house, and eventually established a hermitage or anchorhold (a dwelling that was enclosed so that the hermit or anchoress had virtually no contact with the outside world) in Markyate. Her reputation for holiness soon attracted followers and eventually, her anchorhold was transformed into a priory for nuns, with Christina installed as abbess. Christina's husband, Burhtred, obtained an annulment of their marriage around the time that she became an anchoress at Markyate. There is no evidence that Christina was ever reconciled with her family.[8]

Christina of Markyate's experiences were undoubtedly unusual, even if we take the extremes described in the hagiographical account of her life as exaggerated to enhance her personal piety. Most wealthy and elite families considered the connections between the family and its members who—willingly or not—had embarked on careers in the church to be both important and more than honorable, since it enhanced the prestige of the family in the dominant religious culture.

The relationship between church and laity in Byzantine Christianity was often more formal than that between church and laity in Roman Christianity, as the rituals of the Byzantine Church were far more focused on an authoritarian vision of the church. Sermons, for instance, which had become popular in the west by the twelfth century, were not included in the Eucharistic service until later. On the other hand, the practice of Christianity in the Byzantine Empire was much more a direct family affair than in the west for the simple reason that priests were allowed to marry and have children. As a result, priests were able to pass their livings on to the next generation and the role of priest's wife was very important to the maintenance of the local Christian community, in much the same way as spouses of Protestant ministers and priests play specific, if informal, roles in modern-day Christianity. This could prove to be a detriment to ambitious priests, since bishops were expected to be unmarried and celibate. Married priests who were possible candidates for promotion actually had to divorce their wives and more or less consign them and their children to monasteries in order to be seen as viable candidates.

The participation of the laity in Byzantine Christianity operated on similar levels as occurred in the west. Among elite families, the presence of personal chapels and the employment of chaplains meant that religious practice occurred largely in the privacy of the home. For the rest of the population, religious practice was probably relatively intermittent and depended upon the kinds of labor in which the family engaged. Family devotions were more likely to include very localized celebrations than more public displays of religiosity and the presence of large celebrations, such as the performance of mystery plays, did not occur in the east. On the other hand, literacy was more prevalent in the Byzantine world than in the west, and the Bible used by Orthodox Christians is written in

Greek, the language of the general population, so it is likely that family devotions could involve a great deal more reading of the Bible than occurred in the west.

Christian Religious Structures and the Family

Another way in which elite families contributed to the religious culture of the Christian medieval world was through the mechanism of founding and endowing monasteries and other kinds of religious communities. Most monasteries, convents, priories, nunneries, and canonries were founded by members of the aristocracy or by royal families who did so both because of religious conviction and a desire to found an establishment to which they felt comfortable sending their children and grandchildren. This connection between religiosity and an interest in the careers of younger family members and future generations is marked in the founding of these establishments. In the early Middle Ages, members of royal families, such as Hild, the daughter of the Anglo-Saxon king of Northumbria, founded monasteries—as Hild did of Whitby—in order to have a place to go in retirement. Indeed, Hild was the first abbess of Whitby, which was a dual monastery: both monks and nuns were housed there, with an abbess presiding over all. Moreover, quite a few of Hild's nieces entered Whitby and several of her female kin succeeded her as abbess. In the late thirteenth century, Geoffrey de Geneville, the lord of Trim, Ireland, founded the Augustinian monastery of St. Mary and the Abbey of the Black Friars (the Dominicans) both in his capital city of Trim. He ultimately retired to Black Abbey, living as a monk for the last few years of his life. The royal monasteries of Glastonbury, Amesbury, and Fontevrault in France were all foundations to which sons and especially daughters of kings and queens of England were sent to live. Two of Eleanor of Aquitaine's daughters were dedicated to Fontevrault, while Edward I's and Eleanor of Castile's daughter, Mary, became a nun at Amesbury in 1285, along with her grandmother, dowager queen Eleanor of Provence, and 13 other aristocratic girls. This removal to a monastery did not necessarily affect family ties negatively. Mary enjoyed not only the company of her grandmother at Amesbury, but also was permitted both to receive visits from family members and to leave the nunnery periodically to celebrate holidays with her family. Evidence suggests that these kinds of relationships and the somewhat relaxed attitude toward the inviolability of the cloister were fairly common in the High Middle Ages.

Byzantine imperial and aristocratic families also founded and patronized monasteries and nunneries in order to install family members in them or to become cloistered themselves. In the Byzantine Empire such foundations were, at least in theory, supposed to be far less involved in the family lives of their founders than occurred in the West. The monastic ideal in the east, especially in the early period, included a complete renunciation of family ties by the individual oblate, to the point of never communicating with family members again. In Byzantine saints' lives, the signs of sanctity often include the saint running away from home to become a monk, hermit, or nun or doing so against the strenuous objections of his or her parents, similar to the life of Christina of Markyate. In the later Byzantine period, perhaps as a result of influence from Western-style monasteries established after the Fourth Crusade when westerners conquered Constantinople, these rigorous rules against interactions between monks and nuns and their natal families were often relaxed. Multiple family members might join the same monastic house, and family members were granted visitation rights and even could dine with their cloistered kin. This seems to have been more the case in nunneries than in male monastic houses, but this does not mean that men who dedicated themselves to the religious life completely relinquished their family ties. Some hermits who had established hermitages on remote mountaintops moved female relatives to nunneries nearby to keep in contact with them.[9]

Families in both the Roman and Byzantine Christian cultures most often endowed monastic houses in order to guarantee prayers for the souls of beloved family members. Husbands made grants for the salvation of wives' souls; wives did the same for husbands. All singled out children. A typical donation might resemble the one made by Eve de Cantelou to the canons of Stodleigh, Warwickshire in the mid-thirteenth century. She granted them 100 shillings-worth of land from one of her manors and approved additional grants made "in free alms" by 23 other individuals, all of which were to pay for prayers for the soul of her recently-deceased husband, William.[10] Often these donations were designed to be turned over to the religious community only after the death of the donor, in a system known in the west as *mortmain*—the "dead hand" of the donor releasing the gift into the live hand of the church. In the fourteenth-century *typikon* (a kind of donation charter that included a specific rule for the monks or nuns of the house) for the convent of the Virgin of Sure Hope, the founder, Theodora Synadene, outlined all the grants she was making in order to build the convent, to which she intended to retire and to which she was also dedicating her daughter, Euphrosyne. Included as well were requirements that the nuns pray for the souls of a large number of family members, including her parents, her husband, herself, her daughter, her two sons and their wives, and others less closely related—a total of 15 people in all.[11]

Finally, elite families also expressed their devotion by endowing specific churches in order to defray the costs of things like stained glass windows, the building and decoration of chapels, and the erection of family monuments and funeral effigies. These kinds of endowments were sometimes far more about family pride than about specific religious concerns. When William Longespee, earl of Salisbury by right of his wife, Ela, died,

Ela was instrumental in both the design and the construction of his tomb in the brand-new Salisbury Cathedral. Her intention was apparently to celebrate her husband's life, including his crusading activities, through the display of an elaborate and expensive monument.

Families of lower social status did not have the financial resources to engage in this kind of expensive and elaborate display of family and religious devotion, but they participated in these kinds of acts in smaller ways. Many endowment charters include small gifts made by people with only a little money to donate. Urban confraternities, religious groups connected to the guild system that operated as centers of religious activity and patronage, relied on family donations to help the endowment funds used for everything from the decoration and building of churches to the granting of dowries to poor girls. These small gifts strained the resources of such families, but the pressure to make sacrifices in order to better the afterlives of the beloved departed was great. Certainly, that was the rationale behind the sale of so-called indulgences that began to develop as a church strategy in the later thirteenth century, and reached a peak in the fifteenth century. Indulgences were small cash payments made to the church that granted in return a reduction of the time a soul spent in purgatory. These donations were used to pay for big building projects, such as the rebuilding of St. Peter's Basilica in Rome, and they were a huge part of the environment of late medieval piety. Even the poorest people were prodded to buy indulgences to benefit family members, at first those who were not yet dead, and later, even those who had already died. Friars sent to preach the sale of these indulgences emphasized the torments of souls in purgatory, thereby scaring the people who heard these sermons into donating their life savings in order to free the souls of their loved ones from them. This might seem to display the church at its most cynical, but it also displayed family feeling at its most emotional. If historians in the past have questioned the devotion of parents to their children and vice versa, all one has to do is see the number of people who purchased indulgences for dead and living parents and children to recognize how deep family devotion went.

Jewish Families and Religion

The laws against Jewish public performance of religious devotion that existed throughout the medieval world meant that Judaism was a family-based religion par excellence. In everything from daily prayers to weddings and funerals, Jewish families were at the center of the religion. Each family member had specific roles to play in religious devotion. Jewish women had to maintain their kitchens as kosher; they led the prayers for the beginning of the Sabbath at sundown on Fridays; and they were in charge of the basic religious education of their children. Jewish men were, perhaps ironically, less involved in these family-based activities, but their religious practices and their control of the more formal aspects of religious education involved them in the education of their children in quite direct ways. In addition, since rabbis were expected to marry, the rabbinic household and all its members were dedicated to the maintenance of religious devotion. Synagogues were much more intimate spaces than churches and the celebration of services were much more interactive than those in Christianity. As a result, there was little of the kind of hierarchical structure inherent in medieval Christianity.

Unlike western Christianity, in which all the rituals and forms of religious observance were conducted in Latin, a language that the vast majority of the population never learned or understood, Jews, especially Jewish boys and men, were expected to have at least a rudimentary understanding of Hebrew. Scholarship, literacy, and education were highly valued by the Jewish community and these qualities were particularly valued when they were used in the promotion of religious understanding.

In Christian-dominated regions, religious education was not really separated from secular education in the Jewish communities, and learning began very early: at age five or six for boys. The main focus was study of the Bible and the standard interpretive texts. Medieval Jews celebrated both the creation of their religious texts and the initiation of boys into the community of learners. On the festival of Shavuot, which celebrated the giving of the Torah (the first five books of the Hebrew Bible) to the Israelites, boys about to begin their formal education were presented before the synagogue's Torah scroll. The Ten Commandments were read aloud, the boys were introduced to their teacher, and they were each given a stone tablet on which were carved the first four and last four letters of the Hebrew alphabet and several relevant verses from the Torah. The tablet was also smeared with honey, to symbolize the sweetness of learning, and special cakes were made to commemorate this introduction to religious education. Although there were no similar ceremonies directed to the religious education of girls, they were also taught, albeit at home, so that they had a basic knowledge of Hebrew, as well as learning prayers in their vernacular languages, such as French, English, or Yiddish.

Family participation in religious services in the local synagogue were far more consistent than religious observance by Christians. It was typical for families to attend Friday evening services and then to return home to their Sabbath meal, which began with the female head of the house saying prayers and lighting the Sabbath candles. In the Middle Ages as now, very observant Jews did not use any form of transportation—such as a cart or horse—or carry anything in their hands on the Sabbath, which began at sundown Friday and continued to sundown Saturday.

Public religious participation in medieval Judaism was more or less entirely conducted by men. Only men could form a minyan, the smallest number of men necessary to say certain prayers or perform certain rituals.

In some synagogues, males and females were physically separated, with men and boys sitting or standing on the main floor and women and girls consigned to galleries above. On the other hand, private devotions were often dominated by the women in the family, whose role as governors of the household gave them status in the religious culture as well.

Religious holidays are generally far more family oriented in Judaism than in Christianity. Two exceptions are Yom Kippur (the annual Day of Atonement) and Simchat Torah (the celebration of the completion of reading the Torah in weekly Sabbath services), two days in which the focus is directed more toward community-wide expressions of belief. One essential difference between Christian and Jewish practices is that the main focus of holidays such as Rosh Hashanah (the Jewish New Year) and Passover (the eight-day celebration of the Exodus story of Moses leading the Israelites out of Egypt) is on the family unit. The prayers recited during a Passover seder, for instance, which were organized and standardized in the Middle Ages, focus on the family re-enacting the Exodus through ritualized eating of specific foods, such as, unleavened bread; eggs dipped in salt water; and *haroset,* a dish invented in the thirteenth century made of apples, nuts, vinegar and honey called. Since food preparation was such a large part of holiday celebrations, Jewish women and girls played important roles in maintaining the religious calendar, but in such celebrations most of the prayers were said by the men and boys in the family.

Other holidays were more community oriented, but nevertheless retained this focus on family life. One of the most joyous celebrations in the Jewish calendar in the Middle Ages was Purim, or The Feast of Fools. Purim celebrates the events described in the biblical Book of Esther. In the years following the Babylonian exile of the Jews, the high king of the Persian Empire, Ahasuerus, married Esther, the niece of Mordechai, the leader of the Jews in the Persian capital city of Susa. The king's advisor, Haman, plotted against Mordechai and ultimately, Queen Esther had to save not only her uncle but all the Jews from Haman's evil plan. This story, retold in various ways during the festival of Purim, was celebrated in a way that is similar to the mayhem of the Christian holiday of Carnival. Families ate special food; engaged in silly skits known in Germany as the Purim-shpiel that parodied and satirized this quite serious biblical story; and were required to eat, drink, and be merry well beyond the point of satiation. In regions of the medieval world where Jews were not restricted from public expressions of their religious culture, Purim festivals were far more public and raucous, even including the enacting of mock marriages by boys dressed up as rabbis. The community might also burn effigies of Haman and have bonfires. Purim celebrations in areas where there was considerable hostility against Jews, such as thirteenth-century France, must have been quite muted, thereby restricting the holiday to the more intimate confines of the household.

Even Yom Kippur, the Day of Atonement, although primarily focused on fasting and prayer and usually taking place in synagogue rather than the home, had a family component. The breaking of the day-long fast at sunset was clearly a family celebration in the Middle Ages as much as it is today. Indeed, the relationship between food and Judaism seems to have been just as important to medieval Jewish families as it is in the modern world.

Jewish funerary practices also involved a specifically family component in ways that Christian ceremonies did not. The body was prepared for burial by women in the family, perhaps assisted by the rabbi's wife, as apparently occurred in late twelfth-century Worms, where the Rokeah's wife, Dulcia, engaged in such kinds of funeral preparations.[12] After the burial, the family was required to engage in a weeklong ceremony of public mourning, known as shiva, during which time no one in the family was permitted to cook, clean, or even comb their hair or look into a mirror (these were covered with a cloth to prevent the mourner from seeing his or her reflection), and they were required to sit on low stools rather than cushioned chairs. Other members of the community were expected to take care of the family in mourning. Once the week was over, the family continued to commemorate the recently dead for a year and then commemorate the end of the mourning period with the unveiling of the tombstone. Thus, even in the most public expressions of celebration and mourning, medieval Judaism focused on the family as the center of all life and ritual.

The localized and private nature of Judaism, on the other hand, meant that the kinds of patronage in which elites engaged—the founding of monasteries and the beautification of churches—simply did not exist. Families were sometimes able to act as patrons of synagogues that were being built or renovated, although Christian and Islamic authorities officially forbade such public expressions of devotion because they might encourage gentiles to convert to Judaism. In addition, families often paid for the creation of new Torah scrolls for their communities and contributed to charity to maintain poor and destitute members of the community.

Islam and the Muslim Family

Like Judaism, the practice of Islam is often an intimately personal act with an important family component. Unlike Judaism, however, the extreme gender segregation of Islam probably worked against the kinds of family-based celebrations common in that religion. Although there were many opportunities in which the religion and family life intertwined, from circumcision celebrations to weddings to funerals, the intimacy of the Christian or Jewish family was probably less apparent.

Islam is fundamentally a very simple religion, with very simple rules: believe in God and the uniqueness of Mohammed as the Prophet of God;

pray five times a day; fast during the holy month of Ramadan; tithe to the poor; and make a pilgrimage (Hajj) to Mecca at least once in one's lifetime. These pillars of faith can be completed by individuals whether they are part of a family or not. Nevertheless, family plays a large part in Islam. Muslims are expected to marry and to produce children. Certain celebrations, such as the single evening meal Muslims can eat during Ramadan, when they fast during daylight hours, and the festival of Eid al-Fitr celebrated when Ramadan ends, are more specifically family celebrations, since food preparation and consumption are central to them.

Unlike Christianity, where religious observance could be in competition with secular culture, and Judaism, which was always a minority faith whose membership had to accommodate the legal and social requirements of the dominant culture, Islam oversaw virtually every aspect of a Muslim individual's life. As a result, the very formation and structure of the Muslim family was overseen by Islam. This reality might seem to make understanding the relationship between Islam and the medieval family easier, but in fact it can make it more difficult. The sources for medieval Islam focus on the individual—the Muslim (someone who submits to God)—and the community of believers as a whole—the *umma*—rather than specifically on the family.

Religious education, as discussed in chapter 8, involved memorization of the Quran. This process was always an obligation of boys, but it is not clear how consistently this was required of girls. In some areas, most notably Egypt, it is possible that small schools for girls were founded, whose teachers were women who had achieved a more advanced level of education than was typical. Exceptional girls might even be educated by male scholars and receive certificates of graduation and go on to teach even men.[13] The absence of the kind of religious institutions, such as convents, available to elite Christian women, however, probably meant that the highly educated Muslim female was very rare, indeed.

Unlike Jewish families, in which a wife might take on professions in business in order to support her husband so that he could devote himself to religious scholarship, there is no indication that wives were an important partner to the imam's religious vocation or duties. Nevertheless, a stable family unit must have been valuable to the Muslim cleric, whose position would have prevented him from engaging in manual labor or interacting on a broad scale with secular activities that were considered corrupting.

Although Islamic law governed the lives of Muslims from womb to tomb, it is difficult to connect family activities to the daily rituals of faith, with the exception of the Friday evening meal. Individuals were required to adhere to the five pillars of faith, so that even pilgrimage to Mecca was more likely to be viewed as a personal act than as a family event. Important life stages, however, had significant family components, such as circumcision rituals for boys, weddings, the birth of children, and funerals. The segregation of the sexes, on the other hand, probably influenced the activities of family members, with the males participating in one set of religious rituals and females engaging in others.

Orthodox Islam recognizes only two festivals: Eid al-Fitr, the Feast of Breaking the Fast at the end of the holy month of Ramadan, and Eid al-Adha, the Big Feast or Feast of Sacrifice, which commemorates Abraham's sacrifice of a ram instead of his son Ishmael (Islamic tradition states that God had demanded the sacrifice of Ishmael not Isaac) and takes place just after the period of pilgrimage, or the Hajj. Islam also recognizes two periods of fasting: Ramadan and the Day of Ashura commemorating the Exodus of Moses and the Israelites. Although modern-day Muslims might also celebrate special days such as Muhammad's birthday and his Night Journey to Jerusalem, these were and are condemned by the more conservative religious authorities, so it is not clear whether these celebrations existed in the Middle Ages. Periods of fasting and prayer were and are clearly connected to individual piety, but feasts, as well as the evening breaking of the fast during Ramadan, must have been moments of family solidarity in the Middle Ages, at least among middle class and poorer Muslim families that did not have the wealth to practice polygamy or to physically isolate females in the household.

Like Judaism and unlike Christianity, medieval Islam did not have religious institutions that can be compared to monasteries or nunneries. As will be discussed in more detail in chapter 11, the branch of Islam known as Sufism, which focused on a mystical relationship with God, did support schools for the development of Sufi mystical piety, but these were temporary foundations to which devotees went only for two years or so. Neither was there the elaborate professional hierarchy that existed in medieval Christianity (and continues to this day). This meant that opportunities for patronage were limited to the building and decoration of mosques, although these could be quite elaborate. Some Islamic communities also supported important religious schools, but it is not clear whether these provided outlets for patronage for the elites in the same way that monasteries did for the elites of the Christian cultures. Certainly the commemoration of family members would have played little, if any, part in such patronage.

Conclusion

The religious experiences of medieval families varied significantly depending upon location, social class, and religious adherence. Although all the major religions contained elements that required or encouraged participation of families as groups, the emphasis in Christianity, Judaism, and Islam was always on personal devotion to God, with other considerations taking second place.

In matters of religious law and governance, however, all three faiths oversaw significant aspects of family life, from the formation and dissolution of marriage to the floor plan and contents of their houses to the education of their children. As a result, even when the devotional emphasis was on the individual, religion in the Middle Ages was a family affair.

Notes

1. An excellent Web site describing Byzantine Christmas rituals is "Greek and Cretan Christmas Customs, Greek New Year, and Epiphany Celebrations," http://www.sfakia-crete.com/sfakia-crete/Christmas.html.

2. See Sharon Farmer, "Persuasive Voices: Clerical Images of Medieval Wives," *Speculum* 61, no. 3 (1986): 517–543.

3. From C.G. Coulton, ed. *Life in the Middle Ages* (New York: Macmillan, c. 1910), 4: 133–141 and found at *The Internet Medieval Sourcebook:* "Guibert de Nogent: Autobiography," http://www.fordham.edu/halsall/cource/nogent-auto.html with corrections.

4. Ibid.

5. The life of Catherine of Siena is easy to construct, but it can be difficult to extract an objective biography from the religious hagiography. For two versions, see *The Catholic Encyclopedia* at http://www.newadvent.org/cathen/03447a.htm and "St. Catherine of Siena" by Mary Ann Sullivan, http://www.op.org/domcentral/trad/stcather.htm.

6. This is discussed at greater length in Linda E. Mitchell, "Agnes and Her Sisters: Squabbling and Cooperation in the Extended Medieval Family" in Mitchell, *Portraits of Medieval Women: Family, Marriage, and Politics in England, 1225–1350* (New York: Palgrave Macmillan, 2003), 25–26.

7. This case appears in legal sources of the royal central courts, as well as in the Archbishop of York's register. It is discussed by Michael Althschul in *A Baronial Family in Medieval England: The Clares, 1217–1314* (Baltimore: The Johns Hopkins University Press, 1965), 183–185, and by Linda E. Mitchell, "Like Mother, Like Daughter: The Parallel Careers of Margaret de Quency and Maud de Lacy" in *Portraits of Medieval Women*, 38–39.

8. The "Life of Christina of Markyate" appears in many sources. The standard translation is that of C. H. Talbot, *The Life of Christina of Markyate, a Twelfth-Century Recluse* (Oxford: Oxford University Press, 1959; reprint 1987) and is excerpted at "The Second Nun's Tale," http://www.unc.edu/depts./Chaucer/zatta/2ndnun.html. A brief biography can be found at "The Catholic Forum," http://www.catholic-forum.com/SAINTS/saintc82.htm.

9. This is discussed by Alice-Mary Talbot, "The Byzantine Family and the Monastery," *Dumbarton Oaks Papers* 44 (1990): 119–129.

10. *Liber Feodorum, The Book of Fees Commonly Called Testa de Nevill,* 2 vols. (London: Records Commission, 1920–1923), 1: 1371–Appendix.

11. Talbot, "The Byzantine Family and the Monastery," 124–126.

12. See Kenneth Stow, "The Jewish Family in the Rhineland in the High Middle Ages: Form and Function," *The American Historical Review* 92, no. 5 (1987): 1085–1110, and Stow, *Alienated Minority: The Jews of Medieval Latin Europe* (Cambridge, MA: Harvard, 1992), 197 and chapter 7 in this work.

13. This is discussed in Leila Ahmed, *Women and Gender in Islam: Historical Roots of a Modern Debate* (New Haven: Yale University Press, 1992), 113–115.

10

Families, Labor, and the Laboring Family

Families in the medieval world operated as a team, no matter what their social class, ethnicity, culture, or religion. This teamwork was vital to the family's survival and it extended through marriage, the creation of new families, and the death of family members. In addition, although the medieval definition of labor excluded members of the aristocracy and many of the lower-level landed class (in medieval western terminology, those who fight), we can talk about even that elite level of medieval society as engaging in labor of different kinds. Of course, the most common labor in the medieval world was agricultural, and rural families were by a large margin the greatest number of laborers. Perhaps unsurprisingly, this population is the least represented in the sources. The work of historians who focus on the medieval west have revealed a great deal about peasant life, especially in the High Middle Ages, but comparable material about Byzantine and Muslim peasants does not exist. Jews, on the other hand, were almost entirely confined to cities: not only were they usually forbidden to own land, but Christian regional authorities limited the kinds of jobs Jews were permitted to do. It can sometimes be difficult to uncover factual information about Jewish families and their labor in sources that are often irrationally hostile to the presence of Jews in the economic system but written by people who were dependent upon Jews for essential components of it.

One thing that can be said about every culture and every social class in the medieval world: families worked hard, harder than people in the developed world have to work today. It is important to remember that

manufacturing and agriculture had to be done without any mechaniza-
tion, that housekeeping was performed without any modern-day conveniences. There was no indoor plumbing, no easy ways to boil water,
to automatic ovens, no gas-fired furnaces, no motorized vehicles, no
artificial lights other than candles, oil lamps, and rushes soaked in animal
fat. Roads were primitive and all modes of transportation were unsafe in
one way or another. In order to survive, whether you were a knight or a
peasant, a merchant or a blacksmith you had to work and so did the rest
of your family.

The Elite Family and Labor

Although members of the elite did not get their hands dirty per se,
they did engage in all kinds of work, from warfare to administration,
from overseeing servants and agricultural workers to weaving tapestries and sewing, from writing literature, theology and philosophy, and
science texts, to writing charters and deeds. In our modern-day sense
of the term, this is labor as much as the work of a ditch digger is, only
cleaner and of higher status. Families engaged in all of this labor, with an
efficient division of tasks depending on age, gender, and level of experience. Adult men were involved in warfare, the training of soldiers, and
worked in public administration. Adult women oversaw the running
of the household, which included not only oversight of the servants,
but also administration of the family's estate records. Men worked as
tutors of young children, while women wove cloth, made tapestries, and
improved the comfort level of the home with embellishments such as
embroidered cushions (something essential to make the bare wood furniture comfortable). Elites dedicated to the religious life—both male and
female—copied and illuminated manuscripts, wrote and taught in the
schools and universities of the medieval world, and engaged in the work
of prayer. While many of these pursuits did not directly affect family life,
they were ancillary to the wellbeing of families both in the education of
future generations and the care of souls. Both sexes engaged in creative
pursuits, such as writing romances and poetry and making music, that
entertained the elite family.

One thing elite classes were specifically not supposed to do was work
that dirtied their hands. Even so, it is doubtful that they were able to avoid
such kinds of labor entirely. Men in war had to engage in a variety of tasks
and even mounted knights had to ensure the comfort and safety of their
mounts. Women, except perhaps for the most elite of the elite, probably
cooked, perhaps gardened, and helped servants in housekeeping.

In very elite Muslim families, these divisions of labor were perhaps less
evident. The radical separation of women from men in the home and the
practice of polygamy among the wealthiest worked against the kinds of
teamwork evident among Christian and Jewish families. Nevertheless,

only the very wealthiest men could afford to have more than one wife and an army of servants and slaves, so the working lives of moderately well-off Muslim family members were probably more or less identical to those of Christian elites.

As in less wealthy families, child labor among elites was evident, but was focused less on helping the family economically as it was connected to training for adult life. Young boys and teenagers in the Christian west worked as pages, participating in the ceremonial life of the noble court. The origin of the social designation esquire in medieval England might have come from the duties of young men who were not yet knights, but who had similar social and work obligations in the noble household. Young men throughout the medieval world were expected to pursue their studies—whether military, lay, or religious—diligently. Their training formed the foundations of the elite culture no matter the religious context. The experiences of the Kurdish leader Salah al-Din (Saladin) provide an interesting example. The young Yusuf Ibn Ayyub was born in Tikrit and sent to Damascus to be educated. He was a very diligent student for the 10 years he spent learning both to be a warrior and a good Sunni theologian. As a teenager the young Yusuf accompanied his uncle Skirkuh to Egypt. He was instrumental in overthrowing the Shi'a Fatimid dynasty, earning the title Salah al-Din—the Righteousness of the Faith—and establishing his own family, the Ayyubid dynasty, as the new rulers of Egypt. Clearly, Salah al-Din was a hard worker, and the agenda of furthering his family's power and prestige seems to have one of his main motivations.

Girls and young women from elite families were expected to work hard at their education as well. They assisted their mothers as they trained for their future lives as wives, mothers, and widows. They had to learn their lessons well and gain expertise early, since for most of them marriage followed soon after puberty. Girls were expected to be highly accomplished before they married, not only in the typical domestic labors of cooking, household maintenance, and the like, but also in sewing (elite women usually made the everyday garments of the household), estate management (which involved both literacy and numeracy), and music. Thus a girl's training must have been highly laborious, especially since the period of time in which their education took place was much shorter than that of their brothers.

Elite families, including foster children in some cases, had to operate as a cohesive unit in order to maintain their social and political position. Although this might not seem like a form of labor, it definitely was. When, in 1207, William le Marshal and his pregnant wife Isabella de Clare traveled to Ireland to visit their estates, which Isabella had inherited and William had acquired in marriage, the two arrived in Wexford as partners in the task of consolidating their control over their volatile territory. William was called back to court by King John and Isabella remained in Ireland. According to the biographical poem, *The Story/History of William le Marshal,* which had been commissioned by his and Isabella's children after their deaths, William spoke to his and Isabella's vassals in Ireland before he left.

Lords! See the countess, whom I here present to you; [by right of law] your lady, the daughter [and heir] of the earl who freely enfeoffed you all when he had conquered this land. She remains amongst you, pregnant. Until God permits me to return, I pray you keep her well and [according to right—that is, according to the feudal law], for she is your lady, and I have nothing but through her.[1]

In this speech, William is depicted as emphasizing that Isabella is the rightful lord and that their new family's authority comes from her inheritance. Moreover, as partners in their family enterprise, William and Isabella had to work together to be successful, Although the dynamic duo of William and Isabella were the most elite of an elite class, their experiences were not different from other aristocratic families. Husbands, wives, and children all had to work together to promote family success.

The medieval elite family was thus not merely a biological unit. It encompassed economic, commercial, legal, and landed interests that engaged everyone in the household. While men were away at war or serving in administration, women had to assume their duties in addition to their own. This was not necessarily an unusual circumstance, since men were away frequently. As overseers of the estates, managers of the household, teacher to the children, guider of the servants, and nurturer of infants, the sick, the poor, and the needy, elite women throughout the medieval world had to wear many hats. Their husbands, who had to juggle military, judicial, administrative, and domestic duties, were significantly burdened as well. It is not surprising that chroniclers comment on the one quality that successful kings always seem to have had: the ability to function on very little sleep.

Labor Among Urban Families in the Christian West

The connections between family survival and family labor are far more clear for families below the social level of the aristocracy. Even among the wealthy urban elite, all members of the family were dedicated to their survival, and this connection between dedicated labor and survival was essential among poorer families. Everything from finance and investment, to craft workshops, to the commercial preparation and sale of food operated from family-run businesses defined the commercial economy that was controlled by medieval families. Moreover, all members of the family had specific jobs to do to promote and sustain the family business.

In the city-states of medieval Italy and the urban centers of medieval Flanders, the control of the city government by guilds and guild masters masks to some extent the contributions of other family members in the commercial life of the city. In medieval northern and central Italy, there is substantial evidence that women invested in business, purchased insurance instruments, and engaged in other kinds of money-based transactions in order to advance the family's economic stability. Although they had to do so through male intermediaries, these transactions were clearly initiated by the women involved. Children, especially younger sons, were absorbed into the family business as soon as their basic education was completed. Wealthier families might choose to dedicate one or more children to careers in the church, but generally sons were steered toward careers either directly related to family-owned businesses or useful to the family: as notaries, lawyers, and so on. Daughters might be less directly engaged in the family business, but especially in Italy and Flanders, the marriages of daughters related directly to the continuing success of the family economy. This does not mean that daughters lived lives of leisure—far from it. Daughters were engaged in creating the material contents of their dowries and trousseaus, in learning household maintenance, and in preparing for marriages that were designed more to benefit the family than to provide a love match.

Among the less well-off urban community, the relationship between family survival and work was far more direct. Although the guild system that regulated all kinds of trade and manufacture in medieval western cities and towns identified only the masters and the paid apprentices and journeymen employed by the master, workshops were in fact family affairs, with all members of the family engaged in the work involved. This is particularly the case in trades involving cloth-making and the manufacture of clothing. Historians have determined that a great deal of work completed in the cloth industries was performed by women and girls who were not paid for their labor, and are thereby invisible in the sources, because they were members of the master's family. In addition, such industry often hired in female servants who did not enjoy apprentice status, and so worked long hours for very low wages (usually about half of what men made doing the same kinds of work). These young women were considered members of the household, even though their employment was likely not permanent: there was probably a high turnover of female labor as girls saved enough to be able to return home to their villages and marry.

Other trades had a direct impact on family life. In the urban centers of the Middle Ages, most houses did not have anything beyond basic cooking facilities, so cooked food, bread, beer, dairy products, and other essentials were purchased from vendors rather than prepared at home. Families engaged in commercial food preparation were very common. Indeed, many of the terms used to define the work in these trades—brewster, huckster, regrator—refer specifically to female work. Women all over Europe were the brewers of ale, and the name Brewster retains the professional designation of female brewers. Until the introduction of hops in the fifteenth century, which made it possible for ale to be preserved for longer, beers was brewed locally, but it was an expensive process to do at home. There seems to be a connection between brewing beer and baking bread, with men controlling baking and their wives engaged in brewing, but independent women—especially widows—also brewed beer.[2] Margery Kempe, as mentioned in chapter 7, started a brewing business, but it failed for a variety of reasons that she does not enumerate in her writings. Hucksters and regrators were women who sold prepared food in open marketplaces and in kiosks. The food was prepared by both men and women in the home workshop, but most of the selling was done by women. Again, both wives and widows worked in these jobs, but much of the actual food production was likely to have been done by the rest of the family. In these circumstances, the public face of the family business was female.

Other kinds of food production, especially when done on a large scale or when significant travel was involved, carried another designation beyond huckster or regrator. Men were designated as victualers (pronounced "vittlers"): sellers of foodstuffs used in the preparation of food. Whereas women were more or less in charge of selling prepared food, men were engaged in the selling of food that had traveled some distance to the town, and which was sold in large markets, or shopped from door to door.

More specialized non-textile based industries also included family labor. Book production became commercialized beginning in the thirteenth century with the rise of vernacular literacy and the development of universities. Family workshops appeared in major cities, such as Paris and London, and major university centers such as Oxford, Cambridge, and Bologna in which apprentices and clerks copied manuscripts, other workers illuminated and decorated the margins of the pages, and still other workers created the miniature paintings that illustrated the manuscripts. There is evidence that, although most of the scribal work was likely performed by men and boys, and the highly specialized work of creating miniature paintings was the job of trained professionals, girls and women sometimes also performed the illumination work, especially the decoration of margins, which were often standardized and required the ability to do close, detailed, and repetitive work. Bookbinding was a completely separate business, where the division of labor among family members was more clearly defined. Illustrations of book production from the later Middle Ages show female family members performing all the elaborate sewing of the manuscripts (something that required a very high degree of skill), while men and boys performed the rest of the binding work, known as forwarding, and the decoration of the leather covers, known as finishing. Both men and women sold books from the front of their workshops.

Some professional jobs were also connected, if indirectly, to family-based labor. Physicians, midwives, and barber-surgeons were all medical practitioners who took on apprentices, and who also often expected their children to enter into the family business. In particular, midwives and barber-surgeons carried on traditional work practices. Physicians required advanced training and a professional certificate to be able to practice their trade, so it was less typical for a physician to have a work-shop. Midwives tended not only to the birthing of babies, but also to vir-tually all the medical needs of women throughout the medieval period. Such careers often passed from mother to daughter and it was one of the few respectable jobs that married women could engage in without the oversight of a male. Unfortunately, by the later Middle Ages midwives were becoming increasingly associated with paranoia about so-called uncontrolled women becoming witches and so their status was reduced and it became harder to do their jobs. Barber-surgeons were professional men who cut hair, pulled teeth, and performed surgical procedures such as trepanning (an ancient technique of drilling into the skull to relieve pressure after an injury) and amputating limbs. All of these activities were considered related. Moreover, since they forced the practitioner to get his hands dirty (something physicians did not do), they were considered labor, and therefore regulated by the guild system. Since barber-surgeons were guild-based, they maintained workshops, trained apprentices, and included their families in their businesses. Physicians were considered the theoreticians of the medical profession. They might occasionally perform procedures such as bleeding or examination of a patient's urine, but their university training and certification placed them in a different category from barbers or midwives.

Most of the labor of urban families is hidden. Public documents describ-ing the different guilds and the different kinds of work performed in the city generally mention only the male head of the workshop-household and not the family workforce that included both men and women and boys and girls. Sometimes women are mentioned as heading working households. These were almost always widows, but their children might well have also been working in the family business and they go unmen-tioned in these sources. In addition, unpaid labor such as household maintenance, cooking, gardening, cleaning, and the outfitting of family members is not mentioned in public documents interested in cataloging only paid labor. This does not mean that these activities performed by all members of the family were (and are) not work. Families had to operate as a symbiotic organism in order to survive and no one in the family could slack off and expect the family to survive.

Family, Work, and the Rural Community in the Medieval West

The requirement of every family member's participation is much more obvious when agricultural labor is considered, but this only skims the surface of the intensive labor in which rural families engaged. The rural family's day was devoted to different kinds of work and the division of labor was much more fluid than among more elite or urbanized families. Although men generally did the heaviest farm work—plowing with teams of oxen or horses, blacksmithing, and so on—and also performed more of the administrative work of the manor as stewards, haywards, and other posts, women occasionally appear in the records as performing these jobs even when there were men available to do them. Women were involved in planting, since everyone was needed to broadcast seeds, maintain the crops, and harvest and glean the fields. Indeed, gleaning (picking up by hand the leftover grain in the fields that had fallen after harvesting or that was too low on the plant to be caught by the sickles and other tools used by the harvesters) was specifically left to poor women and widows to do. Since the gleaned grain was not included in the official harvest totals, it was not subject to the same rent obligations as the rest of the harvest. The poorest members of the community were therefore granted the so-called privilege (it was in fact backbreaking labor) of gleaning so that they could use what they had gathered to feed their families. The bulk of women's work, however, was performed around the house: not only cooking and cleaning, but planting, weeding, and harvesting the vegetable garden attached to the house, care of chickens and other livestock used for food, and the spinning of thread and weaving of cloth for the family's use. Men are occasionally mentioned as participating in the latter task, especially as weavers and especially in the winter months when farm work was suspended because of the cold weather, but it was considered a significant drop on the social ladder for men to resort to spinning thread to feed their families.

Some jobs in addition to spinning were also traditionally female. Women were in charge of the dairy, which included the milking of cows, sheep, and goats, and the preparation of cheese and butter. Medieval people did not drink milk except as infants and toddlers, so most of the dairy production was devoted to cheese making. Cheese was much more durable and did not need to be kept cold in order to preserve it. In addition, the remains of cheese making, such as the whey collected after the curds were formed (similar to modern-day cottage cheese or farmer's cheese), was used in cooking and was probably one of the few ways in which fresh dairy products were consumed.

Women, as mentioned above in reference to urban family labor, were also in charge of brewing ale or beer in the centuries before the introduction of hops into the brewing process. As Judith Bennett has discussed, the brewing of ale was considered one of the most female-exclusive tasks, a good reason why the term "brewster" existed in English long before any male-gendered term appeared. Ale did not contain any preservatives, so it had to be consumed within a few days of its production. This meant that every village had to have its resident brewster (also known as an ale-wife) who both produced and sold the ale to the other villagers.

In regions where wine production was an important cash crop, and where the lord's demesne land was taken up with grape vines, families were engaged in all aspects of viniculture together. Men tended the vines, but everyone participated in the harvest, and women and girls were probably more frequently engaged in crushing the grapes in large vats with their feet than were men. Olive production was also a family—indeed, a village-wide—affair, with the harvest employing everyone in the family, and the production of oil involving the entire community.

Children, as mentioned in chapter 9, were not exempted from agricultural labor. Not only were older girls in charge of taking care of younger siblings, but boys and girls both worked in the fields, in the dairy, as herders of animals, and as minders of the cooking fires and the food being prepared on them. Survival of the rural family probably depended upon child labor; without it, there would not have been enough food to feed the family or cloth to dress them.

The Byzantine Economy and the Byzantine Family

One major barrier to discussing the Byzantine family and its economic role in the urban and rural environments is a lack of both primary sources and secondary analysis of them. Although information on the Byzantine economy is rather plentiful, the documents are usually related to imperial administration, such as descriptions of professions, identification of trades for taxation lists, and so on. Unlike the west, where family-based economic systems were quite common, it is not entirely clear whether the guilds that seem to have existed were structured in the same ways as in the west.[3]

One thing is clear: both the Byzantine urban and the rural economies were entirely dependent upon the actions of the family and the cooperative nature of family work. Elite families engaged in both merchant and land-based businesses as investors. Some members of the merchant class were wealthy enough to be considered aristocrats. Men who headed these businesses probably traveled a great deal, leaving household and business management to wives and sons. Masters of workshops, which were likely to be small and located within a domestic environment as they were in the west, must have relied on spouses to take care of apprentices, to assist in the workshop along with the children of the family, and so on.[4]

In other aspects of the Byzantine family economy, it is entirely likely that women supplemented the family income by engaging in work that was different from that of their husbands, sons, and brothers. Like western European urban women, the most typical trades in which Byzantine women engaged were in textiles—spinning, weaving, sewing—and in selling foodstuffs, such as presiding over market stalls selling fruits and vegetables, and even possibly selling food door to door. In addition, a few women in Byzantine cities served the elites as hairdressers, working in both private homes and in the public baths. And, of course, poor women in Byzantine cities always populated the brothels. Even prostitutes might have been working to supplement family rather than personal income.

It is somewhat easier to discuss rural labor in the context of family. Obviously, the peasant family eking out a living on a small farm needed everyone to be engaged in that task. In addition, Byzantine law had retained the late Roman statutes mandating that sons would work the same jobs as their fathers—a system of inherited status dating from the late third century—so often families were, at least officially, tied to the soil or to specific jobs that were considered essential by the government. Peasant families also maintained workshops for the manufacture of craft goods to supplement their income. These could include the making of pottery, textiles, and other essential items. Workshops could engage in blacksmithing and even the production of labor-intensive foods, such as bread and wine, that were too expensive for single family units to produce. Wealthier peasant families who had surplus crops might also become involved in local or middle-distance trade.[5]

Thus, the day to day labor of Byzantine family members was probably not that different from that of their peers in western Europe, or even in the Muslim Middle East. The official perception of labor by the Byzantine authorities, like those of other medieval bureaucracies, minimized the contribution of family members to the economy. Unlike for the west, however, the variety of sources about Byzantine labor culture is limited in such a way as to make it difficult to illuminate the varieties of family-based work.

Families and Work in the Muslim World

The problems historians encounter in trying to uncover the contributions of the family to the Byzantine economy are magnified when trying to do the same for the Islamic world. The deliberate erasure of most female public activity in Islamic sources, and the emphasis on the dominance of males in the economy work against understanding the ways in which family labor contributed to its survival and prosperity. Historians might be able to assume that many elements common to the experience of medieval western Christians, Byzantine Christians, and Jews in the economies of their regions existed also for the lands around the Mediterranean dominated by Islam. Nevertheless, social and cultural differences between Muslims and their neighbors might have been significant enough to alter the relationship between work and the family, and merit discussion, even if many of the conclusions are only speculative.

Among Muslim elites, the kinds of labor poorer families had to perform themselves—household maintenance, cooking, and so forth—were performed by slaves, mostly female. These would have been overseen by both the elite women in the family and possibly by eunuch overseers. Middle class and poor urban families did not have the luxury of always keeping womenfolk from public view, so the entire family was likely to be more involved in the economy. Although men in the family usually purchased the food that was consumed daily, women also shopped in the market-place, or *souk,* for clothing, textiles, and even jewelry. In addition, the food preparation necessary in order for the men to purchase it for their families was probably done by women. Backlashes against the presence of women in these public venues did occur and local magistrates sometimes banned them from the *souks.* When this occurred, however, it hurt the market economy to a great degree, so the bans were often overlooked or lifted.

According to recent research on the labor of women in the medieval Islamic world, there was significant public hostility to any overt involve-ment of women in family-based economic transactions, such as buying and selling land or investment in mercantile ventures. This is not necessarily all that different from the veiled disapproval in official sources concern-ing such activities among women in medieval Italy. This does not mean, however, that women paid attention to this hostility, or that it stopped them from engaging in such practices. Sources for Italy, such as letter col-lections and contracts, describe a significant level of activity by women, especially widows, in investment schemes and merchant ventures. These kinds of sources simply do not exist in any numbers for the Islamic com-munities in the Middle East. Nevertheless, Muslim women did in fact engage in a wide variety of economic activities that enhanced both their personal fortunes and those of their families. These activities were similar in a sense to those of their fathers, husbands, and sons, in that they were jobs specifically geared toward wage-earning. The Islamic authorities, however, mandated considerable gender specificity with respect to the kinds of labor in which women were permitted to be engaged. According to Maya Shatzmiller, from the eleventh to the fifteenth century,

women's participation in the labour market [was] both considerable and diversi-fied. In fact, their involvement and skills seem to have been more sophisticated and wide-ranging than those of medieval European women. The trades and occu-pations which Muslim women exercised, the professional and unskilled tasks they performed and the commercial activities and deals in which they were involved, reflect a high degree of participation, specialization, and division of labour.[6]

Shatzmiller goes on to say that Muslim women dominated the textile industries in particular, having virtual monopolies over the spinning, dying, and embroidery trades. This labor must have been essential for family maintenance, as was that performed by males.

Despite the profound loss of status that appearing in public could confer on Muslim women, poor women in the cities of the Islamic world had no choice but to appear in public in order to do their work. Some women worked as peddlers, a job also performed by men, going door to door to sell items directly to elite households. Women might have had an advan-tage in these jobs over men, since they could enter the women's quarters of the house without endangering the respectability of the women in the family. Poor women also were hired as professional mourners for funerals, although this practice was frowned upon by Islamic authorities.[7]

Perhaps ironically, historians today have been concentrating their efforts on uncovering the presence of women in the labor force of the medieval Islamic world. The jobs in which men engaged are much more evident in the sources and were not significantly different from those of their Christian and Jewish counterparts. Muslim men engaged in all aspects of administration, trade, manufacture, and agriculture. They competed with Jews in certain kinds of long-distance trade, although they had a monopoly on trade through central Asia along the famous Silk Road. Perhaps unlike their peers in other regions, even elite scholars and religious philosophers might engage in commercial activity. The merchant Ibn Battuta is better known for his descriptions of his travels, which took him all over the Mediterranean world, than he is for the products his business transported. The men and boys in a given family tended to cluster in specific trades, with sons following fathers into the business. This is the case, as well, with Muslim men engaged in military professions. The famous Seljuk amir, Nur ad-Din, followed his father Zengi as the ruler of Damascus, a position he won because of his associations with his father, not his military prowess (although he more than proved himself to be an effective military leader afterwards). As mentioned earlier in this chapter, Salah al-Din accompanied his uncle on military campaign to Egypt. Generations of imams, Muslim holy men, came from specific families. This was a given in the medieval economic culture.

In both urban and rural environments, even when the sources deliberately hide the activities of family members in order to highlight the dominance of specific males, survival would have been impossible without the full participation of the entire family. This is certainly the case in agricultural production, which dominated the medieval Islamic economy into at least the twelfth century, at which time more specialized manufacturing might have begun to overtake agricultural production. As invisible as family members might be, and as specific as laws were in attempts to limit female participation in the public labor market, the jobs performed by middle- and lower-class people could not occur in isolation away from family participation.

Division of labour and specialization in agriculture is generally low and unlikely to grow, given the fact that the farmer, with members of his family, or with the help of daily laborers, constitutes a single production unit, responsible for an array of tasks, including ploughing, planting, harvesting, raising animals, and the production and sale of both raw materials and items manufactured in their cottage industries.[8]

This quotation would refer equally well to agricultural labor in the Christian west and Byzantine east as well.

Jewish Families and Work

Like Christian families in medieval western Europe, Jewish families relied on all of their members to work toward the survival of the family. Except for the few areas where Jews were permitted to own land, such as parts of eastern Europe and some portions of the Muslim-controlled Mediterranean, this labor was urban and focused on professions such as long-distance trade, manuscript production, banking and money-lending, and goldsmithing. The Christian demonization of Jews who engaged in currency exchange and other banking fields, as portrayed for instance in Shakespeare's *The Merchant of Venice,* belies the fact that Jewish bankers were instrumental to the survival of the medieval kingdoms.

Jewish family-owned conglomerates operated throughout the Mediterranean and beyond, engaged in long-distance trade especially of textiles, dyes, and perfumes. Letters found in the Cairo *geniza* outline some of these relationships, not just between the great merchant families, but also within families. Multiple generations in the family participated together and close relationships were formed as a result. In one letter from the early eleventh century, the head of one merchant family thanks the elder of another family for his assistance in the business affairs of his two younger brothers, recently established in Cairo.[9] In another letter, from the early thirteenth century, a trader on voyage to India to acquire amber-gris (for making perfume) and spices writes to his wife, who in her letters to him had provided news of the family, while simultaneously berating him for his long absence. The merchant, in his reply, outlines how hard he has been working—a job that apparently included keeping his traveling companions happy with long drinking contests—and enumerates all of the items he will be bringing back home. He also assures his distraught wife that he has been faithful to her and will continue to be so.[10]

One of the most well-known of the Jewish merchant traders is Benjamin of Tudela, who, after he retired from active work and released from being tied down to one place by the death of his wife and the growth to adult-hood of his children, decided to travel through the Mediterranean world. In the years between 1173 and 1185, Benjamin wandered from Spain through southern France, to Italy and Sicily, Constantinople, and the lands of the Middle East. Although particularly interested in the schools of Jewish scholars and sites sacred to Judaism in the places he visited, Benjamin also provides a detailed glimpse of the economic life of Jewish communities at that time. According to his account, divisions of labor tended to follow family lines, with scholars and rabbis, merchants, trad-ers, and even dyers all passing their skills from father to son. This accords well with other sources of Jewish economic history, and indeed, with examples from the other medieval cultures.[11]

One area in which Jews were heavily involved, at least until the thirteenth century, was the production and sale of high-quality cloth, especially silk and Spanish wool. In Mediterranean areas they were engaged as well in olive and wine production. These activities, like those mentioned by Benjamin of Tudela, would have necessitated intensive involvement of virtually all the family.

As membership in guilds became more imbedded in both western and Byzantine commercial law, Jews became more limited in the kinds of trades in which they were legally able to engage. Skilled artisans in metalworking and mining, silk embroidery, goldsmithing, and medicine became increasingly restricted from the early thirteenth century onwards. Many Jewish families were probably pushed into the profession of moneylending out of necessity. In England, for example, virtually the only profession permitted to Jews before their expulsion in 1290 was moneylending.

Both Jewish men and women became moneylenders. It was not initially seen as a respectable trade among Jewish communities, but when their survival depended upon lending money at interest, this became considerably less important. Moneylending was, however, a precarious profession in the medieval West. Jews found themselves boxed in: the church condemned usury, which was defined as making a profit from money transactions, but both the church and the state relied heavily on Jewish bankers and restricted Jews from practicing most other professions except within the enclave of their own communities. In addition, most kings in medieval Europe—in particular kings Edward I of England and Louis IX of France—exploited the Jews shamelessly, not only taxing them to pay for Crusades and other activities, but also granting amnesty to courtiers in debt to Jewish bankers or even appropriating the debts for their own benefit. It is little wonder that Jews began migrating to central Europe, to Bohemia and Poland, even before they were deported from England and France.

Like Christian businesses, Jewish businesses also operated out of the front rooms and ground floors of their houses. In addition to the trades mentioned above, Jews also had to oversee their own food production and preparation because kosher laws demanded that the food consumed by Jews not be polluted by contact with products, such as pork and shellfish, that Jews are forbidden to eat. This was not such an issue in the Muslim world, since followers of Islam are also forbidden to eat pork, but the increasingly strict requirements for maintaining dietary purity meant that Jewish communities had to develop their own supply networks, maintain their own butcher shops, and probably also have their own versions of hucksters and regrators: women who sold prepared food in the marketplace.

Also like Christian businesses, family members were the invisible labor force in all aspects of a given trade. Jewish women were heavily engaged in investment and oversight of the long-distance carrying ventures in which their husbands and sons engaged. Although sons were usually busy with their education until they reached adulthood, thus perhaps making it less likely that they were active in the family business until they had had at least some level of schooling, daughters were probably put to work at fairly young ages, either learning household maintenance and preparing their trousseaux for marriage, or in the shop, the workshop, or studio working directly in the family business.

Unlike the guild system, which effectively kept Christian families engaged in the same kinds of work for generations, Jewish families did not have a political-economic system that mandated such restrictions. Nevertheless, they engaged in similar activities, and businesses became associated with specific families that passed the business from father to son and so on. Marriages were also organized to maintain professional networks, with cousins marrying to establish connections between far-flung branches of the family, rabbinic families intermarrying, and so on.

Families and Untraditional Work

The working family was not always respectable, law-abiding, or sustaining of the dominant culture. Illegal and unrespectable activities were also family affairs. In particular, prostitution was not always a job in which only single women engaged. Brothels or stews (as they were called in England) could be run by married couples or widows, and the women who worked in them were not always unmarried. Children might be employed as procurers, but it is likely that the social culture tried to control such activities. No level of social condemnation or town ordinance could control this particular industry: prostitution was engaged in by both men (as homosexual or transvestite prostitutes) and women; medieval towns and cities were teeming with them and they had an eager and enthusiastic clientele of both lay and (in the case of Christian Europe) clerical men. Even when they were not connected directly to a family (although this was fairly common), prostitutes formed family-style relationships for their domestic arrangements.

Burglary, robbery, and other illegal activities could also be considered in some circumstances family businesses. Stolen property might be hidden in the cupboards of the house—thus implicating the robber's wife as an accessory since she held the keys to the cupboards. Children were employed as pickpockets. Extended family members were often involved in such activities together, with brothers and cousins being engaged in operating teams of robbers along the king's or public highways. In addition, families sometimes engaged in mayhem directed against their lords or overseers. There are many instances in the English public records, for instance, of families who used work as a pretext for poaching in the lord's woods and streams, for illegal gleaning (that is, gathering the leftover grain after the harvest), and even for committing acts of sabotage against the lord's fields. While this might not seem like work, per se, the fact that these activities were illegal does not mean they were intended to do more than help the family survive.

Finally, families throughout the medieval world could engage in vendettas and feuds that would result in serious disruption of the countryside. As Barbara Hanawalt mentioned, "the family that slays together, stays together."[12] Such activities seem to have been on the extreme end of family cohesiveness, but it is not a meaningless claim that such kinds of illegal activities could be considered a family business. The feuds described in Icelandic sagas, such as *Njal's Saga,* and the family conflicts Shakespeare used as the basis for the play *Romeo and Juliet* were common enough to resonate in their literary forms with their audiences. Although this was not necessarily work that was geared toward family financial maintenance, the family-based violence in medieval society certainly claimed family survival as its rationale.

Conclusion

No matter what their religious affiliation or cultural context, medieval families survived by working together, either by a strict division of labor in which all family members had specific tasks to do, or by the somewhat less defined requirements of a family business. Although the sources very often hide or bury such activity, identifying the labor of only the head of the household, the working family, whether elite, urban, middle-class, or peasant, operated as a unit of production. This situation was not relevant just for work outside the family that required everyone's effort. Work internal to the family's success depended on the dedicated labor of every person in the household: from the women's work of food preparation and of spinning thread and weaving cloth to provide adequate clothing for everyone, to the men's work tilling the fields and maintenance of farm equipment.

Notes

1. *Histoire de Guillaume le Maréchal,* ll. 13532–13544 quoted in David Crouch, *William le Marshal* (London: Longmans, 2003), 100. I have used Crouch's translation with some changes, so this version differs slightly from his. I have placed the differences in brackets.

2. Judith M. Bennett, *Ale, Beer, and Brewsters in England: Women's Work in a Changing World* (New York: Oxford University Press, 1999), discusses the process in England whereby men began to take over the professional production of beer after about 1350 because of the introduction of hops into the brewing process.

3. A useful comparison is by Alexander Kazhdan, "The Italian and Late Byzantine City" *Dumbarton Oaks Papers* 49 (1995): 1–22.

4. This is discussed by Alexander Kazhdan, "State, Feudal, and Private Economy in Byzantium" *Dumbarton Oaks Papers* 47 (1993): 83–100, especially 86–87.

5. These are discussed in greater detail by Jacques Lefort, "Rural Economy and Social Relations in the Countryside," *Dumbarton Oaks Papers* 47 (1993): 101–113.

6. Maya Shatzmiller, "Women and Wage Labour in the Medieval Islamic West: Legal Issues in an Economic Context" *Journal of the Economic and Social History of the Orient* 40, no. 2 (1997): 177.

7. Discussed by Leila Ahmed, *Women, Gender, and Islam: Historical Roots of a Modern Debate* (New Haven: Yale University Press, 1992), 118–119.

8. Maya Shatzmiller, *Labour in the Medieval Islamic World* (Leiden, Netherlands: E. J. Brill, 1994), 176–177.

9. S. D. Goitein, ed. and trans., *Letters of Medieval Traders* (Princeton: Princeton University Press, 1973), 73–75.

10. Goitein, *Letters,* 220–226.

11. Benjamin of Tudela, *Itinerary* at "The Travels of Benjamin of Tudela," http://www.sacred-texts.com/jud/mhl/mhl20.htm and *The Itinerary of Benjamin of Tudela: Travels in the Middle Ages,* trans. Marcus Nathan Adler (Malibu: J. Simon/Pangloss Press, 1983; Reprint, Nightingale Resources, 1983–091).

12. See, for example, Barbara Hanawalt (Westman), "The Peasant Family and Crime in Fourteenth-Century England," *The Journal of British Studies* 13, no. 2 (1974): 1–18 for a discussion of this issue. Quotation is from page 16.

11

The Family as Rhetorical Device: Traditional, Transitional, and Non-traditional Families

The family was the basic unit of all social institutions in the Middle Ages, from the royal court to the Benedictine monastery; from the merchant guild to the university. This is not to say that all of these institutions were comprised of family units, but rather that their structures were intended to mimic family relationships. This in turn had an impact on the ways in which people experienced such institutional structures and also affected the ways in which more conventional families interacted with them.

This situation is particularly true of western Christendom and somewhat less true for the Muslim emirates. Even in circumstances that modern-day thinking might not even begin to define as familial, these structures, with their typical tensions and forms of cooperation, resonate in ways that medieval people would have recognized as family-based. In addition, all medieval cultures contained non-traditional—and often condemned—structures that either self-consciously mimicked family relationships or sought to replace traditional families. Again, this deliberate association with family-based systems was more obvious in the medieval West, but such structures existed as well in the Byzantine East and the Muslim world.

The Royal Court and the Royal Family

In the early Middle Ages, the rulers of the Germanic kingdoms deliberately organized their administrations around the familiar structures of family life. The king was, in effect, the head of the family with all the patriarchal rights pertaining to fathers. Kings controlled the marriages of orphans and widows often as their legal guardians. They distributed largess as paternal figures, especially to the needy. Their kingdoms were destined to be divided upon their death on the basis of the partibility of family estates. Queens had maternal roles to fill as well. They held the keys to the treasury, which was housed within their domestic apartments or bedrooms. This meant that queens were effectively the lords chamberlain of the kingdom, in control of its economic life. Queens were expected to monitor the education of minors in wardship to the king as well as of their own children. They oversaw certain manufacturing in the kingdom, such as textile production, since spinning and weaving were associated with women, especially queens. They also patronized and founded monastic houses because they were supposed to oversee the religious education of the kingdom, just as mothers did in private families.

The Anglo-Saxon epic poem *Beowulf* illustrates the ways in which early medieval Germanic kings and queens embodied paternal and maternal roles for their courts. King Hrothgar, to whose court of Heorot Beowulf arrives, is described as a ring giver or treasure giver, which is one of the most complimentary adjectives early medieval people could use for a king or lord. The term "ring giver" encompassed not just the giving of gifts; it referred to the obligations a monarch or chieftain owed his followers, such as financial security and personal safety. Hrothgar's court was in disarray, however, because he was unable to protect his followers from the attacks of Grendel and his mother. Hrothgar's wife, Queen Wealhtheow, also embodied the ideal qualities of motherhood. She welcomes Beowulf to the court, ensures that he is fed and treated well. She is richly dressed and acts as cup bearer to all the men in the hall. Beowulf promises her that he will set the mead-hall to rights by destroying Grendel. As the poem relates, "these words well pleased the royal lady."[1]

Other early medieval sources present kings and, especially, queens as bad parental figures. Gregory of Tours, for example, depicts the Merovingian Queen Fredegund, widow of King Chilperic, as a particularly bad parent. Her particular vice was irrational rage directed at a person giving her bad news. When she was told by her servant that her daughter Rigunth was being mistreated, instead of addressing the problem, Fredegund accused the messenger and his associates of wrongdoing instead. Thus, instead of protecting the helpless, Queen Fredegund made their circumstances worse.[2]

Although the system in place in the early medieval Germanic kingdoms eventually evolved into a more professional administrative structure, the image of the king as father and the queen as mother still resonated with medieval people. Kings operated both as patrons of everything from religious foundations to schools and colleges and as disciplinarians punishing people who misbehaved by breaking the law. Queens deliberately associated themselves with the Virgin Mary, the ultimate mother figure, and encouraged those associations through conspicuous acts of piety, religious patronage, and the grandiose presentation of alms to the poor. Public displays of these paternal and maternal connections were common, and propaganda strove to associate monarchs with images of the good father and good mother. Alternatively, kings who were perceived as bad were characterized as arbitrary or inconsistent parental figures: they punished people on a whim, took bad advice, played favorites among the vassals in their court, and so on. Queens charged with being bad mothers favored one faction over another, promoted favorites, and pushed their own family forward contrary to the interests of the state.

These images can be illustrated by comparing contemporary descriptions of the royal families in thirteenth-century England and France. King Henry III and his wife, Queen Eleanor of Provence, were often criticized for being, in essence, bad parental figures. Henry was thought of as too religious; he spent money lavishly on the renovation of Westminster Abbey church, for instance, and neglected other duties. He was overly fond of his half-siblings and was accused of ignoring the needs of both his biological children and his full siblings. Queen Eleanor promoted the interests of her birth family over those of her family by marriage by arranging marriage alliances between her female cousins and the most eligible bachelors in the kingdom. She was also too emotional to be considered a good mother. As discussed in chapter 7, when her daughter Mary died at a very young age, she was so overcome with grief that she became ill, prompting criticism from some contemporaries. In contrast, Henry's younger brother, Richard earl of Cornwall, and his wife, Isabella la Marshal, are depicted in some chronicles as the perfect parental couple. Richard was disciplined, careful, and clear-headed. He governed his lands not by pettiness or petulance but decisively and consistently. His wife, Isabella, was devoted to him and his ambitions, despite being a member of the most prominent non-royal family in England, the Marshal earls of Pembroke, and she promoted his interests whenever possible. When Isabella died in childbirth, Richard was grief stricken, but this did not prevent him from being an effective advocate for his allies at a time of great unrest in the kingdom.

At the opposite end of the parental spectrum was the royal triangle made by King Louis IX of France, his mother, Dowager Queen Blanche of Castile, and his wife, Queen Marguerite of Provence (the sister of Henry III's wife, Eleanor). Louis had been crowned at age 12 in 1226 when his father, Louis VIII, died, but his mother, Queen Blanche, acted as regent of France until Louis reached his officially majority at age 21. He married Marguerite of Provence shortly before this time, in 1234. This marriage was arranged by his mother; indeed, Marguerite was a cousin of Blanche's. Even though the marriage was her idea, Blanche was apparently so devoted to her son, Louis, that she became horribly jealous of her daughter-in-law when the young couple showed signs of being in love.

The dowager queen was a domineering character and Louis did not really gain any independence from her until she died in 1252.

This royal triangle between king, dowager queen, and queen-consort created difficulties in the context of the rhetoric of monarchs as parental figures. Although Queen Blanche was revered as a devoted mother, she became a rather over-domineering parent to all of France. Louis's attachment to her metaphorical apron strings was perceived as a weakness on his part and that, combined with Blanche's jealousy, was rumored as the reason why Marguerite did not conceive for several years after the wedding. Once Queen Blanche died, however, Louis was transformed into an exemplary father figure for the kingdom. He was very pious, but not perceived as excessively so. He was willing to consult with both his mother and his wife, but chronicles and his official biographer, the Sire de Joinville, claim that he was not overly influenced by them. He was a mentor not only to his own brothers, such as Charles of Anjou, but he even took the English princes, Henry III's sons Edward and Edmund, under his wing—they accompanied Louis on crusade—and he was considered a far better role model than their father. Louis's prowess on the battlefield was lauded (Henry III's attempts at war were disasters) and even though his crusading efforts were abject failures, they were still considered to be honorable acts, especially in comparison to Henry, who had promised but failed to go on crusade.

It is perhaps ironic that in many ways the careers of Henry III and Eleanor of Provence and of Louis IX and Marguerite of Provence paralleled each other so closely, but with so radically different results in the historical record. Perhaps the reason is that the enduring image of Henry is of a timid overly pious person, hiding in terror when his castle was attacked by rebels, but that of Louis is of a fatherly figure casually seated under his favorite tree as he dispensed wisdom and justice. Even though the historical reality was probably a far cry from these rhetorical images, the contrast between bad father and good father would not have gone unnoticed.

Although the events around which medieval chroniclers locate these kinds of portraits were political in focus—rebellions, wars, and so on—the terminology they used was family-based. The insertions of these episodes into the larger political narrative thus encouraged the reader to think of these very prominent people in a family context. This suggests that they felt their readers would relate better to the subjects at hand were they narrated as business conducted within a larger-than-life family. This was also the case with the Byzantine imperial family, which chroniclers consistently depicted in a parental role with respect to their treatment of the people and of their families. The qualities of a good parent—piety, generosity, firmness of discipline, fairness—were emphasized in depictions of so-called good Byzantine emperors and empresses, while the opposite qualities formed the descriptions of those perceived as bad by chroniclers such as Theodoros Skoutariotes and Michael Psellus.[3]

The Monastic Family

The associations made between monastic life and family life in the Middle Ages (and today) could not have been more deliberate. Heads of monastic houses were titled abbots and abbesses (derived from the Hebrew *abba,* meaning "father"). Members of the monastic house were called brothers and sisters. The relationship between the abbot and the monks as described, for instance, in the *Rule of St. Benedict* is seen as that of a father to his children. The abbot is supposed to reward the monks when they have done well, and to chide and punish them when they misbehave. In female religious communities, the relationship between the abbess and the nuns was supposed to be similar: a mother and her daughters. Indeed, one of the more common complaints of nuns was the abbess-mother showing favoritism toward a particular member of the community: a kind of sibling rivalry common to enclosed groups.

The characterization of monasteries as gender-segregated families extended throughout the system in both the western and Byzantine forms of Christianity. In theory, people who dedicated themselves to monastic life were supposed to cut off all associations with the outside world, including those with their birth families. Monasteries self-consciously tried to embody Jesus's command to leave all elements of worldly activity and follow him. The historical reality of the monastic experience was, of course, quite different from the ideal. Monks and nuns retained contact with both their kin and with the outside world. Family members often joined the same monastic house. The patronage structure necessitated frequent communication between monastic houses and their patrons. These realities sometimes conflicted with monasticism's ideals, but monasteries were unable to divorce themselves completely from the secular world.

As monasticism developed, the relationships between the abbot/abbess and their spiritual sons and daughters did change over time. The crusader orders, such as the Knights Templar and the Knights Hospitaller, mimicked feudal relationships in their order. Although the feudal relationship could be likened to a family structure, the Masters' connections with the brothers of the order were far more deliberately authoritarian than the more democratic system of the traditional monastery, in which the monks elect the abbot and prior who govern their house. The Dominicans and Franciscans conceived (at least at first) of their orders as collections of brothers. They tried to avoid strong associations with a father figure, such as existed among the Benedictines and the Cistercians, or in Byzantine monastic orders. In addition, the Franciscans and Dominicans had tertiary orders made of lay men and women who remained active in public life, were permitted to marry, could have children, and never entered a formal monastery except perhaps very late in life. Although both the Franciscans and the Dominicans eventually did conform to more traditional monastic structures, the emphasis on the equality of all members and their original resistance to authoritarian hierarchies, especially among the Franciscans, remained. Even with these kinds of changes in structure, medieval monasticism was still profoundly family-centered and the terminology and relationships encouraged were based on family norms: brothers and sisters isolated from the world and reliant on no one but themselves for their sustenance.

Sufism and the Islamic *Umma*

Islam does not have a real equivalent to the Christian monastery, but an important—and in the Middle Ages controversial—branch of Islam does have some structural similarities: Sufism. Sufism is a mystical form of Islam whose origins are somewhat hazy. Some scholars consider it to have developed entirely out of Islam, while others have suggested that its origins actually lie earlier.[4] Sufi practitioners are divided into orders, each headed by a teacher or wise man. Individuals dedicated themselves to being immersed in religious instruction with a particular teacher or master for a period of time, during which they lived in communities of students. Unlike monasteries, students did not dedicate themselves permanently to these domestic structures. They could move in and out of the Sufi orders at will and still be considered a member. In addition, Sufi orders maintained inns and hostelries for members who traveled, such as the great Muslim philosopher al-Ghazali.

Medieval Sufi orders, although they did not necessarily use the same terminology as the Christian monastic system, did nevertheless operate as paternalistic communities, with the master operating as a father figure. Although there were female Sufis, it is unlikely that they came from non-Sufi families, so there were no female-only communities or orders. In addition, Islam mandated that all Muslims were to be married, if at all possible, so the idea of enclosed communities of people dedicated to chastity had no place within an Islamic context. For this reason, some of the great Sufi leaders formed the basis of generations of Sufi philosophers and teachers, some of them women. Therefore, the traditional family was just as important within Sufism as the ad hoc and temporary family of scholars who attended the Sufi schools.

The Guild and the University

As mentioned in chapter 10, the workshops overseen by guilds were based fundamentally on family structure. Apprentices lived in the homes of their masters, whose wives oversaw their maintenance. Family members usually worked as unpaid but essential labor in the activity of the workshop. The guilds themselves, although perhaps less obvious in their family-based structures than monasteries and nunneries, were nevertheless organized in ways that could be called familial. Although the members of the guild who had attained master status might be considered more or less equals, the journeymen and apprentices under them were clearly categorized as professional children of the masters. In addition, guilds operated as confraternities, literally associations of so-called brothers who engaged in acts of patronage, in sponsoring religious festivals, and who contributed money to the building of special buildings and the beautification of the city. Finally, guilds operated in a sense as marriage brokers for their members, since most guild masters both married the daughters of other guild members and wanted their own daughters and sons to do so as well.

The medieval academic university essentially operated as a guild. Indeed, the term *universitas,* from which the name university comes, is merely the Latin term for a guild. The structure of the university was perhaps more complex than that of a merchant guild, but the educational program was overseen by a structure that was family-oriented. Masters not only taught bachelors (in Latin, *baccalaurei*), who lived in communities called colleges (in Latin, *collegia*), but also often lived with their pupils in order to impose some kind of order on their daily lives. While this probably resembled a modern-day boarding school arrangement more than a modern-day family, the responsibilities of the masters were very like those of fathers in the Middle Ages.

Alternative Models of Families in the Medieval West: The Spiritual Family

Throughout the medieval period the standard family models were challenged by alternatives, usually fueled by religious dissent or unorthodoxy, that proposed different ways of living in families and other kinds of communal groups. In the late antique period (the second through fourth centuries) a form of Christianity called Montanism proposed an end to marriage, the abolition of private property, and the adoption of communal living. Later forms of Christianity that deviated from the orthodox view, such as the Waldensians, also proposed such innovations as the abolition of marriage and private property and the formation of communal systems in which all the members engaged. Beguines and the Brethren of the Common Life were late medieval religious communities that rejected both traditional family and traditional monastic structures. These were not fully accepted forms of religious expression and, as such, any deviation from the norms of family life were usually condemned as well. Nevertheless, they were popular among certain populations that were largely left out of the dominant social systems of the Middle Ages. Other groups, such as the Cathars or Albigensians, completely rejected the norms of medieval society. They were therefore declared heretical and violently suppressed by the religious and civil authorities.

Historians generally agree that a French merchant named Peter Waldo founded the Waldensian movement in the last quarter of the twelfth century. Peter preached against the amassing of wealth, especially by the church, and promoted a life of absolute simplicity and restraint. Although his message was quite similar to that of his contemporary Francis of Assisi, the church authorities did not approve. Peter's movement was declared heretical initially not because his theology ran counter to orthodoxy, but because Peter disobeyed the church's demand that he stop preaching and conform to the official teachings of the church.

Eventually, the Waldensians formed an alternative to traditional Catholic Christianity, one that the church suppressed with considerable violence in the thirteenth and fourteenth centuries. Waldensian preachers—including women—traveled from town to town to meet with co-religionists in secret. They condemned many traditions of the Catholic church, such as the superiority of priests, the existence of purgatory, the obligations inherent in the sacraments, and the taking of oaths. Followers, although they lived in traditional family units, advocated a more communal lifestyle with a significantly decreased emphasis on private property, the prominence of the family, and the institutions of conventional Christianity. This was a direct challenge not only to the dominant church, but also to the civil authorities.

The Beguine movement seems to have begun in Brabant, a region of medieval France that is now part of Belgium, in the early years of the thirteenth century. This might have been something of a spontaneous movement begun perhaps by a priest named Lambert le Begue, who preached that women should live a spiritually active life, or by the first woman associated with the group, Mary of Oignies, who had been an Augustinian nun.[5] What is clear is that the women who joined the Beguine movement rejected traditional medieval notions of family and convent in favor of a somewhat pragmatic alternative: the creation of female-only communities that operated independently of any central authority and that did not require permanent enclosure of any member. Beguine communities appeared in urban areas. They were residences for women that emphasized work and prayer. Members of each *beguinage* pooled their resources, lived communally, and operated by consensus. This was a movement of religious sisters, rather than a family dominated by a mother. One of the most revolutionary aspects of the movement was its ability to absorb women who, for various reasons, might leave the community and return again—or never return—without penalty. This fluidity and flexibility, coupled with the belief among Beguines that women were capable of achieving spiritual enlightenment without the control or oversight of males, led the church to condemn the movement. Beguines resisted church authority and persisted in presenting a female-specific spiritual vision. As a result, the church clamped down hard. Beguinages were forcibly disbanded and, in 1310, one of the great mystical philosophers of the movement, Marguerite Porete, was burned at the stake as a heretic.

The principles espoused by both the Waldensians and the Beguines—that individuals are capable of spiritual growth through prayer and individual effort—finally found grudging acceptance in the Catholic Church with the Brethren of the Common Life, founded in the mid-fourteenth century by the Dutch theologian Geert Groote. The Brethren—including women—were organized in more traditional monastic fashion, but they did not take vows of poverty, chastity, and obedience like conventional monks and nuns. They devoted their lives to prayer and to education, specifically of lay boys and girls in the cities of the medieval Low Countries (modern-day Belgium, The Netherlands, and Luxembourg). Although dedicated to extreme simplicity, the Brethren were theologically orthodox and, for this reason, they were tolerated by the church. Indeed, the great sixteenth-century reformist theologian Erasmus of Rotterdam received his early education at a Brethren school.

Thus, the rhetorical use of family connections in medieval Christianity—mother, father, brother, sister—were common not only among traditional religious groups but also among non-traditional groups. Indeed, the ideal of replacing one's earthly family with a spiritual one probably resonated more among groups opposed to the traditional structures of the church than among those that were a part of it.

Possibly the most violently attacked alternative to orthodox Christianity in the Middle Ages was the group called the Cathars or the Albigensians (named after the town of Albi in southern France, where the movement allegedly began). The Cathars were dualists: they believed that the world and all that is contained therein were created by an evil being, that Jesus and Satan were brothers, and that God, who embodies perfect goodness, is connected to the soul, which is trapped inside the corrupting body. The leaders of the movement were called *perfecti* (the singular form is *perfectus*). They maintained fairly strict bans on eating nearly all kinds of meat, although they ate fish and some kinds of dairy products, because they believed that mammals also had souls and possibly that souls transmigrated from one body to another at death, until released through purification. The *perfecti* also abstained from sexual intercourse and practiced fairly strict forms of self-discipline. Cathars who were near death could choose to purify themselves by refusing to eat. This was thought to both discipline the corrupt body and free the pure soul from the earthly chains binding it. Until death, however, since the body and the world were considered already to be corrupt, Cathars could theoretically be free to engage in activities that the orthodox authorities viewed as sinful: sex outside the confines of marriage, divorce, the taking of multiple partners, and so on. Homosexuality was not banned, either, since all forms of sexual activity were thought to be equally corrupt—an idea that was not uncommon in medieval orthodox Christianity as well, in that all non-procreative sexual activity was considered sinful in varying degrees. Families were considered fluid, with members moving in and out of them at will. Marriage was discouraged and birth control might have been encouraged, in order to prevent procreation. This was a very different view of family from that of the orthodox church, which promoted the creation of families as both the only way to engage in legal sexual behavior and the only way to produce legitimate children.

The Cathar ideal of perfection thus in no way conformed to orthodox belief. As such, it was condemned by the authorities—the papacy and the kings of France, where most of the Cathars were living. Nevertheless, it was hard to eradicate these ideas and it took more than a hundred years to wipe out the Cathars in southern France.[6]

The Cathars might represent an extremely unorthodox perspective on both the world and family life, but they were not unique in their beliefs. The dualist world view has a very long history, beginning with pre-Christian religions such as Zoroastrianism, religions contemporary with early Christianity, such as that of the Manichees in late Roman North Africa, and forms of Christianity known generally as Gnosticism that were declared heretical in the first few centuries of the religion's existence. Indeed, Gnosticism and a dualist worldview influenced orthodox Christianity in many ways. The Gospel of John and the Book of Revelations are so-called moderate Gnostic texts, and the theology of St. Augustine of Hippo was influenced by his early interest in Manicheeism.

The impact of unorthodox or heretical religions movements on family life in the medieval west could be significant, especially in areas where alternative forms of Christianity became popular, as Catharism did in southern France and the Pyrenees region between France and Spain. Not only were traditional family systems encouraged to conform to different attitudes toward their structure, toward sexuality, and toward children, but some systems rejected these categories outright and advocated everything from complete abstinence to rejecting the traditional family to raising children communally. In addition, when some family members converted to a form of Christianity that had been condemned as heretical by church authorities, not only did this tear families apart, but it could endanger everyone, heretic and orthodox alike. The office of the Holy Inquisition, invented by Pope Innocent III in 1215 to combat Catharism, tended not to differentiate between compliant and dissident family members. All people associated with an heretical group were rounded up, imprisoned, interrogated, and punished. People who were excommunicated by the church were supposed to be shunned by the entire community, including family members. This could also have significant repercussions, not only on individuals in a given family, but also on that family's very survival. The religious authorities usually received support from the institutions of the civil authorities in wiping out religion-based alternatives to the dominant culture. Neither group felt it could afford to tolerate such differences because the authoritarian nature of both medieval Christianity and the monarchic political systems in Europe depended upon ingrained demands of absolute obedience.

Unusual Family Arrangements in the Byzantine, Muslim, and Jewish Cultures of the Middle Ages

If the sources for unorthodox family arrangements are thin for the medieval West, they are more or less nonexistent for the rest of the medieval world. In fact, sources are more likely to emphasize simple cultural differences between, say, Christians and Muslims, as being bizarre and unnatural rather than identify truly unusual family arrangements within a given culture. In addition, the rhetoric of the family was so strong in all the medieval cultures and within all the religious systems that the authorities would have been careful to erase irregularities from the records and to insist that people who were worthy to be included in the historical record operated well within the bounds of legally mandated behavior. Finally, although informal and ad hoc living arrangements had to have been common in all regions of the medieval world and among all social classes, it is impossible to reconstruct them without sources that make reference to them. These simply do not exist for most of the medieval world.

Islamic culture, since it did not have any bias against polygamy, was considered by Christians to be highly irregular as to its family arrangements. Thus, the Christian image of the seraglio as a place in which decadent acts of sexual promiscuity ran rampant did not provide an accurate picture of the Muslim polygamous household, which was far more staid and conventional than Christians imagined it to be. Muslims, for their part, thought that the mixing of the sexes in Christian households, where respectable women could meet and talk to men to whom they were not related, was downright bizarre and even unsavory. To them, such behavior meant that Christian men did not have sufficient control of their wives, and Muslims imagined that Christian women were just as sexually promiscuous as Christians imagined Muslim women confined to a harem must be. Of course, the Muslim perception was just as inaccurate as that of the Christian.

Medieval Islam was just as authoritarian as medieval Christianity and just as intolerant of difference, especially differences that influenced lifestyle and social interaction. Homosexuality, for instance, was condemned by Islam as it was by Christianity, even though there is ample evidence that homosexuality existed in both cultures. Some men engaged in same-sex activity, although few were probably exclusively homosexual since all men in Muslim culture were expected to be married. Certainly same-sex partnered households, if they existed, did so in a vacuum: no sources are available to suggest how such a family would operate in the climate of intolerance and hostility with which it would have been met.

In addition, the legal establishment of alternatives to the conventional Muslim family simply did not exist. Islam did not even provide an alternative similar to the Christian monastery, where individuals could form more or less permanent communities dedicated to prayer. Sufi orders did not operate in the same way. Muslims were expected to be married. Men who did not marry were criticized for their anti-social behavior and women who were unmarried were condemned to a subordinate status in the households of their families. The dominance of the family unit as the basis of the society was simply far too important to allow for alternatives.

Jewish communities, especially when faced with persecution and want, might have made some unusual arrangements in order to reinforce a family in danger of extinction. Judaic law, however, already included arrangements that Christians would have found strange, such as the marriage of first cousins, which was very common in the Middle East, and the tradition of the levirate marriage in which a widow marries the brother of her late husband in order to provide an heir for the dead man. Although the levirate marriage was very rarely invoked in medieval Jewish culture, such an arrangement would not have been considered absolutely extraordinary. On the other hand, community authorities would have been careful to inspect the potential groom for evidence that he was interested in the welfare of his bereaved sister-in-law and not solely in the monetary and property that the levirate marriage would have brought. Jewish communities also valued marriage to the exclusion of any other arrangement. Indeed, Jews in the Middle Ages thought the Christian emphasis on chastity was bizarre. This did not mean, however, that they tolerated overt homosexuality: like Christian and Muslim society, Jews refused to recognize same-sex relationships as legitimate. Thus, it is almost impossible to identify relationships that did not follow traditional family structure, even though they certainly must have existed.

In the Byzantine world, even more than in the Christian west, evidence for unorthodox marriage arrangements is virtually nonexistent. Although chronicles did sometimes record the marital abnormalities of emperors desperate for heirs, these were not necessarily illegal or illicit arrangements and chroniclers might include them just in order to present their subjects in a negative light. Sources for people below the level of the Byzantine aristocracy are scarce indeed, so there is no way to know what kinds of unusual family arrangements might have appeared in times of crisis or among specific groups or communities. The kinds of alternatives that existed among western Christian heretical groups such as the Cathars and the Beguines did not exist in the east, either. Byzantine heretical belief systems were far more theologically oriented than socially oriented. Byzantine Christians argued about whether the three elements of the Trinity were coequal, and whether Jesus was fully human before he became fully God, not about the efficacy of the sacraments or whether priestly blessings were necessary for salvation. Even though the Cathars, for instance, gained converts as far from their origins in France as Bosnia, such social heresies did not reach the Byzantine east. In addition, Byzantine monasteries, as discussed in chapter 9, were much farther removed from the center of the social culture than they were in the west. While many were located in and around cities, they were far less intimately connected to the families of their patrons and they were far more focused on separating their members from all family associations. While this probably promoted the monastery and convent as real alternatives to the conventional family, the highly controlled monastic system worked against such loose and flexible arrangements as those found in the Beguine communities. Thus, Byzantine Christianity shared with western Christianity the idea of the monastery as the standard alternative to a more typical family life, but did not contain openings for unorthodox alternatives that western Christianity seems to have offered.

Conclusion

It is entirely likely that medieval people everywhere made family arrangements that were untraditional when circumstances made such arrangements necessary. It is also likely that most of these arrangements were never recorded by the authorities, so we will never know what they might have been. In the cramped and overcrowded medieval cities, people undoubtedly did strategize in their domestic arrangements for their comfort and survival in ways that would have been frowned upon by the church or the Islamic authorities. In the middle years of the fourteenth century, the period of the Black Death, the combination of mass panic and the horrific mortality rate must have prompted many people to alter their living arrangements. In Boccacio's *The Decameron*, for instance, a group of unrelated aristocrats flee Florence in the wake of the plague's arrival and live together in a country villa. Chronicles describing the Black Death claim that parents abandoned children, and children abandoned their parents, in their fear of the contagion. The breakdown of the social order during the epidemic must have been severe, but it was not permanent. Once the danger had more or less passed, traditional family structures reasserted themselves, even when outbreaks of plague returned every 7 to 11 years. The persistence of medieval family structures and their resistance to significant change is not just a phenomenon of traditional cultures. The fact that family structures to this day resemble those of medieval people is a testament to their enduring power.

Notes

1. *Beowulf,* ll. 607–639, trans. Howell D. Chickering, Jr. (Garden City: Anchor Press, 1977), 85.

2. Gregory of Tours, *History of the Franks,* VII.15, trans. Lewis Thorpe (Harmondsworth: Penguin Books, 1974), 399.

3. For examples of their work, see the *Internet Medieval Sourcebook.* For Skoutariotes, "From the Synopsis Chronika: The Emperors of the 11th Century," http://www.fordham.edu/halsall.source.skoutariotes1.html. For Psellus, "Chronographia," http://www.fordham.edu/halsall/basis/psellus-chronographia.html.

4. The Wikipedia article on Sufism is particularly detailed. See http://en.wikipedia.ord/wiki/sufism.

5. See the essay by Elizabeth T. Knuth, "The Beguines," http://www.users.csbsju.edu/~eknuth/xpxx/beguines.html for a good overview of the movement. Also, Abby Stoner, "Sisters Between: Gender and the Medieval Beguines," http://userwww.sfsu.edu~epf/1995/beguine.html. A recent and comprehensive history of the Beguines is Walter Simons, *Cities of Ladies: Beguine Communities in the Medieval Low Countries 1200–1565* (Philadelphia: University of Pennsylvania Press, 2003).

6. For an interesting, if controversial, depiction of the Cathars, see Emmanuel Leroy Ladurie, *Montaillou: The Promised Land of Error* (New York: Vintage Books, 1979). A more recent, and less controversial book on the Cathars is Malcom Barber, *The Cathars: Dualist Heretics in Languedoc in the High Middle Ages* (London: Longman, 2000).

Glossary

Al-Andalus: the Arabic name for the Islamic region of Spain ruled by the caliphate of Cordoba.

Bailey: in castle architecture, the courtyard enclosed by the main wall, in which one finds the keep and other buildings.

Barbican: the main defensive structures of the outer wall of a castle.

Bride price: the goods and money a potential groom had to pay the potential bride and her family in medieval Germanic culture.

Canon law: the law of the church.

Civil Law: refers specifically to Roman law.

Common law: the law of the English kingdom after the Norman Conquest.

Concubine/concubinage: a woman or a relationship with a woman that is considered to be legal, but that is not a permanent marriage.

Consanguinity/consanguineous: in medieval Christianity, referring to the blood relationship of close kin who are forbidden to marry.

Curtain wall: the wall of a castle that is intersected by towers.

Demesne: in medieval manorialism, the land the lord retains for his own income and to produce the grain he and his family consumes.

Diocese: in the Roman period, this was an administrative unit of the imperial government. In the Middle Ages, this was the administrative unit of the Christian church, over which a bishop presided.

Domus: the Latin term for both house and household.

Donjon: the origin of the word "dungeon," this is the French term for "keep" (see below).

Dowager: a widow who has received her dower and is independent of male control.

Dower: in most cultures, the property the groom grants the bride in the event he dies before her. In Islamic law, this is referred to as dowry.

Dowry: in most cultures, the property the bride brings to the wedding.

Endogamy/endogamous: referring to marriage within the kinship or community unit.

Eunuch: a castrated male.

Exogamy/exogamous: referring to marriage outside the kinship or community unit.

Feudalism: the political and military system of the European Middle Ages in which a lord provides a fief to a free person in exchange for oaths of homage and fealty (loyalty), military service, and the performance of other feudal obligations known as dues.

Fief: the grant—in land, moveable property or both—made by a lord to a vassal in exchange for his or her oaths of homage and fealty (loyalty).

Garderobe: a medieval latrine and the origin of the English term "wardrobe."

Geniza: the storage warehouse for Jewish Torah scrolls and other sacred texts, which was also used to house family archives. The main *geniza* of Cairo was found in the 1890s and forms a significant source for Jewish family life in the Middle Ages.

Germanic: referring to the German-speaking Indo-Europeans who migrated into the Roman Empire beginning in the second century C.E. and established independent kingdoms there and in what is now Germany.

Guild: in the Middle Ages, the basic unit of economic production and training. Guilds were run by designated masters who trained apprentices in their craft. Apprentices eventually could become journeymen and, sometimes, masters themselves.

Gyneceum/gynakaia: the Byzantine term used for the women's quarters in a home or palace.

Hadith: the Islamic collection of the sayings of the Prophet Muhammad, his successors, and his family that are not considered sacred, as in the Quranic texts, but still form a main component to the holy texts of Islam.

Iconoclasm: literally, the smashing of icons. In Byzantine culture, the religious movement to ban the worship of religious images that was dominant in the ninth century, but which was overturned.

Jurists: in Roman law, these are professionals who interpret legal judgments.

Keep: also, *donjon*, the main building in a medieval castle, which usually not only housed the domestic apartments of the lord and lady, but also the Great Hall, the storage areas, and other rooms for administrative, military, or domestic use.

Latifundium/latifundia: the Roman plantation system in which the land is worked by slaves and owned by an absentee landlord.

Levirate marriage: in Judaism, the practice of a childless widow marrying her late husband's brother in order to provide the dead man with an heir.

Lineage: the family line.

Lombards: a Germanic group that invaded the Roman Empire around 600 C.E. and established a kingdom and several other states throughout Italy. Also provided the origins of the name for the Italian region called Lombardy.

Machicolation: in architecture, a projection from a wall, made of wood or stone, through which defenders could pour nasty things onto the heads of an invading force.

Manorialism: in medieval Europe, the economic system of land and labor exploitation in which a lord's manor is worked by serfs or villeins, who receive land and dwellings in exchange.

Manumission: the freeing of a slave from servitude or, in Roman law, the freeing of children from paternal authority [see *patria potestas*]. Also referred to as emancipation.

Manus/sine manu: in Roman law, two different kinds of marriage. The term means "hand," and refers to the status of the bride at marriage: whether she is handed over to her husband's family or if her so-called hand remains with that of her natal family.

Maritagium: in English law, the property a bride brought to the marriage. Called dowry on the Continent.

Matrilineal: a system whereby the lines of descent are considered to run through the mother's family line.

Morning gift/*morgengab*: in medieval Germanic culture, the gift granted to the wife by the husband on the morning after the wedding.

Mund/mundium: in Germanic law, the legal personhood of an individual, which is controlled either by him or, in the case of women, by some other male.

Municipia: the Roman term for an administrative center in an imperial province.

Natal: referring to the family of one's birth.

Ostrogoths: a Germanic group that invaded the Roman Empire in the fifth century and established a kingdom in Italy

Partible inheritance: a system of inheritance in which all, or at least some, of the children inherit portions of an estate.

Paterfamilias: in Roman culture, the male head of the household who has supreme power over all members of the household.

Paternalistic: referring to the definition of a political leader or a political system as being father-like.

Patria potestas: a Latin term referring to the authority fathers had over their households.

Patriarchal: refers to a system in which some adult men of elite status rule over lower-status men, all women, and all children, and in which all men are given legal dominance over women and children. This is the dominant social system of the world both historically and, in many places, currently.

Patrilineal: a family structure in which the main lines of descent are considered to pass primarily down the father's family line.

Peristyle house: a common type of house in the Roman and Byzantine empires in which rooms were arranged around an interior central courtyard, which had a covered walkway, or "peristyle" surrounding it.

Polygamy: the taking in marriage of more than one person, such as a man having several wives or a woman having several husbands.

Polygyny: the marriage of a man to more than one woman at the same time.

Primogeniture: the system whereby the eldest son inherits most or all of his father's estate.

Quran: the holy scriptures of the Islamic faith.

Serf: also known as a *villein,* a peasant in the manorial system who is personally free but tied to the land he or she must work for the lord.

Sharia: the system of Islamic law based on the Quran and *Hadith* that is overseen by Islamic judges called *qadis.*

Triclinium: the dining room of a Greek or Byzantine house, referring to the three couches built into the wall, on which the diners reclined.

Umma: the community of believers in Islam.

Usury: the lending of money at excessive interest. In the Middle Ages, the practice of usury was forbidden by the Roman Church.

Vandals: a Germanic group that invaded the Roman Empire in the fifth century and established a kingdom in North Africa.

Vassal: a free man or woman who swears oaths of homage and fealty (loyalty) to a lord in exchange for a fief.

Villein: see "serf."

Visigoths: a Germanic group that invaded the Roman Empire in the fifth century and established a kingdom in Spain.

War band: in medieval Germanic culture, the group of men who formed the private military and administrative force of a chieftain.

Wergeld: in Germanic law, the value placed upon a person's life and limb.

Bibliography and Recommended Further Reading

The texts listed in this bibliography are mentioned specifically because they are accessible to the general reader, and so can provide useful tools for the person interested in reading more about the medieval world in general and medieval families in particular. The more technical or specialized sources referred to in the chapters of this book can be found in the notes for each chapter.

Primary Sources and Source Collections

Bayard, Tania, trans. and ed. *A Medieval Home Companion: Housekeeping in the Fourteenth Century.* New York: HarperCollins Publishers, 1991. This abridged version of the manual of the man known as the *menagier* (or "goodman") of Paris to his young wife provides the reader with valuable information on the medieval household in later medieval Europe.

Geanokoplos, Deno John. *Byzantium: Church, Society, and Civilization Seen Through Contemporary Eyes.* Chicago: University of Chicago Press, 1984. Virtually the only sourcebook available to general readers interested in the history of the Byzantine Empire.

Goodich, Michael, ed. *Other Middle Ages: Witnesses at the Margins of Medieval Society.* Philadelphia: University of Pennsylvania Press, 1998. A collection of sources focusing on the populations not typically covered by source collections: Jews, dissidents, heretics, and other others.

Halsall, Paul, ed. *The Internet Medieval Sourcebook.* http://www.fordham.edu/halsall/sbook.html This massive compendium of primary sources for the Middle Ages includes links to other source collections edited by Halsall, such as the *Internet Ancient History Sourcebook* and sources compiled on specific topics: Byzantine sources, Islamic sources, women's history sources, and so on. This is the most comprehensive portal for medieval sources to exist on the Internet.

General Works on Medieval History

Most general works focus on western Europe, with only occasional references to the Islamic, Byzantine, and Jewish cultures of the Middle Ages. However, the following books are good starting points for information on medieval people.

Backman, Clifford R. *The Worlds of Medieval Europe.* Oxford and New York: Oxford University Press, 2003. This text gives equal time to all the medieval cultures, unlike most general textbooks.

Duby, Georges, ed. *A History of Private Life. Volume II: Revelations of the Medieval World.* Philippe Ariès and Georges Duby, series editors. Arthur Goldhammer, trans. Reprint, Cambridge, MA: Harvard University Press, 2003. This second volume of a multi-volume series provides an overview of private life mostly in Christian western Europe. The volume suffers to some extent from the dominance of Georges Duby's perspective on the position of women, which has been substantially overturned by more recent historical work, but it is a useful introduction to the issues of private space and family life in the Middle Ages.

Newman, Paul B. *Daily Life in the Middle Ages.* Jefferson, NC: McFarland and Company, 2001. A detailed overview especially of the material life of medieval people.

Veyne, Paul, ed. *A History of Private Life. Volume 1: From Pagan Rome to Byzantium.* Philippe Ariès and Georges Duby, series editors. Arthur Goldhammer, trans. Cambridge, MA: Harvard University Press, 1987. This first volume of a multi-volume series provides a somewhat uneven overview. Although some specific issues and conclusions (such as the isolation of women in the Byzantine period) have been significantly debated by many historians, this is still a useful introduction to the private life of ancient and Byzantine people.

General Works on Medieval Women

Family history is often embedded in women's history, so books dealing specifically with women are often useful for gaining information on family life.

Ahmed, Leila. *Women and Gender in Islam: Historical Roots of a Modern Debate.* New Haven: Yale University Press, 1992. Approximately the first half of the book focuses on pre-modern Islam and the position of women in Islamic religion and culture. This is the classic work by one of the most notable scholars on the history of Islamic women.

Baker, Derek, ed. *Medieval Women.* Oxford: Basil Blackwell, 1978. A classic collection of essays, mostly focusing on women in a religious context.

Baskin, Judith R., ed. *Jewish Women in Historical Perspective.* Second Edition. Detroit: Wayne State University Press, 1999. Four essays on Jewish women in late antiquity and the Middle Ages are very useful for general understanding of the role of women in Judaic culture.

Evergates, Theodore, ed. *Aristocratic Women in Medieval France.* Philadelphia: University of Pennsylvania Press, 1999. This collection of essays is accessible to the general reader, and discusses noble women in the context of their families.

Labarge, Margaret Wade. *The Small Sound of a Trumpet: Women in Medieval Life.* Boston: Beacon Press, 1988. An excellent general survey of the history of women in medieval Europe, although there is a strong focus on women's experiences in northern Europe (England and France) and less attention paid to the Mediterranean world.

Mirrer, Louise, ed. *Upon My Husband's Death: Widows in the Literature and Histories of Medieval Europe.* Ann Arbor: University of Michigan Press, 1992. A collection of essays that covers a wide range of widows' experience and their depiction in medieval literature.

Mitchell, Linda E., ed. *Women in Medieval Western European Culture.* New York: Garland Books, 1999. A collection of essays for the general reader, each written by a different expert in the field, that focuses not only on western European (despite the title) but also Byzantine, Islamic, and Jewish women.

Nicol, Donald M. *The Byzantine Lady: Ten Portraits 1250–1500.* Cambridge: Cambridge University Press, 1994. This collection of brief biographies of elite and imperial women focuses on the public activities of these notable figures.

Ward, Jennifer C, *English Noblewomen in the Later Middle Ages.* London: Longman, 1992. This book, part of Longman's "The Medieval World" series, introduces the historical issues surrounding the lives of aristocratic women—and thereby of aristocratic family life—in late medieval England.

Ancient Rome

Bradley, Keith R. *Discovering the Roman Family: Studies in Roman Social History.* New York: Oxford University Press, 1991. This collection of case studies identifies a number of specific issues concerning Roman families, with a concluding essay that serves as both a general overview and an expansion on the previous essays, by looking at the family of the philosopher Cicero.

Dixon, Suzanne. *The Roman Family.* Baltimore: The Johns Hopkins University Press, 1992. This text is virtually the only modern synthesis of the Roman family designed for the non-specialist.

The Byzantine Empire

Gregory, Timothy F. *A History of Byzantium.* Oxford: Blackwell Publishing, 2005. Although focused mostly on political history, like all general works on Byzantine culture, this new study does incorporate new research on social and family issues.

Rautman, Marcus. *Daily Life in the Byzantine Empire.* New York: Greenwood Press, 2006. The only overview of Byzantine society available for the general reader, this very recent text by a noted archaeologist focuses not only on textual sources but material remains as well.

The Islamic World

Lindsay, James E. *Daily Life in the Medieval Islamic World.* New York: Greenwood Press, 2005. This general study of medieval Islamic society is more or less the only text of its kind: one that provides the general reader with informa-tion on medieval Muslim culture that is usually available only to special-ists. Although the references to family life are minimal—and located in a section entitled "Curious and Entertaining Information"—this is a useful introduction to the medieval Islamic world.

Sonbol, Amira El Azhary, ed. *Women, the Family, and Divorce Laws in Islamic History.* Syracuse, NY: Syracuse University Press, 1996. Although the majority of the essays in this collection focus on the post-Ottoman Islamic world—that is, from the sixteenth century—the introduction and the first essay, "Women and Citizenship in the Qur'an," by Barbara Freyer Stowasser, are useful as introductions to issues pertaining to Muslim women and families.

Medieval Jewish Culture

Abrahams, Israel. *Jewish Life in the Middle Ages.* New York: Meridian Books, 1958. Although this text, which was originally published around the year 1900, is quite outdated with respect to the use of sources, it is important as the first general history of medieval Jewish life that used the then recently dis-covered *geniza* records.

Cohen, Mark R. *Under Crescent and Cross: The Jews in the Middle Ages.* Princeton: Princeton University Press, 1994. Although there is very little information on the Jewish family to be found in this text, it is a good general overview of the ways in which Jews interacted in the dominant cultures of the Middle Ages, and the ways in which those cultures interacted with the Jewish populations living in them.

Goitein, S. D. *A Mediterranean Society: An Abridgment in One Volume.* Revised and edited by Jacob Lassner. Berkeley: University of California Press, 1999. This is a very useful abridgment of the massive multi-volume work on Jewish life in medieval Egypt and the southern Mediterranean, based upon Goitein's extensive study of the *geniza* records.

Roth, Norman. *Daily Life of the Jews in the Middle Ages.* Westport, CT: Greenwood Press, 2005. This text, designed for the general reader, is useful especially in its descriptions of the material and economic cultures of medieval Jews.

Stow, Kenneth R. *Alienated Minority: The Jews of Medieval Latin Europe.* Cambridge, MA: Harvard University Press, 1992. This general study, which makes use of new research especially on Jews living in the Rhineland, is a good recent study of medieval Jewish culture in the Christian west.

Western Europe

Fleming, Peter. *Family and Household in Medieval England.* Basingstoke and New York: Palgrave, 2001. A short and general study of family life in England in the high and late Middle Ages.

Hanawalt, Barbara A. *The Ties That Bound: Peasant Families in Medieval England.* New York: Oxford University Press, 1986. One of the books that revolutionized the study of peasant families, this text is based upon a detailed study of the records of coroners, called "coroner's inquests," that identify how specific people died, in order to understand how medieval peasant families lived.

Mitchell, Linda E. *Portraits of Medieval Women: Family, Marriage, and Politics in England 1225–1350.* New York: Palgrave Macmillan, 2003. This series of case studies of aristocratic women and families focuses on specific aspects of women's lives and how they intersected with both the family culture and the political culture in the English kingdom.

Neel, Carol, ed. *Medieval Families: Perspectives on Marriage, Household, and Children.* Medieval Academy Reprints for Teaching. Toronto: University of Toronto Press, 2004. This collection of previously published essays compiles many of the classic works that introduced the study of the medieval family about twenty years ago. The introduction, by the editor, is an excellent road map into the essays themselves and into the field of medieval family history.

Index

About the Author

LINDA E. MITCHELL is Associate Professor of History at Alfred University. She is Hagar Professor of Humanities and Co-chair, Medieval & Renaissance Studies. She contributed to *Events that Changed the World in the Eighteenth Century* (Greenwood, 1997).